LINCOLN FOR PRESIDENT

ALSO BY TIMOTHY S. GOOD

*The Lincoln-Douglas Debates and
the Making of a President* (McFarland, 2008)

Lincoln for President

An Underdog's Path to the 1860 Republican Nomination

Timothy S. Good

To Sara,

8/18/10

McFarland & Company, Inc., Publishers

Jefferson, North Carolina, and London

LIBRARY OF CONGRESS ONLINE CATALOG

Good, Timothy S. (Timothy Sean)
Lincoln for president : an underdog's path to the 1860 Republican
nomination / Timothy S. Good.
p. cm.
Includes bibliographical references and index.

ISBN-13 978-0-7864-3957-7
softcover : 50# alkaline paper ∞

1. Lincoln, Abraham, 1809–1865 — Political career before 1861.
2. Lincoln, Abraham, 1809–1865 — Political and social views.
3. Character — Case Studies.
4. United States. Declaration of Independence.
5. Presidential candidates — United States — Biography.
6. Political campaigns — United States — History —19th century.
7. Presidents — United States — Election —1860.
8. Republican Party (U.S. : 1854–)
9. United States — Politics and government —1857–1861.
I. Title.
E457.G63 2009 973.7092 — dc22 2009002115

British Library cataloguing data are available

Manufactured in the United States of America

On the cover: *Hon. Abraham Lincoln, Republican candidate
for the presidency, 1860,* painted by Thomas Hicks, lith. by
Leopold Grozelier, Boston; Library of Congress. Flag and
Declaration of Independence background ©2009 Shutterstock.

*McFarland & Company, Inc., Publishers
Box 611, Jefferson, North Carolina 28640
www.mcfarlandpub.com*

To my mom:

Thanks for putting up with the history
discussions at the dinner table.

Acknowledgments

I am extremely grateful to the following people for their assistance: Gene Finke; Meredith Berg, professor of history, Valparaiso University; Gaines Foster, professor of history, Louisiana State University; Gerry Prokopowicz, professor of history, East Carolina University and author of *Did Lincoln Own Slaves? And Other Frequently Asked Questions About Abraham Lincoln*; Tim Townsend, historian, Lincoln Home National Historic Site; Tom Trimborn, professor, Truman State University, and author of *Encounters with Lincoln: Images and Words*; Linda Ray, librarian, Bellevue Public Library; my dad; my brother; and, of course, my wife.

Table of Contents

Preface

This is a sequel to my book *The Lincoln-Douglas Debates and the Making of a President*, and it is also the first narrative of Lincoln's first presidential nomination, his *surprising* presidential nomination. In 1860, the Republicans had a plethora of candidates from which to choose — candidates who had achieved far more success in the political arena than Lincoln. In fact, Lincoln's political career prior to 1860 was marked almost completely by failure. Indeed, nothing in his pre–1860 political career could be described as successful. His one term as a congressman was undistinguished. He never served as a judge or a governor or in any statewide office. He campaigned for the United States Senate and lost — twice. By all measures, he possessed no significant political experience, worse, he appeared politically incompetent.

Yet, in 1860 the Republicans chose Abraham Lincoln over William H. Seward, a United States senator and a two-time governor of the most populous state in the Union — New York; Salmon Chase, the governor of Ohio; Simon Cameron, a Pennsylvania senator; and Supreme Court justice Judge McLean, the famous dissenter in the infamous Dred Scott decision.

Lincoln's nomination becomes all the more perplexing as, just twenty-four hours before the balloting began, he did not have the support necessary to prevail. This all leads to the critical question: Why did the Republicans nominate *Lincoln*?

The reason for his surprising nomination is best understood through a narrative of the years from 1858 until 1860, climaxing with an account of the national convention that nominated him. This is a story of a young party struggling to define itself and its goals, both philosophical and political.

There are many fine biographies on the individuals who attended the convention, but few studies that view the convention through the perspective of *multiple* individuals, especially those from the four crucial states — Illinois, Indiana, Pennsylvania and New Jersey — that the Republicans lost in

1856 and that they desperately needed to win in 1860. One can only fully understand how and why the Republicans chose Lincoln through the views of many lenses, and not just one.

Even from the perspective of multiple individuals, the picture is not easily brought into focus. Over time, the convention's story has been entwined and overgrown with mythology. The most prevalent interpretation contends that the delegates were not motivated by integrity or sincere beliefs, but by limited personal goals. This myth suggests that many of the delegates, for the sole purpose of obtaining a cabinet post for their state's "favorite son," sold their votes to the presidential candidates' supporters like a group of auctioneers at a beef market. Willard L. King's *Lincoln's Manager: David Davis*, William E. Baringer's *Lincoln's Rise to Power* and Benjamin P. Thomas's *Abraham Lincoln* all perpetuate this myth.

This interpretation fails on several grounds. The Republican delegates did not arrive in Chicago for the purpose of ensuring that their "favorite son" would become the secretary of the Interior or the postmaster general. The delegates wanted their "favorite son" to become the 16th president of the United States. To view the cabinet appointments as bribes hides the delegates' true motivations and overarching goals.

Other studies, such as Glyndon G. Van Deusen's *William Henry Seward*, John M. Taylor's *William Henry Seward* and Stephen B. Oates' *With Malice Toward None: The Life of Abraham Lincoln* offer another theory. They argue that the Republicans selected Lincoln because he was "less radical" on slavery than other candidates were, especially the most favored candidate, William H. Seward. A close study of the speeches of Seward and Lincoln and, more important, of the reasons that the delegates provided for their support of Lincoln illustrates that this is an erroneous assumption. Lincoln and Seward shared a common hatred of slavery, which they freely expressed in their speeches and writings. Where Lincoln most differed from Seward, where he appeared "less radical," was not in regards to his political philosophy, but in the manner by which he addressed others. Seward had no difficulty in criticizing others, even fellow Republicans. In his speeches, Lincoln never did. He maintained respect for his fellow Republicans, those individuals with whom he disagreed, and even Democrats. Lincoln's moderate style, not his radical views permitted him to earn the delegates' respect, and made him, in their eyes, the most electable candidate. This quality was best stated by Lincoln himself in a letter to one of his supporters: "Be Careful to give no offence." It was not a conclusion that Lincoln followed out of political expediency, but one that defined who he was as a politician, and, more important, as a person.

Two other studies — Doris Kearn Goodwins' *Team of Rivals: The Polit-*

ical Genius of Abraham Lincoln and David Donald's *Lincoln*—do not fully develop this interpretation. Goodwin correctly identifies Lincoln's character as a crucial factor that determined his nomination, but she does not mention that his character proved most critical in the border states of Illinois, Indiana, Pennsylvania and New Jersey. Donald astutely notes the significance of these states, but does not mention the significance of Lincoln's character.

However, all previous biographies and all previous studies have completely ignored one of the most critical aspects of Lincoln's nomination: the primacy of the Declaration of Independence. In the debates at the convention, among a majority of the delegates, the Declaration rose to a prominence that exceeded all other concerns. Above all, the delegates wanted a candidate who upheld the notion that "all men are created equal." While Lincoln did not struggle as much in his 1859–1860 speeches with his loyalty to the Declaration as he did in the 1858 campaign, he did struggle. While his eventual adherence to "all men are created equal" in the 1858 campaign proved to have a negative effect on his political chances of winning the 1858 election, his return to supporting the Declaration in the 1859–1860 period proved essential to his victory at the convention. Had he dispensed with the Declaration, he would not have stood a chance at Chicago.

In contrast to previous interpretations, I contend that the delegates who attended the Republican convention did not behave like a group of political salesman haggling and bartering for offices, but that they conducted themselves as men united in their hatred of slavery's extension and committed to one common goal: choosing the most electable candidate, the one man who stood the greatest chance of becoming the 16th president of the United States, a man who could win the border states, who opposed slavery's extension and firmly believed that the Declaration of Independence's phrase "all men are created equal" meant "all men."

While delegates supporting other candidates held seemingly winning hands with previous elections won, current political offices held, and available campaign funds, Lincoln supporters held only one card, the one card that would trump them all: the character of Lincoln.

The American Declaration of Independence

When in the Course of human events, it becomes necessary for one people to dissolve the political bands which have connected them with another, and to assume among the powers of the earth, the separate and equal station to which the Laws of Nature and of Nature's God entitle them, a decent respect to the opinions of mankind requires that they should declare the causes which impel them to the separation.

We hold these truths to be self-evident, that all men are created equal, that they are endowed by their Creator with certain unalienable Rights, that among these are Life, Liberty and the pursuit of Happiness...

July 4, 1776

1

Before '59

Seventeen days after the election, Lincoln wrote:

I am glad that I made the late race. It gave me a hearing on the great and durable question of the age, which I could have had in no other way; and though I now sink out of view, and shall be forgotten, I believe I have made some marks which will tell for the cause of civil liberty long after I am gone.[1]

He had lost, again.

Despite months of campaigning, dozens of speeches, and hundreds of miles traveled by ship, train and horse across Illinois, on November 2, 1858, the Democratic senator Stephen A. Douglas defeated the Republican candidate Abraham Lincoln for the United States Senate.

This defeat was not Lincoln's first taste of failure.

Three years before, in 1855, he had campaigned for the United States Senate and had come within a hair's breadth of victory. The state legislatures chose the senators and in the Illinois State Legislature, with ninety-nine possible votes, Lincoln garnered forty-five on the first ballot. To succeed, he needed five more votes. He needed to convince just five more legislators to join him, but the five he needed refused to support him. With each succeeding ballot, more and more legislators abandoned Lincoln. After the seventh one, with only fifteen legislators still standing with him, he resigned himself to defeat, and threw his remaining votes to the one remaining anti–Douglas candidate, Lyman Trumbull, who prevailed.

In summarizing this defeat, Lincoln wrote that the "election is over, the Session is ended, and I am not Senator." He had to content himself "with the honor of having been the first choice of a large majority" of the fifty-one legislators who choose an anti–Douglas candidate, but he admitted that it "was rather hard for the 44 to have to surrender to the 5 — and a less good humored man than I, perhaps would not have consented to it — and it would not have been done without my consent. I could not, however, let the whole political result go to ruin, on a point merely personal to myself."[2]

Two years later, in early 1858, he summarized his life and his accomplishments:

> Born, February 12, 1809, in Hardin County, Kentucky.
> Education defective.
> Profession, a lawyer.
> Have been a captain of volunteers in Black Hawk war.
> Postmaster at a very small office.
> Four times a member of the Illinois legislature, and was a member of the lower house of Congress.[3]

In late 1858, he could have added, "Twice defeated for the United States Senate."

And yet, just one day after predicting that he would "be forgotten," he wrote the following: "The fight must go on. We are right, and can not finally fail. There will be another blowup in the so-called democratic party before long.

"In the mean time, let all Republicans stand fast by their guns."[4]

The "fight" to which Lincoln referred, in which he believed that he was in the "right," began in 1854 with the passage of Douglas's Kansas-Nebraska Act. Lincoln was "astounded," "thunderstruck," and "stunned" when he heard of the passage of this law. Douglas's legislation now permitted slavery in territory where it had previously been prohibited by the 1820 Missouri Compromise. Lincoln wrote in the third person: "His profession had almost superseded the thought of politics in his mind, when the repeal of the Missouri compromise aroused him as he had never been before."[5] He was back into politics, and back into the fight.

The same year that Douglas's Kansas-Nebraska Act became law, Lincoln assailed it in a Peoria, Illinois, speech. He first praised what he considered America's cornerstone, the Declaration of Independence, and more specifically, its author. He noted that Thomas Jefferson was "a chief actor in the revolution; then a delegate to Congress; afterwards twice President" and perhaps the "most distinguished politician of our history." He acknowledged that Jefferson had also been a "slave-holder," but that he also conceived the idea of preventing slavery from "ever going into the north-western territory." Banning slavery from the Northwest territory, an area which would eventually become the free states of Ohio, Indiana, Illinois, Michigan and Wisconsin, was precisely what Jefferson "foresaw and intended — the happy home of teeming millions of free, white, prosperous people, and no slave amongst them." The author of the Declaration of Independence, Lincoln argued, had originated the "policy of prohibiting slavery in new territory," and that policy had through "sixty odd of the best years of the republic" worked to the nation's "great and beneficial end."

In contrast, Douglas had justified the Kansas-Nebraska Act based on the principle of popular sovereignty, the idea that the people of the territory should determine whether slavery should be permitted. Lincoln assaulted that proposition. He claimed that the sacred right of self government is "grossly violated" by granting the "liberty of making slaves of other people," a concept that Jefferson had never conceived. Lincoln held that the Missouri Compromise directly applied to the Nebraska territory and therefore prohibited slavery within it. Although Douglas claimed that his act had no effect on the application of the compromise, Lincoln emphatically believed that the act was "the repeal of the Missouri Compromise" and that it was simply wrong. He considered it "wrong in its direct effect" by allowing slavery into Kansas and Nebraska and "wrong in its prospective principle" by allowing slavery to spread beyond its current boundaries.

Appalled by Douglas's apparent indifference to his act's effect, Lincoln confessed that he "can not but hate" this "covert real zeal for the spread of slavery." He expressed his "hate" of it "because of the monstrous injustice of slavery itself ... because it deprives our republican example of its just influence in the world — enables the enemies of free institutions, with plausibility, to taunt us as hypocrites — causes the real friends of freedom to doubt our sincerity, and especially because it forces so many really good men amongst ourselves into an open war with the very fundamental principles of civil liberty — criticizing the Declaration of Independence."

Lincoln also rejected Douglas's popular sovereignty doctrine as a solution to the problem of slavery, for if the white man "governs himself that is self-government; but when he governs himself, and also governs another man, that is more than self-government — that is despotism," something Lincoln termed the "Divine right of Kings." Lincoln further argued that if the "negro is a man" and "'all men are created equal'" then "there can be no moral right" to make "a slave of another." "No man is good enough to govern another man, without that other's consent." This concept is the "leading principle — the sheet anchor of American republicanism." Lincoln warned that no one should be deceived, the "spirit of seventy-six and the spirit of Nebraska are utter antagonisms; and the former is being rapidly displaced by the latter."

Lincoln called for the opponents of the Nebraska act to unite. The act had "soiled" the republican robe and "trailed [it] in the dust. Let us turn and wash it white, in the spirit, if not the blood, of the Revolution." He pleaded for the people to return slavery "to the position our fathers gave it" and let "us re-adopt the Declaration of Independence." May both "north and south —

let all Americans — let all lovers of liberty everywhere — join in the great and good work. If we do this, we shall not only have saved the Union; but we shall have so saved it, as to make, and to keep it, forever worthy of the saving. We shall have so saved it, that the succeeding millions of free happy people, the world over, shall rise up, and call us blessed to the latest generations."[6]

Lincoln's hope for his nation suffered another blow three years later with the Supreme Court's Dred Scott decision. Chief Justice Roger Taney decided against the slave Dred Scott and declared that not only was Scott not permitted to sue in federal court, he also, along with all African Americans, could not become an American citizen.

On June 26, three months later, Lincoln attacked Taney's decision, and the arguments he employed in this speech, like those he had employed in his 1854 Peoria speech, would serve as the foundation for many of his remarks in the Lincoln-Douglas debates. The Dred Scott decision would become, second only to the Kansas-Nebraska Act, a major stimulus to the refinement of Lincoln's views on slavery. The speech also highlighted what Lincoln considered especially grievous about Taney's decision: the chief justice's erroneous interpretation of the Declaration of Independence.

In a speech in Springfield, where two weeks earlier Douglas had spoken on a variety of subjects, including the Dred Scott decision, Lincoln admitted that he had listened to Douglas's speech and he now wished to "assail (politically, not personally)" those who shared the senator's opinions. He denied, as some had charged, that the Republicans were somehow violently resisting the Court. Lincoln claimed that the Republicans believed in "obedience to, and respect for the judicial department of government" and that the Court's "decisions on Constitutional questions, when fully settled, should control, not only the particular cases decided, but the general policy of the country, subject to be disturbed only by amendments of the Constitution" and that any actions beyond these actions "would be revolution."

While acknowledging full respect for the court and stating that the Republicans "offer no resistance to it," Lincoln asserted, "we think the Dred Scott decision is erroneous" in part, because the Taney court had made the decision on the basis of historical facts that were wrong. Taney had declared that "negroes were no part of the people who made, or for whom was made, the Declaration of Independence, or the Constitution of the United States." Lincoln noted that Judge Curtis, in his dissenting opinion, had shown that in five of the thirteen states that formed the Constitution, "free negroes were voters." The people had ordained and established the Constitution and in some states, "colored persons were among those qualified by law to act on the subject."[7]

Lincoln also took issue with Taney's declaration that the "public estimate of the black man is more favorable now than it was in the days of the Revolution." Lincoln countered that this "assumption [was] a mistake" and that it was "grossly incorrect to say or assume." States had withdrawn the right of suffrage for free blacks. In earlier times, "our Declaration of Independence was held sacred by all, and thought to include all; but now, to aid in making the bondage of the negro universal and eternal, it is assailed, and sneered at, and construed, and hawked at, and torn, till, if its framers could rise from their graves, they could not" recognize it at all.

Taney admitted that the Declaration was "broad enough to include the whole human family," but both Taney and Douglas also claimed that it did not include African Americans, because the founders did not "place them on equality with whites." This line of argument, Lincoln asserted, committed "obvious violence to the plain unmistakable language of the Declaration. I think the authors of that notable instrument intended to include all men, but they did not intend to declare all men equal in all respects. They did not mean to say all were equal in color, size, intellect, moral developments, or social capacity. They defined with tolerable distinctness, in what respects they did consider all men created equal — equal in 'certain inalienable rights, among which are life, liberty, and the pursuit of happiness.' This they said, and this [they] meant."

Lincoln recognized that these freedoms were not currently available to all, but that did not weaken the power of the Declaration. The founders "did not mean to assert the obvious untruth, that all were then actually enjoying that equality, nor yet, that they were about to confer it immediately upon them.... They meant simply to declare the right, so that the enforcement of it might follow as fast as circumstances should permit. They meant to set up a standard maxim for free society, which should be familiar to all, and revered by all; constantly looked to, constantly labored for, and even though never perfectly attained, constantly approximated, and thereby constantly spreading and deepening its influence, and augmenting the happiness and value of life to all people of all colors everywhere." The phrase "all men are created equal" was of no use in declaring independence from Great Britain, Lincoln argued, but it did create "a stumbling block to those who" in the future "might seek to turn a free people back into the hateful paths of despotism."

Douglas held a completely counter view, Lincoln asserted. To Douglas, the Declaration applied only to the "'white race,'" specifically "British subjects on this continent." This interpretation, Lincoln believed, made a "mere wreck — mangled ruin" of "our once glorious Declaration" by placing the "French, Germans and other white people of the world" with the "Judge's inferior races."

Lincoln concluded with a summation of the differences between the parties. The Republicans considered the "negro" "a man; [and] that his bondage is cruelly wrong, and the field of his oppression ought not be enlarged." Douglas and the Democrats, Lincoln went to say, reject "negro manhood; deny, or dwarf to insignificance, the wrong of his bondage," "crush all sympathy for him," "cultivate and excite hatred and disgust against him" and then "compliment themselves as Union-savers for doing so" by describing the extension of slavery into the territories as "a sacred right of self-government."[8]

A year later, in 1858, Lincoln had another opportunity to fight Douglas's act and Taney's decision when the Illinois Republicans nominated him as their senatorial candidate. Throughout the summer and the fall of that year, in his speeches and debates, he argued that the Kansas-Nebraska Act and the Dred Scott decision had altered the nation's destiny and had violated the Declaration of Independence, a document which professed the truth that "all men are created equal." On August 17 at Lewistown, Illinois, in a speech which one individual referred to as the "apostrophe of the Declaration of Independence,"[9] Lincoln made this argument.[10] He claimed that the colonial communities, speaking through "their representatives in old Independence Hall, said to the whole world of men: 'We hold these truths to be self-evident: that all men are created equal; that they are endowed by their Creator with certain unalienable rights; that among these are life, liberty, and the pursuit of happiness.' This was their majestic interpretation of the economy of the Universe. This was their lofty, and wise, and noble understanding of the justice of the Creator to His creatures."

This right was not limited, Lincoln contended:

> [It was to be granted] to all His creatures, to the whole great family of man. In their enlightened belief, nothing stamped with the Divine image and likeness was sent into the world to be trodden on, and degraded, and imbruted by its fellows. They grasped not only the whole race of man then living, but they reached forward and seized upon the farthest posterity. They erected a beacon to guide their children and their children's children, and the countless myriads who should inhabit the earth in other ages. Wise statesmen as they were, they knew the tendency of prosperity to breed tyrants, and so they established these great self-evident truths, that when in the distant future some man, some faction, some interest should set up the doctrine that none but rich men, or none but white men, were entitled to life, liberty, and the pursuit of happiness, their posterity might look up again to the Declaration of Independence and take courage to renew the battle which their fathers began — so that truth, and justice, and mercy, and all the humane and Christian virtues might not be extinguished from the land; so that no man would hereafter dare to limit and circumscribe the great principles on which the temple of liberty was being built.

The Declaration was not safe, Lincoln feared. It was under attack by Douglas and Taney, and had already been damaged:

Return to the fountain whose waters spring close by the blood of the Revolution. Think nothing of me — take no thought for the political fate of any man whomsoever — but come back to the truths that are in the Declaration of Independence. You may do anything with me you choose, if you will but heed these sacred principles. You may not only defeat me for the Senate, but you may take me and put me to death. While pretending no indifference to earthly honors, I do claim to be actuated in this contest by something higher than an anxiety for office. I charge you to drop every paltry and insignificant thought for any man's success. It is nothing; I am nothing; Judge Douglas is nothing. But do not destroy that immortal emblem of Humanity — the Declaration of American Independence.[11]

Lincoln though, did not always remain consistent in his defense of the Declaration, and the battle of the 1858 campaign took on a much larger issue that neither of the two candidates could appreciate at the time. The most crucial conflict of the campaign was not between the two candidates, but within Lincoln himself, whether he would speak in favor of his egalitarian interpretation of the Declaration before audiences that did not accept it and whose support he desperately needed, or whether he would abandon it for the sake of winning. Douglas recognized that Lincoln's original stance on the Declaration was a fatal weakness that would turn central Illinois — the crucial area that both Douglas and Lincoln needed to win — against the Republican candidate. In Chicago, to open his campaign against Lincoln, Douglas defended the Dred Scott decision and attacked Lincoln's position. The senator argued that the "negro" had no guaranteed rights. The government was "founded on the white basis" and "was made by the white man, for the benefit of the white man, to be administered by white men, in such manner as they should determine."[12]

Lincoln, at first, remained unaffected by Douglas's assault. The totality of Douglas's philosophy was a direct threat to the nation, Lincoln charged. In Chicago, in response to Douglas, Lincoln claimed that the senator's philosophy of "don't care if slavery is voted up or voted down," his support for the Dred Scott decision, and his position that the "Declaration of Independence did not mean anything at all" were endangering the foundation of the nation. Douglas's opinions would "rub out the sentiment of liberty in the country" if these sentiments were "ratified," "confirmed," "endorsed," "taught to our children, and repeated to them." At their base, Lincoln considered these arguments the same as those "kings have made for enslaving people in all ages of the world." There was significant danger, Lincoln believed, "in taking this old Declaration of Independence, which declares that all men are equal upon principle and making exceptions to it where will it stop. If one man says it does not mean a negro, why not another say it does not mean some other man?"[13]

In his conclusion, Lincoln even took time to attack the idea of "superior" and "inferior" races. He asked that the nation "discard all this quibbling about this man and the other man — this race and that race and the other race being inferior, and therefore they must be placed in an inferior position" and "discard all these things, and unite as one people throughout this land, until we shall once more stand up declaring that all men are created equal."[14] It would be a stance that he would not consistently uphold at all the debates.

When he next spoke at Springfield, just seven days after his Chicago speech, his courage began to fail or his political wisdom began to take hold. There he claimed that African Americans were not equal in all respects. At the first debate, at Ottawa, Lincoln's descent continued. For the first time in the campaign, he embraced the "superior" and "inferior" concept while also arguing for his interpretation of the Declaration of Independence. When he traveled to Freeport in a strong Republican area, though, he dropped the Declaration completely. He maintained this strategy at the southernmost debate, Jonesboro, but at the Charleston debate, in the crucial central area of Illinois, he moved even further from his Chicago remarks by catering to the audience's prejudices. He again spoke of the division of the races based on "superior" and "inferior" lines, but without any mention of the Declaration. At Galesburg in a more northern area, for the first time since Ottawa, he once again referred to the Declaration of Independence but he still advocated for the division of the races. Finally, at Quincy, at the second to last debate, he displayed consistency that had been absent in his remarks when he made the same arguments as he had at Galesburg.[15]

At the last debate at Alton, though, Lincoln once again embraced the Declaration of Independence without the encumbrances of "superior" and "inferior" races. Three years before, Lincoln argued, the following:

> [There had never been a man] "so far as I knew or believed, in the whole world, who had said that the Declaration of Independence did not include negroes in the term 'all men.' I re-assert it to-day. I assert that Judge Douglas and all his friends may search the whole records of the country, and it will be a matter of great astonishment to me if they shall be able to find that one human being three years ago had ever uttered the astounding sentiment that the term 'all men' in the Declaration did not include the negro." Lincoln knew his interpretation was not accepted by all and recalled the "shameful though rather forcible declaration of Pettit of Indiana, upon the floor of the United States Senate, that the Declaration of Independence was in that respect 'a self-evident lie,' rather than a self-evident truth. But I say, with a perfect knowledge of all this hawking at the Declaration without directly attacking it, that three years ago there never had lived a man who had ventured to assail it in the sneaking way of pretending to believe it and then asserting it did not include the negro. I believe that the first man who ever said it was Chief Justice Taney

in the Dred Scott case, and the next to him was our friend Stephen A. Douglas. And now it has become the catch-word of the entire party.

There was a great danger, Lincoln believed, in this interpretation taking hold and becoming permanent. Whenever this "new principle — this new proposition that no human being ever thought of three years ago, — is brought forward, I combat it as having an evil tendency, if not an evil design; I combat it as having a tendency to dehumanize the negro — to take away from him the right of ever striving to be a man. I combat it as being one of the thousand things constantly done in these days to prepare the public mind to make property, and nothing but property, of the negro in all the States of this Union."

Describing the Declaration of Independence as a noble goal, and not an immediate condition, Lincoln argued that the authors had "meant simply to declare the right so that the enforcement of it might follow as fast as circumstances should permit." Equality did not have to exist in the late eighteenth century for the phrase to be considered universally egalitarian. Rather, Lincoln interpreted the founding fathers as intending to "set up a standard maxim for free society which should be familiar to all: constantly looked to, constantly labored for, and even, though never perfectly attained, constantly approximated and thereby constantly spreading and deepening its influence and augmenting the happiness and value of life to all people, of all colors, every where."[16] Lincoln, at the last debate, had returned in a public forum to the philosophy which he personally espoused, and he made no mention, for the first time in three debates, of "superior" and "inferior" races.

Then, six weeks after he made these remarks, he lost. In the crucial central area which he needed to win, Douglas prevailed. One of the few central areas Lincoln won contained Charleston, where he had spoken in favor of racial inequality without mention of the Declaration. In the central area that contained Alton, where he spoke of egalitarianism and the Declaration, Douglas won.

The key to the campaign, though, was not whether Lincoln succeeded on election day, but whether he displayed the courage to speak in favor of the philosophy that he believed when facing an electorate that did not believe it. Although he succumbed to the racism of his day at certain debates, the final one at Alton proved his courage. At the last debate he had defined politicians as those who were indifferent to slavery, such as Douglas, and he described statesmen as those who argued otherwise. To Lincoln, nothing proved the fundamental wrong of slavery more than the Declaration of Independence. When he spoke in favor of the Declaration without mentioning "superior" and "inferior," he stood at Alton not as a politician seeking votes, but as a statesman claiming that "all men" meant "all men."

The defeat devastated Lincoln. A reporter who had attended all the debates and many of Lincoln's speeches wrote: "The next time I saw Mr. Lincoln, after the election, I said to him that I hoped he was not so much disappointed as I had been. This, of course, 'reminded him of a little story.' I have forgotten the story, but it was about an over-grown boy who had met with some mishap, 'stumped' his toe, perhaps, and who said that 'it hurt too much to laugh, and he was too big to cry.'"[17]

Yet Lincoln partially regained his footing, and, in several letters after the election, called on the Republicans to continue. "The fight must go on," he demanded. "We are right, and can not finally fail."[18] Despite this vigorous encouragement to maintain the fight, he believed he would have no part in it. Just two weeks later, he wrote: "I think we have fairly entered upon a durable struggle as to whether this nation is to ultimately become all slave or all free, and though I fall early in the contest, it is nothing if I shall have contributed, in the least degree, to the final rightful result."[19]

2

Seward's "Irrepressible Conflict"

October 25, 1858

Lincoln's defeat in Illinois proved especially depressing for Republicans nationwide. In 1856, their presidential candidate, John C. Frémont, came within four states of prevailing. He lost only the northern states of New Jersey, Pennsylvania, Indiana and Illinois. Had he won Pennsylvania, and carried just two of the remaining three states, the Republicans would have captured the White House in their first attempt.

In all four of these states the Republicans faced a vibrant Democratic Party, and in Illinois and Indiana, the Republicans also faced a significant population of former southerners. In 1860, the Republicans would need a candidate who could appeal to Democrats and former southerners. Instead, the Republican Party's presumed nominee, William H. Seward, appealed to neither.

Seward had, by all measures, enjoyed a fantastic political career. He had lost only one election — over twenty years before, in 1834 — and had since become the dominant Republican in the most populous state in the union, New York. He had served two terms as the governor of that state, from 1839 to 1842, and was then elected senator from New York in 1849 and again in 1855. Some people even advocated him for the Republican Party's presidential nomination in 1856, but wiser minds had prevailed, suggesting that he wait. After 1856, his political friends overtly promoted Seward as the next Republican presidential nominee. His domination of the Republican Party in New York seemed to extend to the entire party.

His politics bordered on the radical. While governor, he opposed the return of two fugitive slaves, an action that had raised the ire of southerners and northern conservatives, but praise from radicals in the North. He pro-

15

vided a house in Auburn, New York, for Harriet Tubman, the famous Underground Railroad conductor, and he and his wife operated their house as a station on the Underground Railroad at least on one occasion and possibly more. All these actions, and the speeches he gave in support of these antislavery activities, had earned him the admiration of many of the Republican Party's most radical elements.[1]

However, throughout the 1850s, while Seward rose to the position of acclaimed leader of the antislavery movement, he continually displayed a fatal flaw in his character. As the nation's sectional crisis became more intense, so did Seward's attacks. He did not limit himself to attacking an issue itself as Lincoln did. He began to insult and threaten those who supported the issue as well. He fought slavery with an unswerving passion and an uninhibited tongue.

On March 11, 1850, Seward propelled himself into the national limelight with his first speech in the United States Senate. The speech was entitled "Freedom in the New Territories," and was better known as the "Higher Law" speech. Seward attacked some of the great legislators of American history, including Henry Clay and Daniel Webster, and began his rise in the antislavery movement.

Seward's argument was simple: let California enter the union as a free state without any concession to the South. Any fugitive slave law, a key provision of the Compromise of 1850, was "unjust, unconstitutional, and immoral." Instead of offering any overtures to the South, Seward demanded that the federal government abolish slavery in the District of Columbia. He argued against those who sought to defend slavery with the Constitution. The document, he declared, "does not *expressly* affirm anything on the subject; all that it contains is two incidental allusions to slaves."

Seward's defining moment occurred over halfway through the speech when he identified the source of his antislavery philosophy. He asserted, "But there is a higher law than the Constitution, which regulates our authority over the domain, and devotes it to the same noble purposes. The territory is a part — no inconsiderable part — of the common heritage of mankind, bestowed upon them by the Creator of the universe. We are his stewards, and must so discharge our trust as to secure in the highest attainable degree, their happiness."[2]

While demonstrating that the Constitution did not support slavery, Seward could find no language within it to attack slavery, so he bypassed the Constitution, and chose another source, one which was not subject to compromise, or to electorates, or legislatures: Holy Scripture. Seward's stance placed him beyond the reach of political discussion on a pedestal where he and his philosophy could stand untouched by any human attacks or assaults.

Seward's speech received great praise in some radical antislavery circles but condemnation from his opponents. Senator John C. Calhoun of South Carolina, as expected, assailed Seward, and one southern newspaper described Seward as an "unscrupulous demagogue." Even members of his own party criticized him. Senator Henry Clay of Kentucky assaulted Seward's philosophy, and Lincoln, who pointed to the Declaration of Independence and not Holy Scripture for his public antislavery stance, later wrote, "I do not endorse his 'Higher Law' doctrine." The most surprising criticism, though, came from Seward's close political confidant, Thurlow Weed, who also disapproved of this notion.[3]

Seward remained undaunted by the disapproval. While Lincoln defined character in his respect of others, Seward defined it as honesty: "The first element of political character, or rather of public character is sincerity." And for Seward, nothing proved more sincere than insulting one's opponent. However, Seward would not mention this "Higher Law" philosophy as a Republican. The divide that the Kansas-Nebraska Act caused for the nation in 1854 also served as a divide for Seward. Instead of a more radical philosophy, Seward, as a Republican, would become more radical in his attacks on the opposition.

In Seward's defense, though, in order to gauge the radical nature of Seward's speech, it is vital to understand the context in which he delivered it. While one could conclude that Seward intended to forsake the entire Constitution, he, in fact, meant only to ignore one particular provision of the Compromise of 1850: the Fugitive Slave Law. He made no overt threats or insults against the South or northern Democrats. His statement had limited applicability. A speech he would deliver eight years later would not.

When Douglas unveiled his Kansas-Nebraska Act, Seward, like Lincoln, vehemently fought against it. Seward perceived that this act would permit slavery to spread unchecked over the western territories. Seward and thirteen senators, out of a total of fifty-two, voted against it. But the conflict in the Senate exposed the flaw in Seward's character, and gave a hint of a speech yet to come. While Lincoln urged all Americans to fight the new law, Seward instead seemed to welcome the new law as an opportunity to fight Americans. Seward delivered a speech in the Senate, in May of 1854, in which he stated, "Come on, then gentlemen of the slave states. Since there is no escaping your challenge, I accept it on behalf of the cause of freedom. We will engage in competition for the virgin soil of Kansas, and God give the victory to the side which is stronger in numbers as it is in right."[4]

During the next two years, Seward's antislavery crusade continued unabated until, with one defining speech, he once again propelled himself to the forefront of the national debate on slavery. In the fall of 1858, a divisive and passionate campaign engulfed New York. Republican candidates constantly begged Seward to speak on their behalf, and he delivered many speeches to help their cause. Of all his speeches, though, one outshone or over-shadowed, depending on one's perspective, all his speeches of that year, and, in many ways, eclipsed all the speeches he had ever given, or ever would give.

The philosophy that Seward would espouse in this speech was not orig-inal. Four months before, on June 16, 1858, Lincoln had spoken of this con-cept in his "House Divided" speech, when he predicted that the nation might become all free. For Lincoln, the speech became a political problem. None of his advisors approved of the speech when he first shared it with them. All expressed disappointment and condemnation; it was far too radical. William Herndon, Lincoln's law partner, admitted that Lincoln's statements were "true," but, he added, "is it wise or politic to say so?" One Republican declared it a "d — d fool utterance," while a more diplomatic individual described it as "ahead of its time." Lincoln had patiently listened to the advice, but made no changes. Lincoln's advisors proved correct. Douglas considered the speech great material for attacks on Lincoln, and referred to it in almost all the debates. Lincoln, on the other hand, mentioned it rarely, only choosing to debate it at those times when Douglas had attacked it.[5]

Despite the difficulty that the philosophy had proved to be for Lincoln, on October 25 Seward faced a friendly crowd at Rochester, New York, and delivered his "Irrepressible Conflict" speech. The speech would expose Seward's radical nature in philosophy and in words. Seward defined himself in this speech, and his view of America, both past and present. Some Amer-icans would praise this speech; others would vilify him for it.

Seward argued that "one of the chief elements of the value of human life is freedom in the pursuit of happiness" and the slave system was not only intol-erable, unjust, and inhuman" toward the slave but also to the "freeman" as well. "The slave system through its power completely controls all government where it is entrenched," he asserted. "In states where the slave system pre-vails, the masters, directly or indirectly, secure all political power, and con-stitute a ruling aristocracy. In states where the free-labor system prevails, universal suffrage necessarily obtains, and the state inevitably becomes, sooner or later, a republic or democracy."

These two tenets made slavery and free labor not only "incongruous," Seward asserted, but also "incompatible. They never have permanently existed together in one country, and they never can.... In the United States, slavery came into collision with free labor at the close of the last century, and fell before it in New England, New York, New Jersey, and Pennsylvania, but triumphed" over free labor in "Virginia, the Carolinas, and Georgia. Indeed, so incompatible are the two systems, that every new State which is organized within our ever-extending domain makes its first political act a choice of the one and the exclusion of the other, even at the cost of civil war...." From the New Yorker's perspective, "these antagonistic systems are continually coming into closer contact, and collision results."

The inevitable collision, Seward predicted, would leave one system dominant:

> Shall I tell you what this collision means? ... It is an irrepressible conflict between opposing and enduring forces, and it means that the United States must and will, sooner or later, become either entirely a slaveholding nation, or entirely a free-labor nation. Either the cotton and rice fields of South Carolina and the sugar plantations of Louisiana will ultimately be tilled by free labor, and Charleston and New Orleans become marts of legitimate merchandise alone, or else the rye-fields and wheat-fields of Massachusetts and New York must again be surrendered by their farmers to slave culture and to the production of slaves, and Boston and New York become once more markets for trade in the bodies and souls of men.

The time of compromise had passed, Seward claimed: "It is the failure to apprehend this great truth that induces so many unsuccessful attempts at final compromises between the slave and free States, and it is the existence of this great fact that renders all such pretended compromises, when made, vain and ephemeral." Seward argued that "our forefathers ... regarded the existence of the servile system in so many of the States with sorrow and shame" and "they knew that one or the other system must exclusively prevail."

Seward, having shelved his "Higher Law" argument, having made no mention of God or Holy Scripture, now reached for the Declaration of Independence, as had Lincoln. He stated that America's forefathers "based the whole structure of the government broadly on the principle that all men are created equal, and therefore free." Seward took issue with the southern congressman who declared the Declaration of Independence as a "self-evident lie" and also with Taney's Dred Scott decision. The forefathers never expected or anticipated "that, within the short period of one hundred years, their descendants would bear to be told by any orator, however popular, that the utterance of that principle were merely a rhetorical rhapsody; or by any judge, however venerated, that it was ... hypocritical and false. By the ordinance of 1787 they dedicated all of the national domain not yet polluted by slavery to free labor immediately, thenceforth and forever; while by the new constitution and laws they invited foreign free labor from all lands under the sun."

As for the African slave trader, they "interdicted the importation of African slave labor, at all times, in all places, and under all circumstances whatsoever." The forefathers "modified this policy of freedom" by permitting slavery to continue in "several States," intending that eventually, those states would "abolish slavery in their own way and at their own pleasure." But, the

Senator claimed, despite their compromises, "the fathers knew that the two systems could not endure within the Union, and expected within a short period slavery would disappear forever."

Both Seward's "Higher Law" speech and his "Irrepressible Conflict" speech exemplify his ability to threaten those with whom he disagreed, but he exhibited a far more radical and threatening nature in his "Irrepressible Conflict" speech. While his "Higher Law" doctrine proved more radical in the source of its philosophy, Holy Scripture, the "Irrepressible Conflict" speech proved more radical and threatening by the action it implied. The "Higher Law" speech targeted only a particular law, while his later speech targeted half the nation. Seward suggested not just ignoring the Fugitive Slave Law in the northern states, but imposing a whole new order on the southern states. Seward's choice of the word "conflict," at a time when a violent conflict engulfed Kansas, also proved a radical choice. The word only fanned the flames of those who believed in the militant nature of Seward and the Republican Party. Seward now seemed to call for an invasion against the South, and he received far more attention and abuse from southerners and northern conservatives than he ever had for his "Higher Law" speech.[6]

Some of Seward's biographers, recognizing the radical nature of Seward's speech, contend that the senator later regretted his "irrespressible conflict" statement, but they offer no convincing evidence to support their claim. One biographer alleges that Seward mentioned his disappointment over that phrase, during the Civil War, to a jailed southern sympathizer who then recorded Seward's supposed statement in a book she wrote in England. Dismissing this highly questionable source, the evidence points to a far different conclusion. Seward and his supporters exhibited great pride in the boldness that had predicted an "irrepressible conflict." Seward never discounted the phrase in any later speeches, and when the New Yorkers arrived in Chicago in 1860 for the convention, they proudly described themselves as the "irrespressibles." It was not Seward's nature to back down or retreat or admit wrong, but it was certainly his nature to pronounce frank statements without regard to the consequences or ramifications.[7]

While his "irrepressible conflict" phrase proved controversial, another part of his speech truly defined the difference between him and Lincoln, and again demonstrated a weakness of Seward's character. At one point in his speech, Seward, the former Whig, forgetting or simply ignoring the known fact that many current Republicans, known as Democratic-Republicans, had previously belonged to the Democratic Party, assaulted not just the current Democratic Party, but the Democratic Party throughout its entire existence: "The history of the Democratic party commits it to the policy of slavery. It has been the Democratic party, and no other agency, which has carried that policy up to its present alarming culmination." Claiming that the Democratic Party originated with President Monroe, Seward alleged that "at that time, in this State, and about that time many others of the free States, the Democratic party deliberately disenfranchised the free colored or African citizen," and the Democratic Party had "continued this disenfranchisement ever since. This was an effective aid to slavery; for, while the slaveholder votes for his slaves against freedom, the freed slave in the free States is prohibited from voting against slavery."

When the United States received territories after the Mexican War, the Democratic Party insisted that only slave states would be admitted from these lands, Seward argued. He recalled that "from 1840 to 1843 good and wise men counseled that Texas should remain outside the Union until she should consent to relinquish her self-instituted slavery; but the Democratic party precipitated her admission into the Union, not only without that condition, but even with a covenant that the State might be divided and reorganized so as to constitute four slave States instead of one." Democrats, he alleged, "refused to admit New Mexico as a free State, and only consented to admit California as a free State on the condition" that slavery would be permitted in "all of New Mexico and Utah" along with "the concession of perpetual slavery in the District of Columbia, and the passage of an unconstitutional, cruel, and humiliating law, for the recapture of fugitive slaves, with a further stipulation that the subject of slavery should never again be agitated in either chamber of Congress." The Kansas-Nebraska Act engineered by Douglas continued the Democratic Party's rampant advocacy for slavery's expansion.

In conclusion, Seward warned that "a revolution" had begun and "revolutions never go backward." "While the government of the United States, under the conduct of the democratic party, has been all that time surrendering one plain and castle after another to slavery, the people of the United States have been no less steadily and perseveringly gathering together the forces with which to recover back again all the fields and all the castles which have been lost, and to confound and overthrow, by one decisive blow, the betrayers of the constitution and freedom forever."[8]

Had Seward limited his criticism to present Democrats, he could be excused, but by criticizing all Democrats, both past and present, he personally and overtly insulted many current Republicans who had abandoned the Democratic Party over the Kansas-Nebraska Act. In this speech, Seward managed to threaten southerners and insult Democrats and even Democratic-Republicans, members of his own party. The only group that Seward left unscathed were Whig Republicans, like himself.

The reaction of one particular Democratic-Republican, Gideon Welles, demonstrates Seward's profound error. Welles, a discreet, highly respected leader of the Connecticut Republicans and one of the leading New England

Republicans who had proudly served as a Democrat prior to 1854, was, according to his biographer, "outraged" by Seward's "distortion of history for the benefit of the Whigs." Seward's assault on Democratic-Republicans seems all the more surprising because both Seward and his closest advisor, Thurlow Weed, had been desperately seeking Welles' support for Seward's presidential candidacy.

Welles was so incensed by Seward's accusation that, in a rare moment, he took pen to paper to publicly attack a fellow Republican in a scathing editorial on New York's *Evening Post*'s front page. "As an old Democratic Republican," Welles began, "I must dissent from some of the doctrinal points of Senator Seward's speech at Rochester on the 25th ult., and deny emphatically that the democratic party, at its origin and for many subsequent years, was committed to the policy of slavery." Welles found it "surprising" that Seward, a former Whig, "could not so far divest himself of old partisan feeling and prejudice as to forbear aspersing so large an element of the Republican party as those democrats who have signalized themselves in resisting the aggressions of slavery."

From Welles' perspective, the Kansas-Nebraska Act had transformed the political landscape, including the Democratic Party. "Of the so-called democratic party of the present day which embraces within its organization almost the whole of the whigs of the slave states, and no inconsiderable portion of them in the free states, I have nothing to say, except that, by whatever name it may be designated, it is not, in its men or measures, to be identified with the democratic party of the days of Jackson." Emphasizing the watershed since the time of Jackson, Welles argued that "the political issues then before the country related to the powers and limitations of the federal government and the practical questions before the country were the bank, internal improvements within the states by the federal government, and duties for protection instead of revenue." Welles believed that "slavery in no form of phase constituted a division between the two great parties."

In his final sentence, his final attack, Welles destroyed any hope that Seward and Weed might gain his support, or perhaps that of any other Democratic-Republican. Seward's "statement of historical facts is not only incorrect but unjust," he wrote, "and his doctrinal views are such as can never meet the approval of A DEMOCRATIC REPUBLICAN." Seward had, once again, demonstrated his ability for bluntness at the expense of political expediency, and by insulting Welles and all other Democratic Republicans, he had vividly displayed an inherent weakness that was distinctly lacking in a certain Republican from Illinois.[9]

One Republican praised Welles' response as "very able even for Gideon Welles." However, for the New York Republicans, the letter was shocking. One Republican was so dispirited about the Connecticut Republican's comments that he arranged a meeting between Seward, Welles and two other Republicans. The meeting was held, but they forged no compromise. Seward had created a wedge between the two men. Welles was in no mood to seek reconciliation, and Seward was in no mood to apologize. Welles later recalled of the meeting, "Of course we had no particular conversation and should not have agreed if we had."[10]

The editors of the *Evening Post,* who published Welles' editorial, added their evaluation to the Seward-Welles controversy by agreeing with Welles, and also agreeing with Seward. The editors commended Welles for correctly identifying "the true period of the formation of the democratic party, and gives a just view of its original objects, and accurate narrative of its gradual degeneracy." However, by focusing solely on Seward's attack on the Democratic Party, the editors thought "that, in one respect," Welles failed "to do justice to Mr. Seward's views. That slavery and freedom are incompatible, as affirmed by Mr. Seward, we believe as implicitly as we believe the incompatibility of any other opposites. If either one of them has the ascendancy in the Union the other must yield." The editors agreed with Seward's contention that "the triumphs of the slave power achieved in the United States with a few years past, have astonished the world." Knowing how easily a militant interpretation could be applied to Seward's speech, they believed that "the time has now arrived in which slavery must begin to decline, not by the effect of any new exercise of the central power, or any disregard of the rights of the states; nor do we perceive that any such means are even hinted at in Mr. Seward's speech; but simply by the effect of its own unpopularity — simply by the force of that general disesteem which the possession of political supremacy in the Union has enabled it so long to resist."

At least one other Republican concurred with the editors of the *Evening Post.* "I agree with Seward in his 'Irrepressible Conflict,'" Lincoln later wrote. He had argued the same philosophy in his "House Divided" speech just four months before, but he never made any statements that agreed with Seward's depiction of the Democratic Party's history.[11]

Despite angering some Republicans, the "Irrepressible Conflict" speech had no immediate effect on Seward's presidential aspirations. He remained the Republican Party's dominant and most popular figure, and the party's expected presidential nominee.

3

Defining a Lincoln Republican Party

November 1858–August 1859

After his defeat in November, Lincoln came to one, simple, inescapable conclusion: his political career had ended. Lincoln continually expressed regret for having lost the election and urged Republicans to continue a fight in which he believed that he would play no part. He had made two unsuccessful attempts since 1854, and could not foresee any possibility of a third.

While Lincoln anticipated no future in politics, Seward, on the other hand, paraded about as the next president of the United States, and not just within the United States. The New York Republican held such high confidence of his destiny that, foregoing the necessity of delivering any speeches in the United States to secure his presidential nomination, he traveled to Europe, Asia and Africa. For seven months, from May until December of 1859, with less than a year remaining until the convention, he remained completely out of the country. Dignitaries in London, Paris, Rome, Egypt, Beirut, Belgium and Holland entertained the person to whom they next expected the crown to fall. He attended audiences with Queen Victoria, the British Prime Minister, King Victor Emanuel of Piedmont-Sardinia, King Leopold I of Belgium, Napoleon III of France, and even Pope Pius IX, who commented on Seward's future expected "higher advancement." In Beirut, Seward even found time to purchase four Arabian horses, three for himself and one for the Republican senator Simon Cameron of Pennsylvania. On the other hand, during these same months, Lincoln remained entirely within the state of Illinois, a vast majority of his time in Springfield, toiling away at a myriad of mundane law cases in his two-man law firm.[1]

Yet his law cases provide insight into a fundamental principle of Lincoln's character — his consistent ability to attack the issue and not the person — as opposed to Seward's tendency to assault the issue and the proponents of the issue. One particular case involving a Revolutionary War veteran's widow best illustrates the difference between them. Lincoln's law partner, William H. Herndon, declared that, in this case, he had never witnessed Lincoln "so wrought up." One day a widow, "crippled and bent with age, came hobbling" into their office to tell her tale. A pension agent had not refunded the widow for a "portion of a fee." Lincoln, "stirred up" by the widow's story, visited the agent and demanded the return of the fee. The agent refused, Lincoln became incensed and took the case. At the trail, he informed the jury:

> Time rolls by, the heroes of '76 have passed away and are encamped on the other shore. The soldier has gone to rest, and now, crippled, blinded, and broken, his widow comes to you and to me, gentlemen of the jury, to right her wrongs. She was not always thus. She was once a beautiful young woman. Her step as elastic, her face as fair, and her voice as sweet as any that rang in the mountains of old Virginia. But now she is poor and defenseless. Out here on the prairies of Illinois, many hundreds of miles away from the scenes of her childhood, she appeals to us, who enjoy the privileges achieved for us by the patriots of the Revolution, for our sympathetic aid and manly protection.

The speech brought tears, indignation, and victory. Lincoln's notes for his presentation were simple: "No contract.— Not professional services.— Unreasonable charge.— Money retained by Def't not given by Pl'ff.— Revolutionary War.— Describe Valley Forge privations.— Ice — Soldiers bleeding feet.— Pl'ff's husband.— Soldier leaving home for army.— Skin Def't.— Close."[2] And skin him he did. He won the case and covered all the widow's costs, including her hotel bill and her transportation home.

And yet he never once personally criticized or attacked the opposition. He kept his focus on the issue in the case, a trait that he also employed in his political life. Where Seward attacked slavery and all Democrats, Lincoln attacked only slavery.

While Seward could focus on his upcoming international trip in November and December of 1858, Lincoln had only his recent defeat to consider, and Republican friends throughout the North wrote him letters of condolence. "Your very kind and complimentary letter of the 15th was received yesterday," Lincoln replied to one, "and for which I sincerely thank you. In the last canvass I strove to do my whole duty both to our cause, and to the kind friends" who had supported him. He hoped that "those friends find no cause to regret that they did not assign that post to other hands." "Even though it has ended in personal defeat," he believed that the "seed has been sown that will yet produce fruit. The fight must go on. Douglas managed to be supported both as the best means to break down, and to uphold the slave power. No ingenuity can long keep those opposing elements in harmony. Another explosion will come before a great while."[3]

To another he wrote, "Well, the election is over; and, in the main point, we are beaten. Still, my view is that the fight must go on. Let no one falter. The question is not half settled." He predicted that "new splits and divisions will soon be upon our adversaries; and we shall [have] fun again."[4] To a third Republican he declared: "The fight must go on. We are right, and can not finally fail. There will be another blow-up in the so-called democratic party before long." He added, "In the mean time, let all Republicans stand fast by their guns."[5] Lincoln wrote in a similar vein to one of the editors of the *Chicago Press and Tribune*, the newspaper which had provided him unflinching support. Lincoln heard that the editor was "feeling like h-ll yet." "Quit that," he admonished him. "You will soon feel better. Another 'blow-up' is coming; and we shall have fun again."[6] Lincoln wrote another supporter: "I expect the result of the election went hard with you. So it did with me, too, perhaps not quite so hard as you may have supposed. I have an abiding faith that we shall beat them in the long run. Step by step the objects of the leaders will become too plain for the people to stand them. I write merely to let you know that I am neither dead nor dying."[7] In all of these letters, he never once expressed a belief that he would become, or hoped to become, a candidate again.

His friends hoped otherwise. When Lincoln failed in his first attempt to win a United States Senate seat, he had thrown his support to Lyman Trumbull, who, despite having served faithfully in the Democratic Party for years, professed abhorrence toward Douglas's Kansas-Nebraska Act. Despite their political differences prior to 1854, Lincoln and Trumbull as Republicans shared common ground. Lincoln even devoted a considerable amount of time defending Trumbull during one of the Lincoln-Douglas debates. After Lincoln's defeat, Trumbull attempted to give Lincoln some direction, some path from his personal despair, by suggesting that he consider seeking a congressional seat. Lincoln completely rejected the idea: "I have not the slightest thought of being a candidate for Congress in this District. I am not spoken of in that connection; and I can scarcely conceive what has misled Mr. Underwood in regard to the matter."

Lincoln also replied to Trumbull concerning speculation that he wanted Trumbull's Senate seat. Some had accused the Democratic-Republicans, including Trumbull, of failing to fully support Lincoln's 1858 campaign, and Lincoln wrote his fellow Republican: "The article mentioned by you, prepared for the *Chicago Journal*, I have not seen; nor do I wish to see it, though I heard of it a month, or more, ago. Any effort to put enmity between you and me is as idle as the wind. I do not for a moment doubt that you, Judd, Cook, Palmer, and the republicans generally, coming from the old democratic ranks, were as sincerely anxious for my success in the late contest as I myself and the old whig republicans were." Lincoln also told Trumbull that he would not seek Trumbull's Senate seat: "I can not conceive it possible for me to be a rival of yours, or to take sides against you in favor of any rival." Lincoln would not consider opposing Trumbull, who shared the same ground with him on the crucial issue of slavery. He simply had no practical political options for either the House of Representatives or the Senate.[8]

But there was the presidency. Lincoln received a letter from a supporter who recommended him for the highest office in the land. Lincoln also brushed aside the suggestion: "I must, in candor, say I do not think myself fit for the Presidency. I certainly am flattered, and gratified, and some partial friends think of me in that connection; but I really think it best for our cause that no concerted effort, such as you suggest, should be made." However, apparently keeping his options open, he added, "Let this be considered confidential."[9]

In response to another Republican who asked for Lincoln's opinion of Ohio governor Chase's abilities, and his own presidential future, Lincoln appeared even less optimistic. "As to Gov. Chase, I have a kind side for him," he admitted, because Chase "was one of the few distinguished men of the nation who gave us, in Illinois, their sympathy last year." However, Lincoln had questions concerning Chase's value as a presidential candidate: "I never saw him, [I] suppose him to be able, and right-minded; but still he may not be the most suitable as a candidate for the Presidency." But he had even more questions about himself: "I must say I do not think myself fit for the Presidency." This time though, he did not request that his statement remain confidential.[10]

Lincoln had denied any interest in seeking a congressional seat, a senate seat, and confessed that he did not have the qualifications for the presidency. He had eliminated all political options. In March of 1859, over a year after he began his campaign against Douglas, he must have admitted that his political career had come to an unimpressive and uninspiring end.

Yet, while Lincoln lost hope for his own political career, he still believed that the Republican Party stood as the nation's only hope, the only force that stood in slavery's path, the only instrument that could halt slavery's spread. But the eight months from January to April of 1859 marked a critical time for the members of the young party. They had to remain united and focused on their common ground. But this was no easy task.

The Republican Party constituted an amalgamation of many different political philosophies. Former Free Soilers advocated an abolitionist creed. Former Democrats and former Whigs harbored opposing opinions on tariffs, internal improvements, and the bank — issues that had divided their parties prior to 1854. To further complicate the task, the Republicans also had to appeal to those voters in the four northern states they had lost in the 1856 presidential election: Illinois, Indiana, Pennsylvania and New Jersey.

From March 1859 until August 1859 Lincoln freely dispensed advice to those party members who contacted him, and he even took the stage once to lead by example. In providing this advice, though, Lincoln became more and more frustrated with the lack of philosophical cohesion among the narrowly focused members of his party.

On January 10, Republican congressman Israel Washburn[11] of New Hampshire, in the House of Representatives, rose to defend the Republican Party. He claimed that "two antagonistic ideas underlie the political movements of the country" which he defined as "the democratic and the aristocratic. The democratic affirms the equal rights of all men; while the aristocratic denies the existence of such rights, and divides mankind into classes — a governing and privileged class, and a governed and disabled class." To Washburn, "The real question before the American people is, which is the true government: that which recognizes the democratic idea, or that which builds upon the aristocratic? I know of no better statement of the former than is to be found in the Declaration of Independence. Say the authors of that great instrument:

> We hold these truths to be self evident, that all men are created equal; that they are endowed by their Creator with certain inalienable rights; that among these are life, liberty, and the pursuit of happiness. That to secure these rights governments are instituted among men, DERIVING THEIR JUST POWERS FROM THE CONSENT OF THE GOVERNED."

Washburn then quoted from a document he considered the antithesis of the Declaration of Independence: Kansas' Lecompton Constitution, written by the proslavery men of that territory: "A practical and authoritative exposition of the latter [aristocratic] is contained in the Lecompton constitution, the seventh article of which reads as follows: 'The right of property is before and higher than any constitutional sanction,' read Washburn, 'and the right of the owner of a slave to such slave and its increase is the same, and as inviolable, as the right of the owner of any property whatever.'"

The Democratic Party abided by the proslavery "doctrines of the Lecompton constitution," he declared: "The Republican party draws its inspiration, its principles, and its lessons of duty, from the Declaration of Independence." He described the "self-styled Democratic party" as "essentially a southern or slaveholders' party. Its policy, in reference to all questions of national or political interest, is dictated by the slaveholders." The Democrats, Washburn asserted, had "yielded" to the slaveholders and pursued numerous policies solely for the slaveholders' benefit. These policies included demanding "the admission of Oregon into the Union as a State, with a constitution which denies to colored persons, although they may be citizens of sovereign States under the constitutions thereof, the right to maintain suits at law for the vindication of any right, or the redress of any wrong."

Washburn continued: "After years of uneasiness and apprehension, it became apparent to the people of the free States that the Democratic party, as it calls itself, had been subsidized by the slaveholders." The congressman also argued that "it was seen that among the organizations of the day there was no one which, from its combined earnestness and liberality, was competent to maintain the cause of liberty and republicanism against the plottings of the slaveholding oligarchy" until the creation of the "REPUBLICAN PARTY." Washburn claimed that "it is suggestive of the better days of the Republic" and "its associations are of liberty, order, and law; it is the name by which the author of the Declaration of Independence, and the father of the Constitution, chose to be known...." He contended that "the party which is worthy to wear it [the name Republican] should hold every lover of liberty, every hater of oppression, every opponent of slavery fanaticism, whether in the North or in the South, for it draws the breath of its life from the Declaration of Independence, and it 'stands in defense of the Constitution.'"[12]

Seeking the Illinois Republican's assessment, Washburn's brother, Elihu, sent Lincoln a copy of the speech. Lincoln replied, "I have just received your brother's speech sent me by yourself. I had read it before; and you will oblige me by presenting him with my respects, and telling him I doubly thank him for making it—first, because the points are so just and well put; and next, because it is so well timed. We needed, from some one who can get the public attention, just such a speech just at this time. His objection to the Oregon constitution because it excludes free negroes, is the only thing I wish he had omitted." Here Lincoln displayed his desire that the Republicans uphold the Declaration of Independence as the ultimate goal, but remain focused on the immediate goal: halting slavery's expansion. Not all Republicans, as Lincoln knew from his time in Illinois, supported his ideas of equality. Illinoisans had approved one of the most stringent Black Codes in the nation, laws that outlawed immigration of free African Americans. However, all Republicans despised Douglas's Kansas-Nebraska Act and slavery's spread into the western territories. Washburn had correctly attacked the Democratic Party and defended the Republicans, but, in Lincoln's opinion, he had overextended himself by speaking against a provision that was not yet universally accepted by all Republicans.[13]

Whether Lincoln personally favored the Black Codes and Oregon's exclusion of free African Americans is best conveyed in a private letter that he wrote to a friend just four years before. His friend had apparently inquired as to whether Lincoln supported the anti-immigrant Know-Nothing party. Lincoln wrote:

> I am not a Know-Nothing. That is certain. How could I be? How can any one who abhors the oppression of negroes, be in favor of degrading classes of white people? Our progress in degeneracy appears to me pretty rapid. As a nation, we begin by declaring that "all men are created equal." We now practically read it "all men are created equal, except negroes." When the Know-Nothings get control, it will read "all men are created equal, except negroes, and foreigners, and catholics." When it comes to this I should prefer emigrating to some country where they make no pretence of loving liberty — to Russia, for instance, where despotism can be taken pure, and without the base alloy of hypocracy.

The Know-Nothings had attempted to oppose recent immigrants by denying them their right to suffrage. Here in this letter Lincoln used the same language from the Declaration of Independence to oppose the denial of suffrage that he used to oppose slavery. This enlightening paragraph demonstrates Lincoln's egalitarian interpretation of the "all men are created equal" phrase by arguing that these words guaranteed freedom *for all people* regardless of color ("negroes"), religion ("catholics"), or place of birth ("foreigners"). Obviously, it would have been a case of gross inconsistency of Lincoln's personal interpretation of the Declaration of Independence if he justified all these freedoms and also believed that the Declaration denied the right for some to live in all states of the nation.[14]

It is worthy of note, though, that when the Senate had debated the admission of Oregon the previous year, Seward voted for the bill although he expressed his "regret" that the state constitution "excludes people of African descent, though free." Lyman Trumbull, as a close political associate of Lincoln's and an Illinois Republican senator, assailed Seward by arguing that it was Congress's duty to "prevent the spread of slavery" into the territories but that as a senator, Trumbull had "no power to prevent Oregon "or any other State" from "dealing with her black population as shall seem to her best." Trumbull correctly understood common ground upon which Republicans stood; Seward did not.[15]

Four weeks after Washburn spoke on March 1, Lincoln, for the first time since his defeat, returned to the stage with a speech in one of the most Republican cities in his state: Chicago. In his remarks, Lincoln focused on the mistakes of his campaign against Douglas and how he wanted to apply those lessons learned to the Republican Party's upcoming 1860 campaign.

His speech marked "the first on which I have appeared before an audience since the campaign of last year," Lincoln reminded them. In referring to the 1858 campaign, he expressed his "thanks for the gallant support that you of the city of Chicago and of Cook County gave to the cause in which we were all engaged in the late momentous struggle in Illinois." He was "gratified that during that canvass and since, however disappointing its termination, there was among my party friends so little fault found in me as to the manner in which I bore my part."

He then, without mentioning it, accepted blame for his "House Divided" philosophy which he first stated in his "House Divided" speech. The philosophy remained a constant issue throughout the 1858 campaign in his speeches and in almost all the debates. The philosophy infuriated some Republicans because Lincoln stated that the nation might become all free. This prediction angered some of his supporters who interpreted it as an "abolitionist" sentiment which could only serve to threaten southerners. One prominent Republican, Judge T. Lyle Dickey, whom Lincoln considered a friend, actually defected to Douglas's campaign and appeared on the platform with Douglas at the first debate.

In discussing this sensitive issue, Lincoln carefully avoided any mention of the defectors whom he knew personally. It was the closest Lincoln would ever come to admitting that he had overreached in that speech. Lincoln suggested that there was a lesson to be learned from his mistake, a lesson from which the Republican Party as a whole could learn — focus on the containment of slavery and do not become distracted and divided on the other minor issues: "I remember in that canvass but one instance of dissatisfaction with my course, and I allude to that, not for the purpose of reviving any matter of dispute or producing any unpleasant feeling, but in order to help get rid of the point upon which that matter of disagreement or dissatisfaction arose." Lincoln indicated his understanding as follows:

> In some speeches I made I said something, or was supposed to have said something, that some very good people, as I really believe them to be, commented upon unfavorably, and said that rather than support one holding such sentiments as I had expressed, the real friends of liberty could afford to wait awhile. I don't want to say anything that shall excite unkind feeling, and I mention this simply to suggest that I am afraid of the effect of that sort of argument. I do not doubt that it comes from good men, but I am afraid of the result upon organized action where great results are in view, if any of us allow ourselves to seek out minor or separate points on which there may be difference of views as to policy and right, and let them keep us from uniting in action upon a great principle in a cause on which we all agree; or are deluded into the belief that all can be brought to consider alike and agree upon every minor point before we unite and press forward in organization, asking the cooperation of all good men in that resistance to the extension of slavery upon which we all agree.

If the Republicans failed to remain united on their common ground, he said, "I am afraid that such methods would result in keeping the friends of liberty waiting longer than we ought to. I say this for the purpose of suggesting that we consider whether it would not be better and wiser, so long as we all agree that this matter of slavery is a moral, political and social wrong, and ought to be treated as a wrong, not to let anything minor or subsidiary to that main principle and purpose make us fail to cooperate."

Horace Greeley, as editor of the *New York Tribune* during the 1858 senate campaign, had urged Republicans to consider supporting Douglas. Lincoln had not forgotten. "One other thing," he stated, "and that again I say in no spirit of unkindness. There was a question amongst Republicans all the time of the canvass of last year, and it has not quite ceased yet, whether it was not the true and better policy for the Republicans to make it their chief object to reelect Judge Douglas to the Senate of the United States." "I differed with those who thought that the true policy," Lincoln acknowledged, "but I have never said an unkind word of any one entertaining that opinion." He believed that "most of them were as sincerely the friends of our cause as I claim to be myself; yet I thought they were mistaken...."

Lincoln, in stark contrast to Seward, stated, "In what I say now there is no unkindness even towards Judge Douglas." However, he warned that "if we, the Republicans of this State, had made Judge Douglas our candidate for the Senate of the United States last year and had elected him, there would to-day be no Republican party in this Union." He argued that "the Republican principle, the profound central truth" lay in their belief "that slavery is wrong and ought to be dealt with as a wrong." That principle, he claimed, "cannot advance at all upon Judge Douglas' ground," for the Senator "does not care whether it is voted up or voted down, as it is simply a question of dollars and cents. Whenever, in any compromise or arrangement or combination that may promise some temporary advantage, we are led upon that ground, then and there the great living principle upon which we have organized as a party is surrendered."[16]

In closing, he advocated one immediate political goal for his party. "I do not wish to be misunderstood upon this subject of slavery," he asserted. "I suppose it may long exist, and perhaps the best way for it to come to an end peaceably is for it to exist for a length of time. But I say that the spread and strengthening and perpetuation of it is an entirely different proposition. There we should in every way resist it as a wrong, treating it as a wrong, with the fixed idea that it must and will come to an end." He pleaded with the Republicans:

> All you have to do is to keep the faith, to remain steadfast to the right, to stand by your banner. Nothing should lead you to leave your guns. Stand together, ready, with match in hand. Allow nothing to turn you to the right or to the left. Remember how long you have been in setting out on the true course; how long you have been in getting your neighbors to understand and

believe as you now do. Stand by your principles; stand by your guns; and victory complete and permanent is sure at the last.[17]

However, Lincoln's speech in Chicago, recorded by a *Chicago Press and Tribune* reporter, never saw the light of day until decades later. Lincoln confessed to the reporter his regret for having made comments that could be interpreted as insulting Greeley, and he requested that the paper not publish the speech. The reporter agreed. The speech and the interchange with the reporter highlighted another Lincoln quality that Seward lacked. Lincoln could admit when he was wrong.[18]

Lincoln's correspondence in the subsequent months continued to espouse the philosophy that he had expressed in his letters and in his Chicago speech. He had been invited to "attend a Festival in Boston" held "in honor of the birth-day of Thomas Jefferson," but, Lincoln regretfully responded, "my engagements are such that I can not attend." While a simple note would have sufficed, he could not pass on the opportunity to extol the wisdom of Jefferson, and his Declaration of Independence and to criticize the Democratic Party. Lincoln remembered "that the Jefferson party was formed upon their supposed superior devotion to the personal rights of men" while "holding the rights of property to be secondary only." Lincoln found it "equally interesting to note how completely the two have changed hands as to the principle upon which they were originally supposed to be divided." The Democratic Party "of to-day hold[s] the liberty of one man to be absolutely nothing, when in conflict with another man's right of property. Republicans, on the contrary, are for both the man and the dollar; but in cases of conflict, the man before the dollar."

"The principles of Jefferson are the definitions and axioms of free society," Lincoln declared. "And yet they are denied, and evaded, with no small show of success. One dashingly calls them 'glittering generalities'; another bluntly calls them 'self evident lies'; and still others insidiously argue that they apply only to 'superior races.' These expressions," he claimed, "differing in form, are identical in object and effect — the supplanting the principles of free government, and restoring those of classification, caste, and legitimacy. They would delight a convocation of crowned heads, plotting against the people. They are the van-guard — the miners, and sappers — of returning despotism. We must repulse them, or they will subjugate us."

He concluded with three evocative sentences. "This is a world of compensations and he who would be no slave, must consent to have no slave. Those who deny freedom to others, deserve it not for themselves; and, under a just God, can not long retain it." Of the author of the Declaration of Independence, he wrote, "All honor to Jefferson — to the man who, in the concrete pressure of a struggle for national independence by a single people, had the coolness, forecast, and capacity to introduce into a merely revolutionary document, an abstract truth, applicable to all men and all times, and so to embalm it there, that to-day, and in all coming days, it shall be a rebuke and a stumbling-block to the very harbingers of re-appearing tyranny and oppression."[19] The Declaration of Independence and the phrase "all men are created equal" remained Lincoln's moral compass.[20]

To a Kansas Republican who requested advice for the state's platform, Lincoln wrote: "The only danger will be the temptation to lower the Republican Standard in order to gather recruits. In my judgment such a step would be a serious mistake — would open a gap through which more would pass out than pass in. And this would be the same, whether the letting down should be in deference to Douglasism, or to the southern opposition element." He feared that either compromise "would surrender the o[b]ject of the Republican organization — the preventing the spread and nationalization of Slavery. This object surrendered, the organization would go to pieces." Despite the line he had drawn, he did "not mean by this, that no southern man must be placed upon our Republican National ticket for 1860. There are many men in the slave states for any one of whom I would cheerfully vote to be either President or Vice President provided he would enable me to do so safely to the Republican cause — without lowering the Republican Standard." If the Republicans compromised, if "a union be attempted on the basis of ignoring the Slavery question, and magnifying other questions which the people just now are really caring nothing about, and it will result in gaining no single electoral vote in the South and losing ev[e]ry one in the North."[21]

Lincoln, though, found himself continually tested with the issue of fusion and compromise. The German Republicans constituted a significant portion of the party whose support was vital for Republican victory, and they were understandably sensitive to any attempts to disenfranchise immigrants, or to withhold citizenship from immigrants. A group of German Republicans composed a letter to Lincoln concerning a Massachusetts constitutional change that intended to place limitations on immigrants.

Lincoln replied: "Your note asking, in behalf of yourself and other German [sic] citizens, whether I am for or against the constitutional provision in regard to naturalized citizens, lately adopted by Massachusetts; and whether I am for or against a fusion of the republicans, and other opposition elements, for the canvass of 1860, is received." He recognized that "Massachusetts is a sovereign and independent state; and it is no privilege of mine to scold her for what she does. Still, if from what she has done, an inference is sought to be drawn as to what I would do, I may, without impropriety, speak out. I say then, that, as I understand the Massachusetts provision, I am against its adoption in Illinois, or in any other place, where I have a right to oppose it." The opinion appeared easy to expect considering Lincoln's interpretation of the Declaration: "Understanding the spirit of our institutions to aim at the elevation of men, I am opposed to whatever tends to degrade them. I have some little notoriety for commiserating the oppressed condition of the negro; and I should be strangely inconsistent if I could favor any project for curtailing the existing rights of white men, even though born in different lands, and speaking different languages from myself."

As for a union with other parties, Lincoln agreed to the idea, conditionally: "As to the matter of fusion, I am for it, if it can be had on republican grounds; and I am not for it on any other terms. A fusion on any other terms, would be as foolish as unprincipled." Not only would he oppose a compromise for philosophical reasons, but for practical ones as well: "It would lose the whole North, while the common enemy would still carry the whole South." However, "the question of men is a different one. There are good patriotic men, and able statesmen, in the South whom I would cheerfully support, if they would now place themselves on republican ground. But I am against letting down the republican standard a hair's breadth."[22]

Lincoln also addressed Republicans concerning the opposition to the Fugitive Slave Law. To Chase, the Ohio Republican governor, Lincoln wrote, "Please pardon the liberty I take in addressing you, as I now do. It appears by the papers that the late Republican State convention of Ohio adopted a Platform, of which the following is one plank, 'A repeal of the atrocious Fugitive Slave Law.'"

Lincoln personally opposed the Fugitive Slave Law. Just four years before, in a private letter to a friend, he made use of the word "hate," a word which rarely appeared in his correspondence. He wrote, "I hate to see the poor creatures hunted down, and caught, and carried back to their stripes, and unrewarded toils." Illinois' stringent Black Codes proved a constant reminder to Lincoln that his personal views were incongruent with a majority of those who resided in his home state. Lincoln's advice to Chase best portrayed his belief that while the ideals expressed in the Declaration of Independence encompassed the final goal — freedom for all — the immediate goal — halting slavery's spread in the territories could be accomplished only by prevailing in 1860, and to fight the Fugitive Slave Law in 1860 would lose the election and their best opportunity to halt slavery's spread.[23]

Lincoln informed Chase that this plank "is already damaging us here. I have no doubt that if that plank be even *introduced* into the next Republican National convention, it will explode it. Once introduced, its supporters and it's [*sic*] opponents will quarrel irreconcilably. The latter believe the U.S. constitution declares that a fugitive slave '*shall be delivered up*'; and they look upon the above plank as dictated by the spirit which declares a fugitive slave '*shall not be delivered up.*'" Lincoln concluded with a plea for a dose of reality: "I enter upon no argument one way or the other; but I assure you the cause of Republicanism is hopeless in Illinois, if it be in any way made responsible for that plank. I hope you can, and will, contribute something to relieve us from it."[24]

Chase then requested Lincoln's views. The lawyer replied with a rather long legal opinion that concluded with his statement that "congress has constitutional authority to enact a Fugitive Slave law" even if he personally opposed the law, although he did not mention his personal opinion in the letter. "But," Lincoln continued, "I did not write you on this subject, with any view of discussing the constitutional question." His intention had been more practical in regard to the upcoming 1860 elections. "My only object was to impress you with what I believe is true, that the introduction of a proposition for repeal of the Fugitive Slave Law, into the next Republican National convention, will explode the convention and the party. Having turned your attention to the point, I wish to do no more."[25]

Lincoln defined to another Republican the only strategy he believed would successfully elect a Republican president in 1860. In referring to the Democratic Party as the "rotten democracy," he wrote, "If the rotten democracy shall be beaten in 1860, it has to be done by the North; no human intervention can deprive them of the South. I do not deny that there are as good men in the South as the North; and I guess we will elect one of them if he will allow us to do so on Republican ground. I think there can be no other ground of Union. For my single self I would be willing to risk some Southern men without a platform; but I am satisfied that is not the case with the Republican party generally."[26]

To another party member, a more radical one, Schuyler Colfax of Indiana, Lincoln expressed complete and utter frustration with the Republicans throughout the nation. He warned "against divisions in the Republican ranks generally, and particularly for the contest of 1860. The point of danger," he knew, "is the temptation in different localities to 'platform' for something which will be popular just there, but which, nevertheless, will be a firebrand elsewhere, and especially in a National convention." He railed against several short-sighted Republican policies such as "the movement against foreigners in Massachusetts; in New-Hampshire, to make obedience to the Fugitive Slave law, punishable as a crime; in Ohio, to repeal the Fugitive Slave law; and squatter sovereignty in Kansas. In these things there is explosive matter enough to blow up half a dozen national conventions, if it gets into them; and what gets rife outside of conventions is very likely to find it's [*sic*] way into them." Lincoln suggested that "what is desirable, if possible, is that in every local convention of Republicans, a point should be made to avoid every-thing which will distract republicans elsewhere." As for the states he had men-tioned, Lincoln advised: "Massachusetts republicans should have looked beyond their noses; and then they could not have failed to see that tilting against foreigners would ruin us in the whole North-West. New Hampshire and Ohio should forbear tilting against the Fugitive Slave law in such way as [to] utterly overwhelm us in Illinois with the change of enmity to the con-stitution itself. Kansas, in her confidence that she can be saved to freedom on 'squatter sovereignty'—ought not to forget that to prevent the spread and nationalization of slavery is a national concern, and must be attended to by the nation." He pleaded, "In a word, in every locality we should look beyond our noses; and at least say nothing on points where it is probable we shall disagree." Colfax replied, "he who could accomplish it, is worthier than Napoleon or [Victor] Emanuel [*sic*]."[27]

The following month Lincoln traveled to Iowa, marking the first time that year that he journeyed outside the state of Illinois. His trip had no polit-ical purpose — he intended to view some property that had been given to him as payment for a debt. While he stayed in Council Bluffs, Iowa, though, he did deliver a political speech but unfortunately only a brief summary of it remains.

Throughout the first six months of 1859 Lincoln consistently delivered one message to his fellow Republicans: focus on halting the expansion of slav-ery and make no statements and no resolutions that would distract from this goal or would anger those who agreed on principle to the restriction of slav-ery. Opposition to Douglas's Kansas-Nebraska Act should remain the com-mon ground upon which the party stood, and with which it would do battle in 1860. The Declaration of Independence was the nation's cornerstone and the ideal to which it should progress, but they should fight the Kansas-Nebraska issue now as the first battle toward the ultimate goal.

Throughout the early months of 1859 Lincoln had remained off the stage and out of public view. But in the fall of that year, he returned to the stage once again, to battle the one person who had brought him back into politics five years before.

4

Douglas Assails the Republicans in Ohio

September 1859

In the fall of 1859, Douglas opened his presidential campaign in the North. He fired his first salvo in a long article titled "The Dividing Line between Federal and Local Authority: Popular Sovereignty in the Territories," which was featured in the most popular national publication of the day, *Harper's Weekly*. After this article, he took to the road to attack his opposition and chose a pivotal northern state — Ohio — for his tour.

Douglas's Harper's article and Ohio speeches would prove critical to Lincoln. In all of Lincoln's political speeches from September of 1859 until the convention, Lincoln, above all other issues, would focus upon and would contradict the philosophy that Douglas argued in the Harper's article and the Ohio speeches.

Douglas opened his article with a declaration: "Under our complex system of government it is the first duty of American statesmen to mark distinctly the dividing line between Federal and Local authority. To do this with accuracy involves an inquiry, not only into the powers and duties of the Federal Government under the Constitution, but also into the rights, privileges and immunities of the people of the Territories, as well as of the States composing the Union." While "the relative powers and functions of the Federal and State governments have become well understood," Douglas found, "the disputed question — involving the right of the people of the Territories to govern themselves in respect to their local affairs and internal polity — remains a fruitful source of partisan strife and sectional controversy. The political organization which was formed in 1854, and has assumed the name of the Republican party, is based on the theory that African slavery, as it exists in

38

this country, is an evil of such magnitude — social, moral, and political — as to justify and require the exertion of the entire power and influence of the Federal Government" to result in slavery's "ultimate extinction."

Douglas argued that the philosophy espoused by Seward and Lincoln constituted the philosophy of the entire party. The Democratic Party believed that the nation could continue peaceably half-free and half-slave; the Republicans did not. The Republicans were the radicals, Douglas alleged, because they predicted a "an irrepressible conflict between freedom and slavery, free labor and slave labor, free States and slave States, which is irreconcilable, and must continue to rage with increasing fury until the one shall become universal by the annihilation of the other." To support his claim, he quoted Seward, or as he described it, "the language of the most eminent and authoritative expounder of their political faith":

> It is an irrepressible conflict between the opposing and enduring forces; and it means that the United States must and will, sooner or later, become entirely a slaveholding nation or entirely a free labor nation. Either the cotton and rice fields of South Carolina, and the sugar plantations of Louisiana, will ultimately be tilled by free labor, and Charleston and New Orleans become marts for legitimate merchandise alone, or else the rye fields and wheat fields of Massachusetts and New York must again be surrendered by their farmers to slave culture and to the production of slaves, and Boston and New York become once more markets for trade in the bodies and souls of men.

Douglas argued that this notion was not unique to Seward, but was held by other Republicans as well. In referring to Lincoln, Douglas wrote: "In the Illinois canvass of 1858 the same proposition was advocated and defended by the distinguished Republican standard-bearer in these words:

> In my opinion it [the slavery agitation] will not cease until a crisis shall have been reached and passed. "A house divided against itself can not stand." I believe that government can not endure permanently half slave and half free. I do not expect the house to fall, but I do expect it will cease to be divided. It will become all one thing or all the other. Either the opponents of slavery will arrest the further spread of it, and place it where the public mind shall rest in the belief that it is in the course of ultimate extinction, or its advocates will push forward till it shall become alike lawful in all the States — old as well as new, North as well as South.

Douglas concluded that these two men, advocating the philosophy of their party, accurately portrayed the Republicans as a party intent on sectional war. "Thus it will be seen, that under the auspices of a political party, which claims sovereignty in Congress over the subject of slavery, there can be no peace on the slavery question — no truce in the sectional strife — no fraternity between the North and South, so long as this Union remains as our fathers made it — divided into free and slave States....

The Democrats adhered to the opposite notion, one of peace, by respecting the rightful authority of territorial residents. "The Democratic party" Douglas contended, "is a unit in its irreconcilable opposition to the doctrines and principles of the Republican party." He admitted, however, that "there are radical differences of opinion in respect to the powers and duties of Congress, and the rights and immunities of the people of the Territories under the Federal Constitution, which seriously disturb its harmony and threaten its integrity."[1]

The solution lay in popular sovereignty and he drew support from the American Revolution. In direct contrast to Lincoln, Douglas claimed that America's cornerstone lay not in the principles of the Declaration of Independence, but in the principle of popular sovereignty. "Our fathers of the Revolution," the senator asserted, "were contending, not for Independence in the first instance, but for the inestimable right of Local Self-Government under the British Constitution; the right of every distinct political community — dependent Colonies, Territories, and Provinces, as well as sovereign States — to make their own local laws, form their own domestic institutions, and manage their own internal affairs their own way." The Americans demanded their freedom when "the government of Great Britain had violated this inalienable right of local self-government by a long series of acts on a great variety of subjects."

Douglas pointed to a 1772 petition passed by the House of Burgesses of Virginia. In it, the Virginians informed the king that "The importation of slaves into the colony from the coast of Africa had long been considered as a trade of great inhumanity; and under its present encouragement we have too much reason to fear will endanger the very existence of your Majesty's American dominions." Douglas pronounced:

> Mark the ominous words! Virginia tells the King of England in 1772, four years prior to the Declaration of Independence, that his Majesty's American dominions are in danger: Not because of the Stamp duties — not because of the tax on Tea — not because of his attempts to collect revenue in America! These have since been deemed sufficient to justify rebellion and revolution. But none of these are referred to by Virginia in her address to the Throne — there being another wrong which, in magnitude and enormity, so far exceeded these and all other causes of complaint that the very existence of his Majesty's American dominions depended upon it! That wrong consisted in forcing African slavery upon a dependent Colony without her consent and in opposition to the wishes of her own people!

Here Douglas destroyed Lincoln's argument by completely supplanting the Declaration of Independence — and the words "all men are created equal" — as America's cornerstone with his "popular sovereignty." The demand for the right of self-government predated the Declaration and was not founded on any universal egalitarian philosophy. "The people of Virginia," Douglas continued, "... still adhered to the doctrine which they held in common with their sister Colonies, that it was the birthright of all freemen — inalienable when formed into political communities — to exercise exclusive legislation in respect to all matters pertaining to their internal polity — slavery not excepted; and rather than surrender this great right they were prepared to withdraw their allegiance from the Crown."

Douglas, knowing the Republicans intended to force the territories into the nation as free states, assailed that right with historical precedence. He referred to a clause in the Constitution of Virginia which demanded that the colony have the right to exclude slavery, and that the denial of that right by Great Britain became "one of the reasons for separation." Most important, this constitution "was adopted on the 12th day of June, 1776, three weeks and one day previous to the Declaration of Independence." It had remained "in force as a part of the Constitution for a period of fifty-four years, was re-adopted, without alteration" by the Virginians in their 1830 Constitution and again approved by the Virginians in the 1850 Constitution. "At this day," Douglas continued, "[this provision]" "remains a portion of the fundamental law of Virginia — proclaiming to the world and to posterity that one of the reasons for separating from Great Britain was 'the inhuman use of the Royal negative in refusing us [the Colony of Virginia] permission to exclude slavery from us by law'!"

In vouching for popular sovereignty as incorporated in the Kansas-Nebraska Act, Lincoln followed the founders' legacy, Douglas maintained. "This exposition of the history of these measures shows conclusively that the authors of the Compromise Measures of 1850, and of the Kansas-Nebraska Act of 1854, as well as the members of the Continental Congress of 1774, and the founders of our system of government subsequent to the Revolution, regarded the people of the Territories and Colonies as political communities which were entitled to a free and exclusive power of legislation in their Provincial Legislatures...." In countering Lincoln, the most important phrase in the sentence was "subsequent to the Revolution," which effectively rebuffed Lincoln's assertion that the Declaration of Independence established the United States. Douglas confirmed: "The principle, under our political system, is that every distinct political community, loyal to the Constitution and the Union, is entitled to all the rights, privileges, and immunities of self-government in respect to their local concerns and internal polity, subject only to the Constitution of the United States."

Lest anyone attack Douglas's proposition as having basis in Virginia alone, the Senator maintained that "the legislation of Virginia on this subject may be taken as a fair sample of the legislative enactments of each of the thirteen Colonies, showing conclusively that slavery was regarded by them all as a domestic question to be regulated and determined by each Colony to suit itself, without the intervention of the British Parliament.... Each Colony passed a series of enactments, beginning at an early period of its history and running down to the commencement of the Revolution, either protecting, regulating, or restraining African slavery within its respective limits and in accordance with their wishes and supposed interests."

Therefore, the issue upon which the Colonies and Great Britain differed found its source not in the principle that "all men are created equal." The "issue upon which the Declaration of Independence was founded and the battles of the Revolution were fought," Douglas argued, "...involved the specific claim on the part of the Colonies — denied by the King and Parliament — to the exclusive right of legislation touching all local and internal concerns, *slavery included*." This exclusive right "being the principle involved in the contest, a majority of the Colonies refused to permit their Delegates to sign the Declaration of Independence except upon the distinct condition and express reservation to each Colony of the exclusive right to manage and control its local concerns and police regulations without the intervention of any general Congress which might be established for the United Colonies."

In applying this principle to the nation's current crisis in respect to the territories, Douglas believed it was "important that this Jeffersonian Plan of government for the Territories should be carefully considered for many obvious reasons" because, after all, this plan "was drawn by the author of the Declaration of Independence." The Jeffersonian Plan, according to Douglas, "stood on the Statute Book when the Convention assembled at Philadelphia in 1787 and proceeded to form the Constitution of the United States" and "embodies and carries out the ideas and principles of the fathers of the Revolution — that the people of every separate political community (dependent Colonies, Provinces, and Territories as well as sovereign States) have an inalienable right to govern themselves in respect to their internal polity...."

However, what Douglas did not mention proved to be as significant as what he did mention. In his entire essay, he avoided any direct reference to "all men are created equal," upon which he and Lincoln had devoted so much of their time in the debates. Douglas may have considered the literal meaning of the phrase simply too difficult to counter, and therefore tossed it aside. He also failed to discuss Jefferson's support for the prohibition of slavery in the northwest territory. Lincoln had used this act to support his contention that the founders and Jefferson were opposed to slavery, and sought to place it on a path of eventual termination. Finally, despite his constant mention of "Popular Sovereignty" throughout the debates, he avoided the phrase in the entire essay. He sought to frame the argument on a national basis that would have interest in all states by redefining the argument as not simply the rights of those in the territories, but the rights of all states. This argument could persuade the southern Democrats to support him as the best Democrat to oppose the Republicans. He further hoped that the argument would also demonstrate to the northern Democrats that he did not intend to simply placate the proslavery forces by permitting slavery to freely expand into the territories, and perhaps into the North as well.

The same month *Harper's Weekly* published his essay, Douglas swung through central and southern Ohio intending to galvanize support for his presidential aspirations. He first spoke at Columbus on September 7 and made an argument strikingly similar to one which justified "states rights." Douglas announced that it was not his "intention to enter into an examination of any one question pertaining to the local and domestic policy of your own State, because, in regard to the interests and concerns of your State, I hold my political action bound by that great principle of the Nebraska bill which tells every political community to regulate its own affairs and mind its own business, and not to interfere with those of its neighbors." Further, the "Democratic party holds that it is the right of the people of every State, of every Territory, and every political community within this Confederacy to decide that question to suit themselves." However, "We are told by the leaders of the Republican party that there is an irrepressible conflict between freedom and slavery, free labor and slave labor, free States and slave States, and that it is their intention to continue to excite, agitate and divide the country until slavery shall be abolished or established throughout the country. In other words, the Republican Party holds that there must be uniformity in the local institutions of all the States and Territories of the Union." Douglas pointed to the two Republicans he most enjoyed quoting to support his argument: "Mr. Seward, in his Rochester speech, says that it is an irrepressible conflict between enduring forces, and must last until uniformity shall be established. Mr. Lincoln, in the Illinois canvass of last year, compared it to a house divided against itself which could not stand, and said that this Union could not permanently endure divided into free and slave States, as our fathers made it."

Douglas, continuing to refer to the ideas propagated in his *Harper's Weekly* essay, referred to the American Revolution. "The American Colonies," the senator asserted, "claimed the right in their Colonial legislatures to regulate the slavery question, and all other matters affecting their internal policy, to suit themselves, without the interference of the British Parliament, or any other power on earth." In again attempting to undermine the Declaration of Independence, Douglas maintained "that they as Colonies had the exclusive right to decide all questions of Territorial policy, slavery included, to suit themselves." Then, after this right had been established as the cause of revolution, "the Declaration of Independence was put forth, and all the battles of the Revolution were fought in vindication of that great principle."

Douglas, in attempting to hold the middle ground, portrayed the slavery issue in a fashion that would be acceptable to his antislavery audience. "Under that great principle of popular sovereignty," he declared, "one half of the original slaveholding States have since abolished slavery." However, he said "This result was not accomplished by the Wilmot Proviso, or by the Ordinance of 1787, or by the Republican platform, or by the action of Congress but it was abolished by the free and voluntary action of the people in each State, acting as they pleased."

The senator pounded away at the assertion, which Lincoln had argued many times in the debates, that the states of the Northwest Territory had been determined free by Congress: "I have often been told in Illinois by the Republicans, and I suppose you have heard the same here, that Illinois is a free State because of the sagacity of our fathers in adopting the Ordinance of 1787. I have heard of people assembling in the Western Reserve of Ohio, and celebrating with great pomp and veneration the 13th of July because it was the day on which the Ordinance of 1787 was passed, prohibiting slavery northwest of the Ohio River; and the learned speakers would tell the present generation that you are a free State in Ohio because of that Ordinance." Douglas rebuffed this interpretation of history: "I should not have the same respect for my fellow citizens of Ohio, which I do so sincerely entertain, if I thought that you were free merely because you could not help it." The senator asserted, "Gentlemen of Ohio, you are a free State because you chose to be free."

The Republicans had created this argument among free and slave only for the sake of national disunion, Douglas alleged. "Why should the North be arrayed against the South, and the South against the North?" he asked. "These geographical parties are of recent origin. They were unknown in the times of the Revolution when our liberties were first established." If anyone attended a Republican meeting, Douglas asserted, they would hear "orators" who "will deal in appeals to the Southern passions and Southern prejudices against Northern people and Northern institutions." Douglas questioned, "What is the object of these men now in thus fanning the flames of sectional strife at the North and the South, dividing the people by a geographical line, and making them enemies...?" The Republicans only intended "sectional strife and discord."

Douglas saw nothing but Republicans' hatred of the South manifested in their platform: "Take their platform from the beginning to the end, and it has a negro under every plank. There is not a white plank in their entire platform." The Republican language elicited an equally negative response from those it attacked, Douglas maintained: "It is all armed against the South, and if you go South among the fire-eaters of Louisiana you will find their petitions aimed as directly against the North." The senator's party took a far more positive, patriotic position: "Now, the Democratic party desires to harmonize all conflicting interests and passions in the Republic upon that great principle which underlies all our institutions, and declares that the people in every State and Territory shall be free to decide the slavery question, and every other question for themselves."

In conclusion, Douglas, referring to his great hope of manifest destiny, declared, "We are bound to extend and spread until we absorb the entire continent of America, including the adjacent islands, and become one grand ocean-bound republic. I do not care whether you like it or not; you cannot help it! It is the decree of Providence." Douglas believed that "this continent was set apart as an asylum for the oppressed of the whole world, and as a nursery for liberty — and here the people are collecting from all parts of the world, and taking shelter under the shadows of the great tree of Liberty. This emigration cannot be stopped, and you must have more land." He pleaded, "Let America have a policy of harmony with her destiny. Let us be what our numbers and what our position require us to be — not only an example to the friends of liberty, but a terror to the oppressors of man throughout the world. Let America have a firm, fixed policy abroad as well as at home; but, above all, let our policy at home be that which serves and preserves liberty — liberty at the fireside — liberty in the regulation of our local and domestic concerns." In referring to himself and the Democratic Party, his plea ended with "Now, my friends, why should not all conservative men — all lovers of peace and of the law — all friends of the Union — rally in support of these great principles upon which our Union was formed, and from the maintenance of which can you alone expect harmony and peace."

Douglas traveled farther south, to Cincinnati, for his next speech. Here, he spoke more boldly, especially in his attacks on two Republicans: William Seward and Abraham Lincoln. The senator still maintained that "the Democratic party is the only political organization in this country which can preserve the peace, the harmony, and the fraternity of this glorious Union." He believed that "there ever has been — there ever will be — two parties in this country: the one is founded on the great fundamental principle of self-government, which underlies all our institutions; the other is the antagonism of the Democratic party." To Douglas, "the great question which separates the Democratic party from the Opposition party at the present time involves the slavery question, the Opposition party contending that the slavery question is a federal question to be determined and controlled by federal authority, and the Democratic party holding that the slavery question is a local question...."

In developing his argument that his party — and he as the expected Democratic presidential nominee — remained the only choice to counter the disunionists, Douglas charged "that the Southern Opposition party and the Northern Republican party advocate the same principle — that of Congressional intervention on the subject of slavery — and differ only as to the application of that principle." While these two forces promulgated contrasting philosophies, the Democratic Party stood "firmly by the principle of non-intervention by Congress with slavery anywhere, and popular sovereignty in the States and Territories alike."

Later he turned his attacks to Seward and Lincoln. Douglas claimed that Seward, "the most eminent and authoritative expounder of Republican principles," contended that "there is an 'irrepressible conflict' between freedom and slavery, free labor and slave labor, free States and slave States, which must continue to rage until the States all become free or all become slave." The senator further argued that Seward "when he uttered that sentiment ought to have felt bound by a sense of justice and courtesy to have acknowledged that he borrowed the sentiment from an eminent leader of his own party. Three months previous to Mr. Seward's Rochester speech, Mr. Abraham Lincoln, of Illinois, in making a speech accepting a nomination of the Republican party of his State, had announced the same principle in more explicit and emphatic language." By describing this conflict as one that would "rage" between the sections, Douglas, for the first time in September 1859, grabbed what had been implied by Seward and Lincoln and described it in the most belligerent terms. The "real purpose" of the Republican Party, Douglas asserted, forced the States to "become all free or all slave; that they can not endure part free and part slave; that the contest must continue and increase in fury until the one class of States has been annihilated by the complete triumph of the other." Douglas emphatically rejected this philosophy of "uniformity": "I assert that the framers of the Constitution neither contemplated nor desired uniformity in respect to the local and domestic institutions of the several States."

In bringing his speech to an end, Douglas declared that he stood "tonight, as I have stood for ten years, vindicating this great and inestimable right of local self-government in all political communities — States as well as Territories." The Whig party had advocated this right but "Mr. Seward and Governor Chase and Mr. Sumner and others concluded to strangle the old Whig party and abolitionize its Northern forces." These men "found it necessary to abolish the party, to dissolve its organization, and change its name before they could repudiate the doctrine of non-intervention and popular sovereignty." To bring the Whigs into the new party, they "tied cords around their hands and feet, blindfolded them, and led them into the abolition camp for

Father Giddings to christen them in the abolition faith." Henry Clay would not have been so led, Douglas alleged. He reminded the audience "of the last speech of Henry Clay" when he asserted "that if the day ever came, as he apprehended it must soon, when the Whig party would be reduced to a miserable abolition faction, that he would join the Democracy [the Democratic party] and uphold the Constitution."

A week later Douglas arrived in Wooster, Ohio, the final stop in his Ohio campaign trip. Here, he reiterated the themes that he had stated in the previous speeches, displaying the confidence and consistency that had become his reputation. "It is not my purpose to discuss any question pertaining to your internal policy or domestic concerns," he declared. "Those questions are matters for you to determine for yourselves, without the interference of anybody outside the limits of your State." This policy of noninterference by the Democratic Party made it "the only political organization that can preserve the peace, harmony, and unity of this great confederacy." Douglas lowered the slavery issue from a moral plain to "simply a proposition of whether slavery is a federal or a local question. The Democratic party stands upon the issue that slavery is a local question, existing in the several States under the laws thereof, by State authority and not by virtue of the Constitution of the United States." Employing historical precedent to bolster his argument, the senator saw commonalities between the Kansas struggle and the earlier conflict between the colonies and Great Britain. In both instances it was a question of whether people had the right to determine how to resolve local and domestic matters. The Republican Party, Douglas argued, "in denying the right of the people of a Territory to manage their own domestic affairs, claim the power of Congress to occupy the identical position that George III and the Tories of the Revolution occupied towards the American Colonies." A territory, "with its executive, legislative, and judicial departments," Douglas claimed, has "the inalienable right to govern" itself "in respect" to its "local and domestic concerns."

The senator proudly gave special attention to himself for upholding domestic and local rights: "The Kansas-Nebraska Bill was introduced and passed for the purpose of carrying out that same principle; I am author of that bill." Like a martyr, he had suffered for taking this stand: "I have been pretty genteelly abused for being the author of it. I have seen the time when I could travel from Boston to Chicago by the light of my own effigy, and all along the Western Reserve of Ohio I could find my effigy upon every tree we passed." He asked, "And for what was all this abuse heaped upon my devoted head?— simply because I had introduced into Congress, and helped pass a bill declaring that it was the true intent and meaning of the act not to legislate slavery into any State or Territory nor to exclude it there from, but to leave the people thereof perfectly free to form and regulate their domestic institutions in their own way, subject only to the Constitution of the United States."

However, in his attempt to bypass any discussion on the morality of slavery, Douglas found himself, the experienced debater, in a rare moment, on the defensive. Someone interrupted him, shouting, "Is slavery a Christian institution?" The senator quickly replied, "I do not know of any tribunal on earth that can decide the question of the morality of slavery or any other institution. I deal with slavery as a political question involving questions of public policy. I deal with slavery under the Constitution, and that is all I have to do with it." Douglas reminded the heckler that "when the Constitution was being framed, a party arose in the Convention demanding the instant prohibition of the African slave trade upon moral and religious grounds." The person in the crowd correctly responded, "That does not answer my question." Douglas, obviously irritated at the question, and the interruption, shot back, "My dear sir, I take my own time to answer the question, and you ought to be very thankful that I did not rebuke your impertinence in interrupting me." Then he countered: "The Convention which framed the Constitution decided that the slave trade might continue until the year 1808, from and after which time it was, and would be, abolished" and "thus the moral and religious ground is waived under the Constitution leaving each State to have it as long as it pleases and abolish it when it pleases." He had, once again, avoided the issue of slavery's morality.

He concluded the speech with a rousing call for Ohio to stand in the ranks of the Democrats:

> I appeal to you again. If you wish to win the battle next year, give a little hope and encouragement to your sister States by electing the Democratic ticket this year. I am satisfied that you are to win the great struggle in 1860, and I wish you now just to make Ohio an offset to some of the Republican triumphs in the old Republican States by redeeming your State and putting her at the head of the Democratic column. Illinois feels rather uncomfortable in her isolated position. She stands the only Northern State which from the beginning has never failed to cast her electoral vote for a Democratic President — the only Northern state that has never been conquered by the unholy combination of Republicanism and its kindred isms. You left us alone and we maintained the battle last year single-handed. We now say to Ohio, the oldest of the Northwestern States and the one entitled to take the lead, rally, bring yourself into line, and take command of the entire Northwest. Illinois does not claim the lead, Ohio is entitled to it. Redeem her from Republicanism, Chaseism, and Giddings-ism, and come back to your first love, the Democracy. Whenever you do that Illinois will follow you. If you do not throw off the shackles, we will maintain the fight single-handed and keep the Democratic flag waving in triumph over one Northwestern State at least.[2]

As Douglas rode away from Wooster, he could have picked up a newspaper and discovered that he was once again being pursued. An old adversary had been invited to Ohio to counter him. The Ohio Republicans had not asked their Republican governor, or Pennsylvania's Republican governor, or even the heralded Republican senator from New York to follow Douglas. Instead, they requested the one man who had stood toe-to-toe with the Little Giant in 1858. They wanted, and received, Abraham Lincoln. Douglas had made his argument to the people of Ohio, and now it was Lincoln's turn.

5

Lincoln Assails Douglas in Ohio and Indiana

September 1859

Every time Lincoln stood before a crowd and delivered a speech to remain a viable candidate for the Republican presidential nomination, he had to accomplish three crucial goals. First, he had to remain faithful to the Declaration of Independence. Second, he had to argue that the non-extension of slavery was the party's immediate goal. And finally, he had to make these arguments without insulting Democrats and Southerners. Democrats comprised a significant portion of the population in all four northern states that the Republicans lost in 1856, and many former southerners had emigrated to two of those states, Illinois and Indiana. While he consistently succeeded in upholding the last two goals, even suggesting that a southerner could head the Republican ticket, he failed to consistently uphold the first and most important goal.

Nothing placed Lincoln's nomination for president more in jeopardy than one speech he delivered in Ohio in 1859. No one issue would prove more crucial to the Republicans at the nominating convention than the Declaration of Independence. That document would prove the most important filter for the convention delegates. Lincoln could not have fully foreseen, in September of 1859, the critical importance of that document, but to ensure the possibility of his nomination, he had to maintain full allegiance to the sentiments of the Declaration of Independence. But in his first major speech since the debates, Lincoln slipped, and slipped badly, and nearly ended all hope that he would ever become president.

In the 1858 campaign, Lincoln had fought an internal battle between what he defined as the ideals of a statesman versus those of a politician. As a statesman, he clearly and emphatically spoke of the promise embodied in the Declaration of Independence, in the phrase "all men are created equal." As a politician he occasionally demurred, preferring to advocate for a separation of the races on the basis that the white race should hold the superior position while the black race should remain the inferior one. For three consecutive debates, at the fourth, fifth, and sixth, he argued for the superior and inferior. However, at the fifth and sixth debates, ignoring the obvious incongruence of the Declaration of Independence and the racial inequality, he also claimed that "all men are created equal." In these three debates Lincoln appeared to have fully accepted the concept of superior and inferior as a permanent part of his public statements.

At Alton though, at the final debate, he dispensed with the superior and inferior concept and instead spoke boldly of the Declaration of Independence without the encumbrances of racial inequality. This debate represented a significant break from the previous three debates, and from that debate in October of 1858 until September of 1859, in all his letters and speeches he maintained firm allegiance to the phrase "all men are created equal." Alton clearly represented a significant turn for Lincoln back to the philosophy that he had so regularly espoused prior to his campaign with Douglas. However, at Columbus, Ohio, in the first speech of his tour, he dug up the old philosophy that he had previously buried on the banks of the Mississippi.

In beginning his speech, Lincoln noted that he had "read an article" in the pro–Douglas *Ohio Statesman* that morning, "in which, among other statements, I find the following: 'In debating with Senator Douglas during the memorable contest of last fall, Mr. Lincoln declared in favor of negro suffrage, and attempted to defend that vile conception against the Little Giant.'" This allegation demanded a response, Lincoln believed, so he quoted directly from the debates to counter it. He referred to his comments at Ottawa, at the first debate, where he stated, "'Now, gentlemen, I don't want to read at any greater length, but this is the true complexion of all I have ever said in regard to the institution of slavery and the black race. This is the whole of it; and anything that argues me into this idea of perfect social and political equality with the negro, is but a specious and fantastic arrangement of words....'"

Lincoln was not through with his rebuttal though. He then quoted from the fourth debate, the Charleston debate:

> I will say, then, that I am not, nor ever have been, in favor of bringing about in any way the social and political equality of the white and black races; that I am not, nor ever have been, in favor of making voters or jurors of negroes, nor of qualifying them to hold office, or intermarry with the white people; and I will say in addition to this that there is a physical difference between

the white and black races which I believe will forever forbid the two races living together in social and political equality. And inasmuch as they can not so
live, while they do remain together there must be the position of superior and
inferior, and I, as much as any other man, am in favor of having the superior position assigned to the white race.[1]

Lincoln asserted, "I did not at any time say I was in favor of negro suffrage; but the absolute proof that twice — once substantially, and once
expressly — I declared against it." He had, at least at the beginning of his
speech, dispensed with the promises of the Declaration of Independence.

He then focused on the issue upon which he believed all Republicans
could agree, and upon which he hoped the majority of northerners could
agree: opposition to the Kansas-Nebraska Act. Douglas' legislation "was a
very great change; for the law thus repealed was of more than thirty-years'
standing. Following rapidly upon the heels of this action of Congress, a decision of the Supreme Court is made by which it is declared that Congress, if
it desires to prohibit the spread of slavery into the Territories, has no Constitutional power to do so. Not only so, but that decision lays down principles which, if pushed to their logical conclusion — I say pushed to their logical
conclusion — would decide that the constitutions of free States, forbidding
slavery, are themselves unconstitutional."

However, slavery's expansion did not represent the greatest threat to the
nation. He did not believe that "the revival of the African slave trade, or the
passage of a Congressional slave code" or even "the declaring of a second Dred
Scott decision making [slavery] lawful in all the States" represented the "chief
danger" to the party. Rather, "the most imminent danger," Lincoln asserted,
"that now threatens that purpose is that insidious Douglas Popular Sovereignty." While he admitted that "this government of the United States under
which we live" was based on "genuine popular sovereignty," Douglas' popular sovereignty represented something far different. The leading Democrat
advocated "a principle ... that if one man chooses to make a slave of another
man, neither that other man nor anybody else has a right to object." This
policy had permitted slavery into the territories and for which "there is no
power or right to interfere."

Lincoln rebuffed several of the statements in Douglas' *Harper's Magazine* essay. He found it necessary to again defend his "House Divided" speech,
which Douglas had attacked "in almost all his speeches since it was uttered."
Lincoln also argued that the nation had maintained peace on the slavery question "from the adoption of the Constitution down to 1820" because "our
fathers" supported "a policy restricting the spread of slavery" and "the whole
country looked forward to the ultimate extinction of the institution." Since
Douglas's Kansas-Nebraska Act though, Lincoln, quoting one of his former

speeches, alleged "that the "'agitation has not only not ceased, but has constantly augmented.'"

Lincoln also took issue with Douglas's indifference to slavery. Douglas, Lincoln contended, maintained "that there is no moral question about it, but that it is altogether a matter of dollars and cents." Lincoln ventured to say, "I suppose the institution of slavery really looks small to him. He is so put up by nature that a lash upon his back would hurt him, but a lash upon anybody else's back does not hurt him."

Lincoln further refuted Douglas's proposition that the current Democratic Party espoused Jefferson's philosophy: "He ought to remember that there was once in this country a man by the name of Thomas Jefferson, supposed to be a Democrat — a man whose principles and policy are not very prevalent amongst Democrats today." Jefferson, Lincoln argued, "did not take exactly this view of the insignificance of the element of slavery which our friend Judge Douglas does." Rather, Lincoln recalled that "in contemplation of this thing, we all know he was led to exclaim, 'I tremble for my country when I remember that God is just!'" Jefferson perceived a "danger to this country — danger of the avenging justice of God in that little, unimportant popular sovereignty question of Judge Douglas." Jefferson "supposed there was a question of God's eternal justice wrapped up in the enslaving of any race of men, or any man, and that those who did so braved the arm of Jehovah — that when a nation thus dared the Almighty every friend of that nation had cause to dread His wrath. Choose ye between Jefferson and Douglas," Lincoln asserted, "as to what is the true view of this element among us."

"There are two main objects, as I understand it, of this *Harper's Magazine* essay," he claimed. "One was to show, if possible, that the men of our Revolutionary times were in favor of his popular sovereignty; and the other was to show that the Dred Scott decision had not entirely squelched out this popular sovereignty." Lincoln easily dispensed with Douglas's first proposition, asserting that the Illinois senator "selects part of the history of the United States upon the subject of slavery, and treats it as the whole, omitting from his historical sketch the legislation of Congress in regard to the admission of Missouri, by which the Missouri Compromise was established, and slavery excluded from a country half as large as the present United States." Lincoln did acknowledge that the compromise "was not made by the men of the Revolution" but those men had prohibited slavery in the Northwest Territory and that "the provision excluding slavery was inserted and passed unanimously...." "Begin with the men of the Revolution and go down for sixty entire years," Lincoln argued, "and until the last scrap of that Territory comes into the Union in the form of the State of Wisconsin — everything was made to conform with the Ordinance of 1787 excluding slavery from that vast extent of country." "Indiana once or twice, if not Ohio, petitioned the general government for the privilege of suspending that provision and allowing them to have slaves," Lincoln recalled, but "a report made by Mr. Randolph of Virginia, himself a slaveholder, was directly against it, and the action was to refuse them the privilege of violating the Ordinance of 1787."

Lincoln found Douglas's version of history simply astounding: "And hence I ask how extraordinary a thing it is that a man who has occupied a position upon the floor of the Senate of the United States, who is now in his third term, and who looks to see the government of this whole country fall into his own hands, pretending to give a truthful and accurate history of the slavery question in this country, should so entirely ignore the whole of that portion of our history — the most important of all."

Lincoln also assailed Douglas's interpretation of the Dred Scott decision. "I think myself, and I repeat it here, that this decision does not merely carry slavery into the Territories, but by its logical conclusion it carries it into the States in which we live." Taney's "decision says that the right of property in a slave is affirmed in that Constitution, which is the supreme law of the land...."

Lincoln then, apparently having spoken longer than he intended, admitted, "I must hasten to a conclusion." After briefly contending that Douglas's popular sovereignty would inevitably result in the reopening of the African slave trade, Lincoln returned to the document that he considered his nation's cornerstone and her greatest hope. Although he did not acknowledge the obvious contradiction between his opening statements regarding "superior" and "inferior" races and the phrase "all men are created equal," Lincoln spoke in favor of the Declaration of Independence. "Now let me call your attention to one thing that has really happened, which shows this gradual and steady debauching of public opinion, this course of preparation for the revival of the slave trade, for the Territorial slave code, and the new Dred Scott decision that is to carry slavery into the free States. Did you ever, five years ago, hear of anybody in the world saying that the negro had no share in the Declaration of Independence; that it did not mean negroes at all; and when 'all men' were spoken of, negroes were not included?"

Lincoln thought not, and in so doing, placed the blame for this change of public opinion on the Kansas-Nebraska Act. "I am satisfied that five years ago that proposition was not put upon paper by any living being anywhere. I have been unable at any time to find a man in an audience who would declare that he had ever know anybody saying so five years ago. But last year," Lincoln claimed, "there was not a Douglas popular sovereign in Illinois who did not say it. Is there one in Ohio but declares his firm belief that the Declaration of Independence did not mean negroes at all?" He supposed "that all now express the belief that the Declaration of Independence never did mean negroes. I call upon one of them to say that he said it five years ago." Lincoln feared that "that there has been a change wrought in you, and a very significant change it is, being no less than changing the negro, in your estimation, from the rank of a man to that of a brute. They are taking him down, and placing him, when spoken of, among reptiles and crocodiles, as Judge Douglas himself expresses it."

If public sentiment accepted Douglas's proposition, Lincoln believed that it would fundamentally contradict the philosophy upon which the nation had been founded. The result would fulfill the "words prophetically spoken by Mr. Clay many, many years ago ... when he told an audience that if they would repress all tendencies to liberty and ultimate emancipation, they must go back to the era of our independence, and muzzle the cannon which thundered its annual joyous return on the Fourth of July; they must blow out the moral lights around us; they must penetrate the human soul and eradicate the love of liberty; but until they did these things, and other eloquently enumerated by him, they could not repress all tendencies to ultimate emancipation."

The following day Lincoln traveled south to Dayton, Ohio, where he spoke for two hours and also gave brief remarks later at Hamilton, Ohio. Unfortunately, neither one of these speeches were recorded. The next day, September 18, Lincoln delivered an address in southern Ohio, in Cincinnati.[2]

Before this southern Ohio audience, he defended the "House Divided" speech, defined his Republican philosophy, attacked Douglas as pro-slavery, defended the Declaration of Independence, spoke to southerners, and called on the Republicans to stand on principle when choosing candidates for the upcoming elections. Most critical, he accomplished these goals without insulting or personally attacking his opposition. In beginning his remarks, Lincoln found himself crossing well worn ground. He had, once again, as he had many times before, to defend his "House Divided" speech. He realized that when Douglas had spoken in the city days before, that he "had reminded you, or informed you, if you had never before heard it, that I had once in my life declared it as my opinion that this government cannot 'endure permanently, half slave and half free; that a house divided against itself cannot stand,' and, as I had expressed it, I did not expect the house to fall; that I did not expect the Union to be dissolved; but that I did expect that it would cease to be divided; that it would become all one thing or all the other; that either the opponents of slavery would arrest the further spread of it, and place it where the public mind would rest in the belief that it was on the course of ultimate extinction; or the friends of slavery will push it forward until it becomes alike lawful in all the States old and new, free as well as slave." Lincoln, perhaps with some exasperation, admitted that he "did, fifteen months ago, express

that opinion, and upon many occasions Judge Douglas has denounced it, and
has greatly, intentionally or unintentionally, misrepresented my purpose in the
expression of that opinion."

Lincoln, "without having seen a report" of Douglas's speech, presumed
"that he alluded also to that opinion, in different language, having been
expressed at a subsequent time by Governor Seward of New York" in which
Douglas argued "that there was something couched in this opinion which led
to making of an entire uniformity of the local institutions of the various States
of the Union...." Lincoln also presumed that Douglas "insisted that this was
a declaration of war between the free and slave States — that it was the sound-
ing to the onset of continual war between the different States, the slave and
free States."

Lincoln had responded to this allegation numerous times but found it
necessary to defend them again. "When I made that reply to him — when I
told him on the question of declaring war between the different States of the
Union, that I had not said I did not expect any peace upon this question until
slavery was exterminated...." Lincoln had only "expected peace when that
institution was put where the public mind should rest in the belief that it was
in course of ultimate extinction...." To calm those who feared a belligerent
intention in his words, Lincoln assured the audience that he "neither then
had, nor have, or ever had, any purpose in any way of interfering with the
institution of slavery, where it exists," although it was his personal belief that,
if restricted, slavery would eventually die a natural death.

To calm those southerners who interpreted his comments as a call for
invasion, Lincoln decided "to address a portion of what I have to say to the
Kentuckians" since he found himself speaking on the banks of the river, just
across from Kentucky: "I say, then, in the first place, to the Kentuckians, that
I am what they call, as I understand it, a 'Black Republican.'" As a "'Black
Republican'" Lincoln defined himself as one who believed that "slavery is
wrong, morally and politically. I desire that it should be no further spread in
these United States, and I should not object if it should gradually terminate
in the whole Union." He understood that Kentuckians "differ radically with
me upon this proposition; that you believe slavery is a good thing; that slavery is right; that it ought to be extended and perpetuated in this Union." And
while the difference existed, Lincoln expressed a lack of hope that any discussion would change their minds: "Now, there being this broad difference
between us, I do not pretend, in addressing myself to you Kentuckians, to
attempt proselyting [sic] you," for "that would be a vain effort."

Instead, Lincoln sought to prove to the Kentuckians that if they wished
to protect slavery, they "ought to nominate for the next Presidency, at
Charleston, my distinguished friend Judge Douglas." As a shaper of public

opinion, Douglas "is not only the man that promises you in advance a hold upon the North and support in the North, but that he constantly molds public opinion to your ends." Douglas helped mold "public opinion," Lincoln alleged, through the "well-established fact" that "the Judge never says your institution of slavery is wrong; he never says it is right." Douglas "leaves himself at perfect liberty to do all in your favor which he would be hindered from doing if he were to declare the thing to be wrong." Lincoln feared that "whenever your minds are brought to adopt his argument ... if any man wants it, it is wrong to him not to let him have it."

Slavery was "morally" wrong, Lincoln claimed, and to prove that allegation he pointed to the Declaration of Independence. Lincoln believed that "it is safe to assert that five years ago no living man had expressed the opinion that the negro had no share in the Declaration of Independence." Believing so passionately on this issue, he followed that sentence with "Let me state that again: five years ago no living man had expressed the opinion that the negro had no share in the Declaration of Independence. If there is in this audience any man who ever knew of that opinion being put upon paper as much as five years ago, I will be obliged to him now or at a subsequent time to show it." Since the passage of the Kansas-Nebraska Act, Douglas "had got his entire party, so far as I know, without exception, to join in saying that the negro has no share in the Declaration of Independence." This represented "a vast change in the northern public sentiment upon that question"—a change that obliterated any rights and any hope for African Americans. "Of what tendency is that change?" Lincoln asked. "The tendency of that change is to bring the public mind to the conclusion that when men are spoken of, the negro is not meant; that when negroes are spoken of, brutes alone are contemplated."[3]

To those who, like Douglas, predicted the disunion of the nation with the election of a Republican, Lincoln cautioned that the South could not prevail: "I often hear it intimated that you mean to divide the Union whenever a Republican, or anything like it, is elected President of the United States." Lincoln asked, "Will you make war upon us and kill us all? Why, gentlemen, I think you are as gallant and as brave men as live; that you can fight as bravely in a good cause, man for man, as any other people living; that you have shown yourselves capable of this upon various occasions...." However, Lincoln believed the North had the upper hand. "Man for man, you are not better than we are, and there are not so many of you as there are of us. You will never make much of a hand whipping us." He admitted that "If we were fewer in numbers than you, I think that you could whip us; if we were equal, it would likely be a drawn battle; but being inferior in numbers, you will make nothing by attempting to master us."[4]

Lincoln then turned from advising the southerners to advising the northerners, or more specifically, the Republicans in respect to the restraints by which the Republican Party must conform, and, in so doing, he provided a public definition of a Lincoln republican: "I say that we must not interfere with the institution of slavery in the States where it exists because the Constitution forbids it, and the general welfare does not require us to do so." He recommended that "we must not withhold an efficient fugitive slave law, because the Constitution requires us, as I understand it, not to withhold such a law." Despite these restraints, Lincoln firmly asserted that "we must prevent the outspreading of the institution [of slavery] because neither the Constitution nor general welfare requires us to extend it." He also demanded that "we must prevent the revival of the African slave trade and the enacting by Congress of a Territorial slave code. We must prevent each of these things being done by either congresses or courts. The people of these United States are the rightful masters of both congresses and courts, not to overthrow the Constitution, but to overthrow the men who pervert that Constitution."[5]

He spoke frankly concerning the upcoming election. "We must hold conventions; we must adopt platforms," "we must nominate candidates and we must carry elections." But he cautioned, "In all these things, I think that we ought to keep in view our real purpose, and in none do anything that stands adverse to our purpose." If the Republicans compromised on principle, if they "shall adopt a platform that fails to recognize or express our purpose, or elect a man that declares himself inimical to our purpose, we not only take nothing by our success, but we tacitly admit that we act upon no other principle than a desire to" win, "by which, in the end, our apparent success is really an injury to us."

Lincoln specified how this dangerous compromise could occur. "I know that it is very desirable with me, as with everybody else, that all the elements of the Opposition shall unite in the next Presidential election and in all future time." While he admitted that he was "anxious" for unification of the opposition, he cautioned that "there are things seriously to be considered in relation to that matter. If the terms can be arranged, I am in favor of the union." He feared a compromise that could result in complete defeat. "But suppose we shall take up some man, and put him upon one end or the other of the ticket, who declares himself against us in regard to the prevention of slavery — who turns up his nose and says he is tired of hearing anything more about it, who is more against us than against the enemy — what will be the issue?" The ticket would lead to certain defeat, he predicted. "If we nominate him upon that ground, he will not carry a slave State; and not only so, but that portion of our men who are high-strung upon that principle" of slavery "will not go for him, and he won't get a single electoral vote anywhere, except, perhaps, in the State of Maryland."

"After saying this much," Lincoln wanted to "say a little on the other side." While certain northern candidates could be disastrous for the party, the Republicans could recruit one from the other part of the country. "There are plenty of men in the slave States that are altogether good enough for me to be either President or Vice-President, provided they will profess their sympathy with our purpose and will place themselves on the ground that our men, upon principle, can vote for them." In the South, Lincoln alleged, there were "good men in their character for intelligence and talent and integrity. If such a one will place himself upon the right ground, I am for his occupying one place upon the next Republican or Opposition ticket." The Republicans stood on principle, Lincoln claimed, not on the home state of any potential candidate. "But unless he does so place himself" on the Republican philosophy, "I think it a matter of perfect nonsense to attempt to bring about a union [of the opposition] upon any other basis; that if a union be made," by compromising on principle, "the elements will scatter so that there can be no success for such a ticket, nor anything like success."

Lincoln had, once again, assailed Douglas and his popular sovereignty, defined a Lincoln republican, placed the Declaration of Independence at the forefront of his speech, and most important, had made no mention of "superior" and "inferior." The final speech of his tour, in the divided state of Indiana, a state which had failed to support the Republicans in 1856, and whose support was critical in 1860, would prove whether the Lincoln of Columbus or the Lincoln of Cincinnati, represented the true Lincoln.[6]

He did not escape Ohio without praise or criticism though. The Republican *Cincinnati Gazette* reported that Lincoln delivered a "fresh and original" speech "which will be found interesting and unanswerable." The Democratic *Cincinnati Enquirer* thought otherwise. The newspaper described it as "not worth reading" and that it was "in a single expressive word, *trash* — trash from beginning to end; trash without one solitary oasis to relieve the dreary waste...." The *Enquirer* reminded its readers that "Mr. Lincoln was a candidate against Mr. Douglas" and that "upon this fact stands his reputation — all that he ever had" and owed "his entire significance to that antagonism. Without Douglas Lincoln would be nothing."[7]

At Indianapolis, the capital of a state that resembled central and southern Illinois where the Democrats had defeated the Republicans in the 1858 elections, Lincoln, as he had at the last debate in Alton in 1858, dispelled with favoring public opinion, and spoke boldly about his nation's cornerstone, the Declaration of Independence, without the encumbrances of "superior" and "inferior."

His arguments would have been familiar to anyone who had heard his speeches in Ohio. He responded to Douglas's attacks to both his "House Divided" speech and Seward's "Irrepressible Conflict" speech and argued that, opposed to Douglas's assertion that the nation could continue half-slave and half-free, the nation had been founded on the premise of limiting slavery. The founding fathers' provisions for the eventual end of the African slave trade and the prohibition of slavery in the Northwest Territory proved their anti-slavery nature. He also contended that because of the prohibition of slavery in the Northwest Territory, slavery declined in Illinois but not in Missouri. Lincoln repeated his discussion of free labor versus slavery, arguing that "the hired laborer, with his ability to become an employer, must have every precedence over him who labors under the inducement of force."

Of all the topics he covered though, the most crucial aspect of Lincoln's Indianapolis speech was his conclusion. He ended the speech with a defense of the Declaration, a speech in which he had made no mention of "superior" and "inferior" races. And, he made this argument in a state where the division of the races would have been far more accepted than any comments on equality. In conclusion, Lincoln argued that "there was a feature in connection to Douglas's Popular Sovereignty, that was more dangerous than anything else...." Douglas intended his doctrine to result in the "debauching of public sentiment. The maxims he taught in regard to the institution of slavery, and by relative operation upon the principle of liberty itself, were more pernicious than anything else." Lincoln recalled that "the Judge said he did not care whether slavery was voted up or voted down. That was as much as to say, that he does not believe it to be wrong." However, "this was not the opinion held by the good men of the Revolution," nor was it "the expressed opinion of Mr. Jefferson." Douglas "tells us that the Declaration of Independence never meant negroes, and not only does he tell us so, but every follower joins in and says that the Declaration does not apply to negroes." Lincoln turned and looked at the Democrat Governor Willard, who was in the audience, and asked whether "he would have the boldness to say that the Declaration did not include negroes as well as whites?" Lincoln claimed that "he never heard any one say so, and he had asked thousands. No President had ever said so — no head of any department, nor a member of Congress."

"And yet," Lincoln asserted, "you allow this man to debauch public sentiment among you." In referring to Douglas's Kansas-Nebraska Act, he argued, "You have taken the negro out of the catalogue of man, when you had not thought of such a thing five years ago. Five years ago no living man expressed the opinion that the negro had no share in the Declaration of Independence. But within that space Douglas had got his entire party, almost without exception, to join in saying that the negro has no share in the

Declaration." Douglas's "tendency of that change, that debauchery in public sentiment is to bring the public mind to the conclusion that when white men are spoken of, the negro is not meant, and when negroes are spoken of, brutes alone are contemplated." Lincoln argued that the "change had already depressed the black man in the estimation of Douglas himself, and the negro was thus being debased from the condition of a man of some sort to that of a brute."[8]

Lincoln had started this campaign at Columbus with advocacy for the inequality of the races, and he ended the campaign at Indianapolis with a firm statement for the equality of the races based on the Declaration of Independence. Never again would Lincoln repeat his statements on the separation of the races. The steady rise that he had begun at the Galesburg debate in 1858 and reached its most courageous form at Alton had continued with only Columbus as a temporary setback. After Columbus, he threw his sentiments on racial inequality into the fires of the Declaration of Independence. "All men are created equal" would remain as his moral compass for the rest of his life.

6

Lincoln Invades Seward Country: The Cooper Union Address in New York

September 1859–February 1860

Lincoln's popularity was growing. Throughout the last three months of 1859, he concentrated on his law practice, but politics kept intervening. During this time, Lincoln received an intriguing proposal from a Republican presidential candidate, he confirmed a speech-making trip to New York, he accepted an invitation to speak in Wisconsin, and he took to the road again to visit the territory which had come to define a nation's destiny as well as his own.

Lincoln traveled, by invitation, to the Republican bastion of Wisconsin, a state that had overwhelmingly supported Fremont in 1856 (55 percent to 44 percent) and was expected to support the 1860 Republican candidate with the same enthusiasm. The Wisconsin State Agricultural Society, because of Lincoln's popularity from the 1858 debates, invited him to speak in Milwaukee, Wisconsin, on September 30. This speech proved unusual for Lincoln in that, while he discussed the benefits of free labor, he primarily focused on the benefits of agriculture, not a topic for which he was renowned. Lincoln delivered two other speeches in Wisconsin and, according to the summaries provided in the newspapers, he returned to the same themes he had expressed in Ohio.[1]

The Pennsylvanians, like the Wisconsinites, had begun to appreciate Lincoln's strength. A supporter of Pennsylvania senator Cameron wrote him with a surprising and intriguing offer. The Pennsylvania Republicans were rallying behind their favorite son, Cameron, as their presidential candidate, a person who would naturally carry the Keystone state, and they wanted as their vice presidential candidate Lincoln, a person who could bring Illinois into the Republican fold. Lincoln agreed that "it certainly is important to secure Pennsylvania for the Republicans, in the next Presidential contest; and not unimportant to, also, secure Illinois. As to the ticket you name, I shall be heartily for it, after it shall have been fairly nominated by a Republican national convention; and I can not be committed to it before." He would "labor faithfully in the ranks, unless, as I think not probable, the judgment of the party shall assign me a different position." Lincoln admitted that "if the Republicans of the great State of Pennsylvania, shall present Mr. Cameron as their candidate for the Presidency, such an endorsement of his fitness for the place, could scarcely be deemed insufficient." Lincoln wanted to remain neutral. "Still, as I would not like the public to know, so I would not like myself to know I had entered a combination with any man, to the prejudice of all others whose friends respectively may consider them preferable."[2] Lincoln had played his hand carefully in not endorsing anybody, and in complementing the Cameron supporters. He would not, at this point, hitch to anyone.

That same month, giving him some further confidence in his growing reputation within the Republican Party, he received a letter from eastern Republicans confirming his plans for an upcoming speech in New York. This speech would give him his first opportunity to impress New York and New England Republicans, delegates who would carry significant influence at the convention.[3] But before he traveled east, Lincoln accepted an invitation to travel west, to the territory that had received so much of the nation's attention since 1854, and over which controversy had, in many ways, propelled him to the nation's center stage.

Lincoln delivered numerous speeches in his Kansas tour, of which only some survive today. He continued his defiant stand toward Douglas and popular sovereignty, but his most crucial comments concerned John Brown, who had two months before attempted to foment a violent slave insurrection at Harpers Ferry, Virginia. His raid failed, leaving over a dozen people dead. However, Brown had support in Kansas, throughout the North, and among some Republicans. Lincoln, though, had no desire for the Republicans to achieve their goals through force of arms. "Your Territory has had a marked history — no other Territory has ever had such a history," Lincoln stated in his first speech. He did not wholly support those who had fought against the slavery forces, or those who revered John Brown. "There had been strife and bloodshed here, both parties had been guilty of outrages." Lincoln "had his opinions as to the relative guilt of the parties, but, "displaying his hatred for mob rule, and opposition to the rule of law, he "would not say who had been most to blame." To the lawyer, "One fact was certain — there had been loss of life, destruction of property; our material interests had been retarded. Was this desirable? There is a peaceful way of settling these questions — the way adopted by government until a recent period."[4]

Lincoln considered John Brown's Harpers Ferry raid "wrong for two reasons. It was a violation of law and it was, as all such attacks must be, futile as far as any effect it might have on the extinction of a great evil." "We have a means provided for the expression of our belief in regard to Slavery," Lincoln asserted, "it is through the ballot box — the peaceful method provided by the Constitution. John Brown has shown great courage, rare unselfishness, as even Gov. Wise testifies. But no man, North or South, can approve of violence or crime."[5]

During Lincoln's visit, another event galvanized the people of Kansas. On December 2, John Brown was hanged in western Virginia. The following day Lincoln spoke at Leavenworth.

Lincoln attacked slavery and attacked the Kansas-Nebraska Act; but once again, in the shadow of Brown's death, his most potent comments focused upon the former Kansas resident. Lincoln again rejected the actions of John Brown, and specifically addressed the secessionist southerners.

> While you [southerners] elect [the] President, we submit, neither breaking nor attempting to break up the Union. If we shall constitutionally elect a President, it will be our duty to see that you submit. Old John Brown has just been executed for treason against a state. We cannot object, even though he agreed with us in thinking slavery wrong. That cannot excuse violence, bloodshed, and treason. It could avail him nothing that he might think himself right. So if constitutionally we elect a President, and therefore you undertake to destroy the Union, it will be our duty to deal with you as old John Brown has been dealt with. We shall try to do our duty. We hope and believe that in no section will a majority so act as to render such extreme measures necessary.

While he agreed with "Brown's hatred of slavery," Lincoln "emphatically denounced" the attack on Harpers Ferry. Instead, he pointed to slavery as the cause of the "uprisings" and referred to Nat Turner's rebellion in which "fifty-eight whites" were murdered as proof that these "upheavings" would occur where slavery existed.[6]

Two days later, he departed Kansas.

When he returned to Illinois in December 1859, he had only five months remaining to convince as many Republicans as possible to support him for the Republican presidential nomination. Since his defeat the previous year, his standing within the party had not substantially improved, and more important, he had not yet decided to run. However, in late 1859, his fortune and his perspective began to change. From December 1859 to March 1860, he would deliver a speech in New York at the request of eastern Republicans, would deliver speeches throughout New England (both areas filled with fervent Seward Republicans, and during this time period a few of his supporters began to quietly take action on behalf of his presidential nomination) if he ever decided to run.

This four month period began with several positive letters. First, some Illinois Republicans were fervently working for his nomination and saw their first opportunity to assist their candidate by lobbying for the convention to be held in Illinois, specifically the passionately pro–Lincoln city of Chicago. Norman Judd, a former Democrat who had become a close political associate of Lincoln's, had communicated this strategy to Lincoln, and while Lincoln displayed great respect for Judd's political ability in the past, most notably in conceiving the idea of debating Douglas in 1858, he disagreed with Judd's opinion on the nomination's location: "I find some of our friends here, attach more consequence to getting the National convention into our State than I did, or do." As for the time of the convention, he strongly urged the Republicans to schedule their convention after the Democratic one in Charleston, South Carolina, or, as he wrote, "after the Charleston fandango; and I think, within bounds of reason, the later the better." Concerning the selection of the Illinois delegates, he firmly asserted that they must select delegates at a convention where they could be convinced to vote as a unit, as opposed to selection by districts which would potentially scatter the Illinois votes among multiple candidates.[7]

Lincoln's confidence in his national standing increased further when he received great news from Ohio. Having labored unsuccessfully since the end of 1858 to find a publisher for the 1858 debates, his persistence had finally paid off. Lincoln wrote the publisher:

> Your letter of the 7th ... both requesting of me, for publication in permanent form, copies of the political debates between Senator Douglas and myself, last year, has been received. With my grateful acknowledgments to both you and them, for the very flattering terms in which the request is communicated, I transmit you the copies. The copies I send you are reported and printed, by the respective friends of Senator Douglas and myself, at the time — that is, his by his friends, and mine by mine. It would be an unwarrantable liberty for us to change a word or a letter in his, and the changes I have made in mine, you perceive, are verbal only, and very few in number. I wish the reprint to be precisely as the copies I send, without any comment whatever.

In sending the letter, Lincoln could finally have confidence that the debates which had brought him such acclaim in the North would be available in printed form.[8]

A Pennsylvania newspaper reporter provided more favorable news when he requested an autobiography from Lincoln. So, in the last month of 1859, for only the second time in his life, Lincoln sat down and wrote about himself. The request, and the article for which the request was intended, again demonstrated the national popularity that the Lincoln-Douglas debates had given Lincoln. His first autobiography, the five line version which included the line "Education defective," reflected his attitude toward his life in 1858. Now, one year later, he took more time and provided more information but with honest admittance that his past was worth little attention.

Lincoln introduced his letter with a couple of paragraphs: "Herewith is a little sketch, as you requested. There is not much of it, for the reason, I suppose, that there is not much of me." "If any thing be made out of it, I wish it to be modest, and not to go beyond the material. If it were thought necessary to incorporate any thing from any of my speeches, I suppose there would be no objection." Lincoln added one note of caution to the reporter. Although he could incorporate material written by Lincoln, the article itself "must not appear to have been written by myself."

Lincoln continued with the "not much of me" theme throughout the autobiography. "I was born Feb. 12, 1809, in Hardin County, Kentucky"; "My parents were both born in Virginia" but "of undistinguished families — second families, perhaps I should say." His mother "died in my tenth year" and "my paternal grandfather, Abraham Lincoln, emigrated from Rockingham County, Virginia, to Kentucky, about 1781 or 2, where, a year or two later, he was killed by Indians." To dispense with any romantic notion of this death, he added that his grandfather was not killed "in battle, but by stealth" and when attacked, he was not in any great endeavor, but simply "laboring to open a farm in the forest."

When he turned to the subject of his father, the humility, not forced or created, continued. "My father, at the death of his father, was but six years of age; and he grew up litterally [sic] without education. He removed from Kentucky to what is now Spencer county, Indiana, in my eighth year. We reached our new home about the time the State came in the Union. It was a wild region, with many bears and other wild animals still in the woods. There I grew up."

Lincoln, perhaps painfully, recalled his almost complete lack of learning. "There were some schools, so called; but no qualification was ever required of a teacher, beyond 'readin, writin, and cipherin,' to the Rule of Three. If a straggler supposed to understand latin, happened to sojourn in the neighborhood, he was looked upon as a wizzard [sic]. There was absolutely nothing to excite ambition for education." As a result of this exposure, or lack thereof, "When I came of age I did not know much. Still somehow, I could read, write, and cipher to the Rule of Three; but that was all. I have not been to school since. The little advance I now have upon this store of education, I have picked up from time to time under the pressure of necessity."

As for his early years in Illinois, he thought they were also of little note. "I was raised to farm work, which I continued till I was twenty two. At twenty one I came to Illinois [and after one year moved to New Salem] where I remained a year as a sort of Clerk in a store."

His military service could have provided some measure of pride, but he mentioned it only because of the manner by which he became a leader of his group. "Then came the Black-Hawk war; and I was elected a Captain of Volunteers — a success which gave me more pleasure than any I have had since." With this first success, he campaigned that "same year (1832)" for the state legislature and "was beaten" in that campaign but recalled that, with his recent defeat of 1858 in mind, a defeat that had occurred in the state legislature and not by general election, it was "the only time I have been beaten by the people." In the next "three succeeding biennial elections, I was elected to the Legislature. I was not a candidate afterwards. During this Legislative period I had studied law, and removed to Springfield to practice it. In 1846 I was once elected to the lower House of Congress. Was not a candidate for re-election. From 1849 to 1854, both inclusive, practiced law more assiduously than ever before. Always a whig in politics, and generally on the whig electoral tickets, making active canvasses."

He admitted that during this time he "was losing interest in politics, when the repeal of the Missouri Compromise aroused me again." Ending his narrative there, in 1854, Lincoln simply added, "What I have done since then is pretty well known."

Almost like a postscript, he wrote, "If any personal description of me is thought desirable, it may be said, I am, in height, six feet, four inches, nearly; lean in flesh, weighing, on an average, one hundred and eighty pounds; dark complexion, with coarse black hair, and grey eyes — no other marks or brands recollected."[9]

To appreciate Lincoln's autobiography and his modesty, one must consider Seward's approach to his autobiographies. When letters were sent requesting information on past and present members of Congress in preparation for the *Dictionary of the United States Congress*, Seward, like Lincoln, responded to the request. Lincoln described his education as "defective" in the first instance and "when I came of age I did not know much." Seward had "graduated at Union College in 1820; was admitted to the bar in 1822, and entered upon the practice of his profession at Auburn, in his native State, the following year." Seward had received formal education at the collegiate level; Lincoln had not. Politically, Seward had been "elected to the New York

Senate" in 1830 at only the age of twenty-one. Lincoln, at that age, was performing farm work. Four years after his entry into politics, the Whig Party nominated Seward as "their candidate for Governor of the State," but Seward admitted that this attempt "failed." Four years later, at thirty-seven years of age, "on a second nomination for the same office, he was elected." At the same age, Lincoln was, for the first time, "elected to the lower House of Congress" and remained for just one two-year term, while Seward won election for a second two-year term as Governor.

In neither of his two autobiographical statements had Lincoln delved into policy or accomplishments, but Seward did. The New Yorker had "upheld the system of internal improvements, and devoted himself to reforming and improving the system of public education." Seward had attacked the Know-Nothings, and all those opposing new immigrants, many of which were Catholic, and for which he expressed a great deal of pride. "His plan for taking the management of the public schools in New York out of the hands of the Public School Society, and subjecting them to the control of the State, caused considerable feeling on the subject at the time, and gave rise to an animated contest between the Protestants, who maintained the existing system, and the Roman Catholics, who favored the change."

Many New Yorkers had appealed to Seward to serve another gubernatorial term, but "on the expiration of his second term in office, Mr. Seward declined to be a candidate for re-election, and resumed the practice of his profession at Auburn, in 1843." Lincoln could not state the same for his term in Congress, as his popularity had suffered significantly due to his less than enthusiastic support for the Mexican War.

Finally, Seward wrote that "he was chosen United States Senator for six years" and "he was re-elected in 1855, and still holds the position." Lincoln, of course, by ending his second autobiography in 1854, made no mention of his two failed attempts at becoming a United States senator.

However, the autobiography that Seward wrote for the *Dictionary of the United States Congress* was not his only, nor by far, his longest one. In 1855, in what his biographer aptly termed a "campaign biography," Seward, on his own initiative and against the advice of his most trusted political advisor, Weed, published, not a longer article on himself, but rather an entire four hundred page book-length autobiography titled *The Life of William H. Seward*.[10]

Despite the encouragement Lincoln had received, one meeting dampened all the positive news. On February 8, Lincoln met with a man whom he considered a friend, who had been instrumental in the formation of the Illinois Republican Party, and who was considered one of the leading Illinois Republicans: Orville Browning. Browning, residing in central Illinois, the crucial area Lincoln lost in 1858, could provide insight as to which candidate would best prevail in 1860. Browning recorded in his diary that the two of them "had a free talk about the Presidency. He thinks I may be right in supposing Mr[.] [Edward] Bates to be the strongest and best man we can run — and that there is a large class of voters in all the free States that would go for Mr[.] Bates, and for no other man. He says it is not improbable that by the time the National convention meets in Chicago he may be of [the] opinion that the very best thing that can be done will be to nominate Mr[.] Bates."[11]

Two weeks after this discouraging meeting, Lincoln boarded a train and headed east. His destination was the most populous city in the most populous state in the union, New York City, New York, in Seward's home state.

The republicans who invited Lincoln had invited two other speakers before him: Cassius Clay and Frank P. Blair, Jr. What brought this group of Republicans together, and what instigated their invitation to the speakers was one simple, shared feeling: they despised Seward. They desperately wanted to propel some other candidate to the forefront to compete with the presumed nominee.[12]

Blair, the first speaker, an advocate of Bates, focused on the issue of disunionism. He described John Brown as a "maniac" and chastised both the Democratic Party and the abolition movement as parties for "disunion." He called for Republicans to focus on the "border States holding slaves" who "have the reins in their hands which will control those Southern leaders who now avow the design of making disunion the element of their power." He naturally asserted that Missouri, where Bates resided, holds "the important position ... both as a border and a frontier State" and "she will add her strength to those members of the Confederacy that approve themselves most devoted to the Constitution and the Union...."[13]

Cassius Clay from Kentucky took a different approach. Clay, as an antislavery man in the slave state of Kentucky, had literally fought and bled for the cause. At one point, anticipating an attack on his home, he fortified it with weapons and defenses. In 1843, he became embroiled in a fight with a proslavery politician. The proslavery politician shot Clay in the chest. Clay repeatedly stabbed his assailant in the skull. Clay lived; his assailant died. In Clay's Cooper Union speech, he declared, "They can't drive me out, gentlemen ... it is not safe to put down 'Cash' Clay!" "Put me at the head of the United States" and as for the South, "I will whip them." The audience erupted into great applause after this comment as one supporter yelled, "All in favor of Mr. Clay being the nominee for the next Presidency, please say 'Aye.'"[14]

Lincoln arrived in New York on February 25, ten days after Clay's speech, and two days later he addressed what was arguably the most influential assembly of Republicans to which he had ever spoken.

To emphasize their common ground, Lincoln chose a familiar target: Stephen Douglas, a man whom he had battled against since 1854. Lincoln had pursued the Little Giant throughout the 1858 campaign and pursued him through Ohio one year later, and now, six years after Douglas's Kansas-Nebraska Act, he took to another stage to combat Douglas again.

This time he focused narrowly on one point that Douglas had recently perpetuated in the Ohio campaign. Douglas had attempted to undermine the promise of the Declaration of Independence by completely ignoring it, preferring to found his argument on the opinions of those who signed the Constitution. Lincoln accepted the challenge. If Douglas intended to prove the correctness of popular sovereignty on the basis of the signers the Constitution alone, Lincoln was willing to fight him on that battleground, believing that even there, on the basis of a document which permitted slavery, Lincoln could prove that the signers were antislavery.

Lincoln began by recalling that in Douglas's "speech last autumn, at Columbus, Ohio, as reported in 'The New-York Times,' Senator Douglas said: 'Our fathers, when they framed the Government under which we live, understood this question just as well, and even better, than we do now.'" Lincoln "fully" endorsed this proposition, and he accepted it "as a text for this discourse. I so adopt it because it furnishes a precise and an agreed starting point for a discussion between Republicans and that wing of the Democracy headed by Senator Douglas. It simply leaves the inquiry: '*What was the understanding those fathers had of the question mentioned?*'" This led Lincoln to the question, "What is the frame of Government under which we live?" He argued that "the answer must be: 'The Constitution of the United States.'"

The lawyer then carefully and methodically constructed his argument about the Constitution's signers through a series of questions, an approach he had employed many times in the small towns and courtrooms of Illinois. Douglas was the prosecutor, the Republicans were the jury, and the founding fathers, the defendants. Lincoln intended to prove that the founding fathers were not, like Douglas, guilty of ambivalence toward slavery.

"Who were our fathers that framed the Constitution?" he asked. "I suppose the 'thirty-nine' who signed the original instrument may be fairly called our fathers who framed that part of the present Government.... I take these 'thirty-nine' for the present, as being 'our fathers who framed the Government under which we live.'" Upon these "thirty-nine" signers of the Constitution, Lincoln built his case. The key question, he argued, "is this: Does the proper division of local from federal authority, or anything in the Constitution, forbid *our Federal Government* to control as to slavery in *our Federal Territories*?" Lincoln properly recognized the solid demarcation between him and his adversary on this issue: "Upon this, Senator Douglas holds the affirmative, and Republicans the negative."

The lawyer proposed an examination of the "thirty-nine" as to how "any of them, ever acted upon this question; and if they did, how they acted upon it...." Lincoln cited six examples to prove his case, three of which merit mention: the Ordinance of 1787, the organization of the Territory of Mississippi, and the organization of the Louisiana Purchase. He first focused on "the Ordinance of '87," which included "the prohibition of slavery in the Northwestern Territory." The act had been passed in 1789 by "the first Congress which sat under the Constitution" and "the bill for this act was reported by one of the 'thirty-nine'...." The act "went through all its stages without a word of opposition, and finally passed both branches without yeas and nays, which is equivalent to an unanimous passage. In this Congress there were sixteen of the thirty-nine fathers who framed the Constitution." Lincoln asserted that "this shows that, in their understanding, no line dividing local from federal authority, nor anything in the Constitution, properly forbade Congress to prohibit slavery in the federal territory...." The legislation received its final approval from none other than "George Washington, another of the 'thirty-nine' [who] was then President of the United States, and, as such, approved and signed the bill; thus completing its validity as a law, and thus showing that, in his understanding, no line dividing local from federal authority, nor anything in the Constitution, forbade the Federal Government to control as to slavery in federal territory."[15]

Douglas had consistently argued that the federal government should leave slavery alone in the territories, especially when slavery then existed in the territories. Lincoln rejected this proposition with historical precedence. When "slavery was then actually in the ceded country," Congress, on taking charge of these countries, did not absolutely prohibit slavery within them. But they did interfere with it — take control of it — even there, to a certain extent." Lincoln referred his audience to 1798 when "Congress organized the Territory of Mississippi. In the act of organization, they prohibited the bringing of slaves into the Territory" from outside the United States "and giving freedom to slaves so brought. This act passed both branches of Congress without yeas or nays. In that Congress were three of the 'thirty-nine' who framed the original Constitution."

The United States faced the question again in regards to the Louisiana Purchase. "In 1803," Lincoln noted, "the Federal Government purchased the Louisiana country.... Congress did not, in the Territorial Act, prohibit slavery; but they did interfere with it — take control of it — in a more marked and extensive way than they did in the case of Mississippi." Congress applied restrictions similar to those which had been applied to the Mississippi Territory. Lincoln again claimed that "this act also was passed without yeas or nays. In the Congress which passed it, there were two of the 'thirty-nine.'"

On the question of whether the federal government had the right to interfere with slavery in the territories, Lincoln cited six examples to prove that a total of "twenty-three" of the founders supported Lincoln's philosophy, "leaving sixteen not shown to have acted upon it in any way." He asserted that "we have twenty-three out of our thirty-nine fathers 'who framed the Government under which we live,' who have, upon their official responsibility and their corporal oaths, acted upon the very question which the text affirms they 'understood just as well, and even better than we do now;' and twenty-one of them — a clear majority of the whole 'thirty-nine' — so acting upon it as to make them guilty of gross political impropriety and willful perjury, if, in their understanding, any proper division between local and federal authority, or anything in the Constitution they had made themselves, and sworn to support, forbade the Federal Government to control as to slavery in the federal territories." Lincoln, on this point, in summation, stated, "Thus the twenty-one acted; and, as actions speak louder than words, so actions, under such responsibility, speak still louder."

Lincoln admitted that "the remaining sixteen of the 'thirty-nine,' so far as I have discovered, have left no record of their understanding upon the direct question of federal control of slavery in the federal territories." However, he argued that "there is much reason to believe that their understanding upon that question would not have appeared different from that of their twenty-three compeers, had it been manifested at all." Of the sixteen, "several of the most noted anti-slavery men of those times — as Dr. Franklin, Alexander Hamilton and Gouverneur Morris" were included in the sixteen "while there was not one now known to have been otherwise, unless it may be John Rutledge, of South Carolina." He declared:

> It is surely safe to assume that the thirty-nine framers of the original Constitution, and the seventy-six members of the Congress which framed the amendments thereto, taken together, do certainly include those who may be fairly called 'our fathers who framed the Government under which we live.' I defy any man to show that any one of them ever, in his whole life, declared that, in his understanding, any proper division of local from federal authority, or any part of the Constitution, forbade the Federal Government to control as to slavery in the federal territories. I go a step further. I defy any one to show that any living man in the whole world ever did, prior to the beginning of the present century (and I might almost say prior to the beginning of the last half of the present century,) declare that, in his understanding, any proper division of local from federal authority, or any part of the Constitution, forbade the Federal Government to control as to slavery in the federal territories. To those who now so declare, I give, not only "our fathers who framed

the Government under which we live," but with them all other living men within the century in which it was framed, among whom to search, and they shall not be able to find evidence of a single man agreeing with them.

In concluding this point, Lincoln demanded that "as those fathers marked it, so let it be again marked, as an evil not to be extended, but to be tolerated and protected only because of and so far as its actual presence among us makes that toleration and protection a necessity. Let all the guaranties those fathers gave it, be, not grudgingly, but fully and fairly maintained. For this Republicans contend, and with this, so far as I know or believe, they will be content."

While Lincoln spoke to the Republicans, and to some extent all northerners, he then, surprisingly, turned his attention to another audience, one that vehemently rejected every conclusion he had made and was not present among the Republicans that night: "And now, if they would listen — as I suppose they will not — I would address a few words to the Southern people."

The southern people, he said, had claimed that they were "conservative — eminently conservative," while the Republicans were "revolutionary, destructive, or something of the sort. What is conservatism? Is it not adherence to the old and tried, against the new and untried? We stick to, contend for, the identical old policy on the point in controversy which was adopted by 'our fathers who framed the Government under which we live;' while you with one accord reject, and scout, and spit upon that old policy, and insist upon substituting something new."

The philosophy of the southern people varied considerably, Lincoln knew. "Some of you are for reviving the foreign slave trade; some for a Congressional Slave-Code for the Territories; some for Congress forbidding the Territories to prohibit within their limits; some for maintaining Slavery in the Territories through the judiciary...." Others in the South even agreed with Douglas, supporting "the 'gur-reat pur-rinciple' that 'if one man would enslave another, no third man should object,' fantastically called 'Popular Sovereignty.'" Lincoln claimed though, that there was "never a man among you in favor of federal prohibition of slavery in federal territories, according to the practice of 'our fathers who framed the Government under which we live.' Not one of all your various plans can show a precedent or an advocate in the century within which our Government originated. Consider then, whether your claim of conservatism for yourselves, and your charge of destructiveness against us, are based on the most clear and stable foundations."

The South Lincoln believed, accused the Republicans of creating the slavery agitation: "Again, you say we have made the slavery question more prominent than it formerly was. We deny it. We admit that it is more prominent, but we deny that we made it so. It was not we, but you, who discarded the old policy of the fathers. We resisted, and still resist, your innovation; and thence comes the greater prominence of the question." Lincoln asked, in reference to the change that had occurred with the Kansas-Nebraska Act, "Would you have that question reduced to its former proportions? Go back to that old policy. What has been will be again, under the same conditions. If you would have the peace of the old times, readopt the precepts and policy of the old times."

Lincoln also rejected the accusation by the South that the Republicans had fomented slave insurrections. "Slave insurrections are no more common now than they were before the Republican party was organized," Lincoln declared. In reference to Nat Turner's rebellion, he asked, "What induced the Southampton insurrection, twenty-eight years ago, in which, at least three times as many lives were lost as at Harper's Ferry? You can scarcely stretch your very elastic fancy to the conclusion that Southampton was 'got up by Black Republicanism.' In the present state of things in the United States, I do not think a general, or even a very extensive slave insurrection, is possible. The indispensable concert of action cannot be attained. The slaves have no means of rapid communication; nor can be supplied, the indispensable connecting trains."

Jefferson would have sided with the Republicans, Lincoln argued. "In the language of Mr. Jefferson, uttered many years ago, 'It is still in our power to direct the process of emancipation, and deportation peaceably, and in such slow degrees, as that the evil will wear off insensibly'" so that the nation would be "'filled up by free white laborers.'" However, Jefferson's proposition did not demand that the federal government interfere with slavery where it then existed. "Mr. Jefferson did not mean to say, nor do I, that the power of emancipation is in the Federal Government. He spoke of Virginia; and, as to the power of emancipation, I speak of the slaveholding States only. The Federal Government, however, as we insist, has the power of restraining the extension of the institution — the power to insure that a slave insurrection shall never occur on any American soil which is now free from slavery."

Lincoln also disagreed with the proposition, accepted by many southerners, that John Brown's raid equaled a slave rebellion. "John Brown's effort was peculiar. It was not a slave insurrection. It was an attempt by white men to get up a revolt among slaves, in which the slaves refused to participate. In fact, it was so absurd that the slaves, with all their ignorance, saw plainly enough it could not succeed." Lincoln dismissed the entire venture. "That affair, in its philosophy, corresponds with the many attempts, related in history, at the assassination of kings and emperors. An enthusiast broods over the oppression of a people till he fancies himself commissioned by Heaven to liberate them. He ventures the attempt, which ends in little else than his own execution."

Brown's raid had only increased talk of secession in the South. The final insult, which many southerners considered grounds for secession, would occur with the election of a Republican president. Lincoln found no justification for secession based on the occurrence. "But you will not abide the election of a Republican President! In that supposed event, you say, you will destroy the Union; and then, you say, the great crime of having destroyed it will be upon us! That is cool. A highwayman holds a pistol to my ear, and mutters through his teeth, 'Stand and deliver, or I shall kill you, and then you will be a murderer!'"

Despite the wild southern accusations, Lincoln, unlike Seward, recommended caution to his party faithful. "A few words now to Republicans. It is exceedingly desirable that all parts of this great Confederacy shall be at peace, and in harmony, one with another. Let us Republicans do our part to have it so. Even though much provoked, let us do nothing through passion and ill temper. Even though the southern people will not so much as listen to us, let us calmly consider their demands, and yield to them if, in our deliberate view of our duty, we possibly can." However, Lincoln would not yield on the immorality of slavery. Slavery constituted the "whole controversy" with the South "thinking it right, and our thinking it wrong," Lincoln maintained. "Thinking it right, as they do, they are not to blame for desiring its full recognition, as being right; but, thinking it wrong, as we do, can we yield to them? Can we cast our votes with their view, and against our own? In view of our moral, social, and political responsibilities, can we do this?"

Despite the Republicans' conviction of slavery's immorality, Lincoln urged restraint. "Wrong as we think slavery is, we can yet afford to let it alone where it is, because that much is due to the necessity arising from its actual presence in the nation; but can we, while our votes will prevent it, allow it to spread into the National Territories, and to overrun us here in these Free States? If our sense of duty forbids this, then let us stand by our duty, fearlessly and effectively." Lincoln, in considering Douglas, warned that the Republicans should not "be diverted" by any "contrivances such as groping for some middle ground between the right and the wrong, vain as the search for a man who should be neither a living man nor a dead man — such as a policy of 'don't care' on a question about which all true men do care — such as Union appeals beseeching true Union men to yield to Disunionists...."

In his final paragraph, he demanded determination and vigilance. "Neither let us be slandered from our duty by false accusations against us, nor frightened from it by menaces of destruction to the Government nor of dungeons to ourselves. LET US HAVE FAITH THAT RIGHT MAKES MIGHT, AND IN THAT FAITH, LET US, TO THE END, DARE TO DO OUR DUTY AS WE UNDERSTAND IT."

7

The True Lincoln: In New England

February–March 1860

In New York, Lincoln had omitted the Declaration of Independence. In his entire Cooper Union speech, he had not mentioned the document once. He had demonstrated the antislavery beliefs of the founders, but he had avoided the far more crucial question: *Why* did the founding fathers create and enact antislavery legislation? Lincoln's New England speeches would indicate whether his Cooper Union speech represented a new strategy that would ignore the promise of "all men are created equal" or whether the Cooper Union speech represented the anomaly.

Lincoln delivered speeches at numerous New England towns. The day after Cooper Union he spoke at Providence, Rhode Island, and then on February 29 he visited his eldest son, Robert Todd Lincoln, at Exeter, New Hampshire, where Robert was attending school. On March 1, Lincoln delivered speeches at Concord and Manchester, New Hampshire. He returned to Exeter on March 1 and spent some more time with his son the following day. Bypassing Massachusetts, which had no upcoming elections, he traveled south to Connecticut.[1]

Most of Lincoln's speeches are lost to history; reporters summarized some of them while others only quoted certain passages. However, one speech was recorded almost in its entirety at Hartford, Connecticut, and another speech at New Haven, Connecticut, was recorded verbatim. Both of these speeches provide a more comprehensive and more accurate depiction of Lincoln's philosophy than his Cooper Union speech.[2]

Before speaking in Hartford, Connecticut, however, Lincoln took time to visit with a notable New England Republican who attended Lincoln's Hartford speech, and who would attend the nominating convention in Chicago as the Connecticut delegation chairman: Gideon Welles. The Democratic-Republican was one of five men who constituted the escort for Lincoln in Hartford, and sat close to the stage, reflecting his position in the party. Welles apparently approved of the speech, his biographer noting that although he found nothing new in Lincoln's address, he stood with the rest of the audience members when they enthusiastically applauded the westerner.[3]

In Hartford, the two men conversed for an extended time at a small downtown bookstore. The two continued their discussion later at the office of Welles' Hartford, Connecticut, newspaper, the *Evening Press*, the same newspaper in which Welles had attacked Seward's "Irrepressible Conflict" speech. Although no record exists concerning Lincoln's impression of Welles, Welles must have been impressed by Lincoln. Welles' *Evening Press* described Lincoln's speech as "earnest, strong, honest, simple in style and clear as crystal in his logic." Although Welles' biographer admits that the author of the compliment is not known, this praise of a former Whig was rare for a paper that had clear leanings toward the Democratic-Republican wing of the party.[4]

Lincoln captured the nation's current struggle in the first sentence of his Hartford, Connecticut, speech: "Slavery is the great political question of the nation. Though all desire its settlement, it still remains the all-pervading question of the day. It has been so especially for the past six years. It is indeed older than the revolution, rising, subsiding, then rising again, till '54, since which time it has been constantly augmenting." Lincoln asked, "Why, when all desire to have this controversy settled, can we not settle it satisfactorily?" "One reason," he answered, "is, we want it settled in different ways, and neither has a decided majority. In my humble opinion, the importance and magnitude of the question is underrated, even by our wisest men. If I be right, the first thing is to get a just estimate of the evil — then we can provide a cure."

The evil, Lincoln argued, constituted "one-sixth, and a little more, of the population of the United States" which "are slaves — looked upon as property, as nothing but property. The cash value of these slaves, at a moderate estimate is $2,000,000,000" which "has a vast influence on the minds of its owners." He contended that "public opinion is founded, to a great extent, on a property basis. What lessens the value of property is opposed, what enhances its value is favored. Public opinion at the South regards slaves as property and insists upon treating them like other property."

Public opinion in the North, Lincoln maintained, stood in direct opposition to the South on this issue. "The free states" profess "the equality of men. We think slavery is morally wrong, and a direct violation of that principle. We all think it wrong. It is clearly proved, I think, by natural theology, apart from revelation. Every man, black, white or yellow, has a mouth to be fed and two hands with which to feed it — and that bread should be allowed to go to that mouth without controversy." To Lincoln, slavery was "wrong in its effect upon white people and free labor" and "it is the only thing that threatens the Union." He then exhibited common ground with Seward with the sentence, "It makes what Senator Seward has been much abused for calling an 'irrepressible conflict.'"

Lincoln attacked Douglas's solution to the slavery problem, his proposition of indifference toward slavery, and embraced an old friend, the Declaration of Independence. Douglas had developed a principle of "don't care" about slavery which Lincoln rejected because "every body does care." He questioned, "Is there a Democrat, especially one of the Douglas wing, but will declare that the Declaration of Independence has no application to the negro?" Lincoln had "asked this question in large audiences where they were in the habit of answering right out, but no one would say otherwise." Lincoln recalled that "not one" of the Democrats "said it five years ago. I have never heard it till I heard it from the lips of Judge Douglas." Some "boldly took the bull by the horns and said the Declaration of Independence was not true! They didn't sneak around the question." He asserted that he "heard first from Douglas that the Declaration did not apply to black men. Not a man of them said it till then — they all say it now."

Douglas had argued that a choice had to be made between the white and black races. Lincoln rejected that opinion. "The proposition that there is a struggle between the white man and the negro contains a falsehood. There is no struggle. If there was," Lincoln admitted, "I should be for the white man," but I have never had to struggle to keep a negro from enslaving me, nor did a negro ever have to fight to keep me from enslaving him." However, Lincoln did not believe that this necessitated an attack on the South. "If the Republicans, who think slavery is wrong, get possession of the general government, we may not root out the evil at once, but may at least prevent its extension."

Lincoln, in contrast to Seward, had established a pattern of seeking to maintain the allegiance of all Republicans, especially those who had formerly identified themselves as Democrats. Now, in Hartford, he even appealed to those who continued to maintain allegiance to the Democratic Party. "We want those [Democrats] who think slavery wrong to quit voting with those who think it right." Lincoln believed that "if those democrats really think slavery wrong they will be much pleased when earnest men in the slave states take up a plan of gradual emancipation and go to work energetically and very kindly to get rid of the evil."

Lincoln also renewed his argument that the founders were opposed to slavery as evidenced in the Constitution, and in the prohibition of the slave trade after 1808. In conclusion, he denied Republican involvement in the John Brown raid and stated, in similar language to his Cooper Union address, "If slavery is right, it ought to be extended; if not, it ought to be restricted — there is no middle ground. Wrong as we think it, we can afford to let it alone where it of necessity now exists; but we cannot afford to extend it into free territory and around our own homes. Let us stand against it!" And finally, in response to those who opposed the Republicans by wrapping themselves in the banner of unionism and ignoring slavery, Lincoln rebuffed them. "The 'Union' arrangements are all a humbug — they reverse scriptural order, calling the righteous and not sinners to repentance. Let us not be slandered or intimidated to turn from our duty. Eternal right makes might — as we understand our duty, let us do it!"[5]

The following day, on March 6, he spoke at New Haven, Connecticut. Here, unlike at Cooper Union, Lincoln did not focus solely on the specific issue of secession or the demarcation between federal and state authority, but covered the fundamental issue that led to the talk of secession, the morality of slavery. In so doing, Lincoln again grounded his philosophy in the Declaration of Independence. He claimed that "if the Republican party of this nation shall ever have the national house entrusted to its keeping, it will be the duty of that party to attend to all the affairs of national house-keeping." The Republicans "will then be compelled to attend to other questions, besides this question which now assumes an overwhelming importance — the question of Slavery." "The question of Slavery is the question, the all absorbing topic of the day" and one which "the whole American people ... wish ... settled — wish it out of the way."

Douglas had a solution to the issue when in 1854 he inaugurated a "new policy ... with the avowed object and confident promise that it would entirely and forever put an end to the Slavery agitation. It was again and again declared that under this policy, when once successfully established, the country would be forever rid of this whole question. Yet under the operation of that policy this agitation has not only not ceased, but it has been constantly augmented." Lincoln argued that "this question" of slavery "is one of national importance, and we cannot help dealing with it; we must do something about it whether we will or not. We cannot avoid it."

Lincoln again admitted, in referring to several American leaders, including Douglas, that "the causes of these repeated failures is that our best and greatest men have greatly underestimated the size of this question." He asked his audience to "look at the magnitude of this subject! One sixth of our population, in round numbers — not quite one sixth, and yet more than a seventh, — about one sixth of the whole population of the United States are slaves!" The slaveowners "consider them property" and "the effect upon the minds of the owners is that of property, and nothing else — it induces them to insist upon all that will favorably affect its value as property, to demand laws and institutions to make it durable, lasting and universal. The effect on the minds of the owners is to persuade them that there is no wrong in it. The slaveholder does not like to be considered a mean fellow, for holding himself and sets about arguing himself into the belief that Slavery is right." From Lincoln's perspective, "the property influences his mind."

"But here in Connecticut," he continued, "[and in] the North Slavery does not exist, and we see it through no such medium. To us it appears natural to think that slaves are human beings; men, not property; that some of the things, at least, stated about men in the Declaration of Independence apply to them as well as to us." Lincoln may have originally intended the former sentence to end with "apply to them" but he placed African Americans on equal plane with all others when he added "as well as to us." He dispelled any doubt as to his egalitarianism when he asserted "that this Charter of Freedom applies to the slave as well as to ourselves, that the class of arguments put forward to batter down that idea, are also calculated to break down the very idea of free government, even for white men, and to undermine the very foundations of free society."

Lincoln, though, reiterated the conservative approach, what he believed currently achievable. "We think Slavery a great moral wrong, and while we do not claim the right to touch it where it exists, we wish to treat it as a wrong in the Territories, where our votes will reach it. We think that a respect for ourselves, a regard for future generations and for the God that made us, require that we put down this wrong where our votes will properly reach it. We think that species of labor an injury to free white men — in short, we think Slavery a great moral, social and political evil, tolerable only because, and so as its actual existence makes it necessary to tolerate it, and that beyond that, it ought to be treated as a wrong."

He again displayed great respect toward Seward and again emphasized the common ground with the New Yorker by repeating the favorable comments that he had previously made at Hartford: "Now these two ideas, that property idea that Slavery is right, and the idea that it is wrong, come into collision, and do actually produce that irrepressible conflict which Mr. Seward has been so roundly abused for mentioning." Lincoln, giving further concurrence with Seward's opinion, asserted, "The two ideas conflict, and must conflict."

Lincoln also rejected any accusation that the Republicans were the source of disunion, arguing instead that the conflict developed from the issue of slavery. He asked, "[D]oes anything in any way endanger the perpetuity of this

Union but that single thing, Slavery?" The Republicans rightfully "claim that we are the only true Union men, and we put to them this one proposition: What ever endangered this Union, save and except Slavery?" Lincoln questioned, "Can any man believe that the way to save the Union is to extend and increase the only thing that threatens the Union, and to suffer it to grow bigger and bigger?"

In combating slavery, Lincoln did not "wish to be misunderstood" because he did not "mean that we ought to attack it where it exists. To me it seems that if we were to form a government anew, in view of the actual presence of Slavery we should find it necessary to frame just such a government as our fathers did; giving to the slaveholder the entire control where the system was established, while we possessed the power to restrain it from going outside those limits." Lincoln argued that "from the necessities of the case we should be compelled to form just such a government as our blessed fathers gave us; and, surely, if they have so made it, that adds another reason why we should let Slavery alone where it exists."

Lincoln then took aim at a familiar opponent. "Now I have spoken of a policy based on the idea that Slavery is wrong, and a policy based upon the idea that it is right. But an effort has been made for a policy that shall treat it as neither right or wrong. It is based upon utter indifference. Its leading advocate has said 'I don't care whether it be voted up or voted down.'" Lincoln categorized "this policy, the plausible sugar-coated name of which is 'popular sovereignty.'" Douglas's policy, Lincoln believed, "stands in the way of a permanent settlement of the question." He rebuffed the idea that popular sovereignty would become "the permanent policy of the country" because "there is nobody that 'don't care.' All the people do care!" Douglas could succeed "if the people can be brought round to say honestly 'we don't care.'"

Lincoln brought the issue to its fundamental basis by raising the standard of the Declaration of Independence in the face of Douglas's popular sovereignty. He warned, "Remember what a long stride has been taken since the repeal of the Missouri Compromise! Do you know of any Democrat, of either branch of the party — do you know one who declares that he believes that the Declaration of Independence has any application to the negro? Judge Taney declares that it has not, and Judge Douglas even vilifies me personally and scolds me roundly for saying that the Declaration applies to all men, and that negroes are men." He asked, "Is there a Democrat here who does not deny that the Declaration applies to a negro? Do any of you know of one? Well, I have tried before perhaps fifty audiences, some larger and some smaller than this, to find one such Democrat, and never yet have I found one who said I did not place him right in that. I must assume that Democrats hold that, and now, not one of these Democrats can show that he said that five years ago!"

Lincoln pointed to Douglas's Kansas-Nebraska Act as the source for the repudiation of the Declaration of Independence. "I venture to defy the whole party to produce one man that ever uttered the belief that the Declaration did not apply to negroes, before the repeal of the Missouri Compromise! Four or five years ago we all thought the negroes were men, and that when 'all men' were named, negroes were included." Now Douglas's party rejected that notion. "But the whole Democratic party has deliberately taken negroes from the class of men and put them in the class of brutes."

Lincoln then tackled four specific charges that had been made against his party: Seward's "irrepressible conflict," John Brown, the "revolutionary" nature of the Republicans and the Republicans as the source of disunionism. "There is 'the irrepressible conflict.' How they rail at Seward for that saying! They repeat it constantly; and although the proof has been thrust under their noses again and again, that almost every good man since the formation of our government has uttered that same sentiment...." To Lincoln, Seward was correct. "Another is John Brown!" he exclaimed. "You stir up insurrections, you invade the South! John Brown! Harper's Ferry! Why, John Brown was not a Republican! You have never implicated a single Republican in that Harper's Ferry enterprise" but "still insist that our doctrines and declarations necessarily lead to such results. We do not believe it."

As to the charge that the Republicans were "revolutionaries," Lincoln flatly rejected the accusation by asserting the opposite, that the Republicans were the conservatives. "What is conservatism? Is it not adherence to the old and tried, against the new and tried?" While Lincoln recognized that the some of the Republicans' opponents supported "reviving the foreign slave-trade," or were "for maintaining Slavery in the Territories through the Judiciary" or "for the 'gur-reat pur-rin-ciple' that 'if one man would enslave another, no third man should object,' fantastically called 'Popular Sovereignty'"; none of the Republicans' opponents support the "Federal prohibition of Slavery in Federal Territories," which was "the practice of our fathers who framed the Government under which we live." None of the Republicans' opponents' "plans can show a precedent or an advocate in the century within which our Government originated. And yet you draw yourselves up and say 'We are eminently conservative!'" Lincoln unquestionably believed that it was the Republicans who advocated the principles of the founding fathers and therefore deserved the title of "conservatives."

Lincoln brushed aside the charges that the Republicans were the cause of disunionism by urging the Republicans to support the union: "It is exceedingly desirable that all parts of this great Confederacy shall be at peace, and in harmony, one with another. Let us Republicans do our part to have it so. Even though much provoked, let us do nothing through passion and ill temper." Despite the South's expressed indifference, and in some cases outright hatred of his party, Lincoln, unlike Seward, recommended patience and respect. "Even though the Southern people will not so much as listen to us, let us calmly consider their demands, and yield to them if, in our deliberate view of our duty, we possibly can."

However, Lincoln urged that the Republicans not compromise with the opposition on the immorality of slavery, a compromise which Lincoln considered a form of capitulation, for the opposition would only respect a compromise by which the Republicans ceased calling "slavery wrong, and join[ed] them in calling it right." Then, he said, the Republicans must follow Douglas by "suppressing all declarations that Slavery is wrong, whether made in politics, in presses, in pulpits, or in private. We must arrest and return their fugitive slaves with greedy pleasure." The Republicans would then, like the pro-slavery forces, align themselves against the slave. The Republicans' opposition "whenever a slave runs away [means] they will overlook the obvious fact that he ran because he was oppressed, and declare he was stolen off. Whenever a master cuts his slaves with the lash, and they cry out under it, he will overlook the obvious fact that the negroes cry out because they are hurt, and insist that they were put up to it by some rascally abolitionist."

The Republicans, despite all the charges and accusations, must stand firm, Lincoln insisted. "Let us be diverted by none of those sophistical contrivances wherewith we are so industriously plied and belabored — contrivances such as groping for some middle ground between the right and the wrong, vain as the search for a man who should be neither a living man nor a dead man — such as a policy of 'don't care' on question about which all true men care — such as Union appeal beseeching true Union men to yield to Disunionists, reversing the divine rule, and calling, not the sinners, but the righteous to repentance — such as invocations of Washington, imploring men to unsay what Washington did." In a slight change from his Cooper Union conclusion, Lincoln added, "Neither let us be slandered from our duty by false accusations against us, nor frightened from it by menaces of destruction to the Government, nor of dungeons to ourselves. Let us have faith that right makes might; and in that faith, let us, to the end, dare to do our duty, as we understand it."

At Hartford and New Haven, Lincoln complimented Seward, urged respect for Democrats and for the South, but most important, he returned to the Declaration of Independence. Although the Cooper Union Address may have received more publicity in 1860 and more attention from historians today, it was his Connecticut speeches that properly defined who he was and for what he stood. His hope for his nation was not found in the Constitution but in the Declaration of Independence, in the words "all men are created equal," that the promises of the Declaration, as he stated at New Haven, "apply to them as well as to us."

Lincoln visited five other New England cities after his New Haven speech before returning to New York. From there, on March 12, seventeen days after arriving in New York, he returned home.

Lincoln wrote his wife:

> I have been unable to escape this toil. If I had foreseen it, I think I would not have come east at all. The speech at New York, being within my calculation before I started, went off possibly well and gave me no trouble whatever. The difficulty was to make nine others, before reading audiences who had already seen all my ideas in print.[6]

In terms of improving his standing as a presidential candidate, the trip proved a failure. He did not win the support of any state delegation. The Cooper Union address had no effect on the New York Republican Party, which remained steadfastly behind Seward. Lincoln even failed to impress Horace Greeley, one of the leading anti–Seward Republicans, who had no intention of advocating for Lincoln. Most disappointing of all, Welles, the leader of the Connecticut delegation with whom Lincoln had held two meetings, remained firmly behind Chase. Lincoln had, since the 1858 debates, made speeches in Iowa, Ohio, Indiana, Wisconsin, Kansas, New York, Rhode Island, New Hampshire and Connecticut, and in none of those states could he count on any significant support.

Lincoln historian Ida Tarbell described it best: "Up to the opening of the convention in May there was, in fact, no specially prominent mention of Lincoln by the Eastern press. Greeley, intent on undermining Seward, though as yet nobody perceived him to be so, printed in the New York weekly 'Tribune'— the paper which went to the country at large — correspondence [which favored nine candidates] but not Lincoln. The New York 'Herald' of May 1, in discussing" potential candidates noted six Republicans, but not Lincoln. On May 10, an editorial titled "The Nomination at Chicago" in the *Independent* listed six Republicans "but it did not mention Lincoln." Tarbell found that Lincoln's "most conspicuous Eastern recognition before the convention was in 'Harpers Weekly' of May 12th, his face being included in a double page of portraits of 'eleven prominent candidates for the Republican presidential nomination at Chicago.' Brief biographical sketches appeared in the same number — the last and shortest of them being of Lincoln."[7]

His Illinois supporters could only hope to have more success at the convention than Lincoln had cultivated on the road.

8

Preparing for the Convention

April–May 1860

"Toward the end of 1859 the question of Presidential candidates began to be mooted," the German Republican Gustave Koerner wrote in his memoirs. "Seward, however, seemed to be the choice of most of the Northern and Northwestern States":

> In point of ability he certainly had no superior. He was a man of long political experience, had been a power in his own State, whose governor had been, and was the acknowledged leader of the Republican party in Congress. Seward was a man, not only of considerable general information, but of much thought, a subtle reasoner, a skillful debater, and at times a great orator. He was of a social and rather jovial disposition, fond of good living, and in conversation often bluntly original. Radical in theory, he was conservative in action, and in this particular misunderstood by both parties. He showed much aptitude in diplomacy.... Seward had just returned from a tour through Europe and parts of Asia, and had been shown great attention by leading statesmen and otherwise distinguished persons. The German element was particularly enthusiastic for Seward.

However, "of Republican candidates there was no lack." Koerner considered Chase "at least equal to Seward, as far as natural genius was concerned" and "radical in action as well as in thought. The great State of Ohio was for him, and he had friends in almost every other State." The large state of Pennsylvania urged her favorite son, Cameron, and Missouri rallied behind Edward Bates, a former tacit supporter of the Know-Nothings. Koerner found it "strange" that in Missouri Bates, "was most strongly supported by the Germans, who were really almost the only Republicans in the State." Furthermore, Bates, "being an old-line conservative Whig, and having presided over the Whig Fillmore Convention in 1856, which endorsed, not the platform, but Fillmore, the nominee of the Native American Convention ... had very many friends amongst the Republicans or People's party, as it was called in Pennsylvania, and was considered very strong in Indiana." Bates had associated with the Republicans since 1856 and Koerner, the German Republican, belatedly admitted that he had several admirable qualities: "He was an upright man, a prominent lawyer, a most eloquent orator." Despite these qualities, and no doubt because of his association with the Know-Nothings, Koerner believed that Bates was "by no means qualified to be the leader of such a party as the young Republican party then was."

The Illinois Republicans pursued a quiet strategy in regard to Lincoln, Koerner noted. They believed "that the best policy for the party in our State was to keep Lincoln in the background for the present, or at least not to push his claims to any extent. The friends of Seward, Bates, Cameron and Chase would fight against each other, and necessarily damage the candidates they upheld. Lincoln, being out of the struggle in a measure, would be let alone, and, when brought forward at the proper time, would meet with no embittered enemies." This was easily accomplished since Lincoln was considered far less prominent than his competition. In fact, the only state whose support he could hope to garner before the convention was his home state.

First, the Illinois Republicans wanted the convention in Illinois, Koerner recalled. Judd, working on Lincoln's behalf, "after a long combat" helped convince the National Central Committee, which met in New York, to select Chicago "as the place for the National Presidential Convention," while "Seward's friends pleaded strongly for some city in New York; Chase's, for Cleveland or Columbus, Ohio; Bates's, for St. Louis." The National Central Committee members chose Chicago because they considered it "a sort of neutral ground" since "Lincoln was not considered a candidate in the first instance, but only as a possible one in case of failure to select one of the more prominent candidates."[1]

Despite Seward's deserved status as front-runner, if not presumed nominee, other Republicans drew attention to themselves as possible candidates. Cassius Clay, in a rather bold move, actually wrote to Thurlow Weed, Seward's confidant and political manager, suggesting that he, and not Seward, should be the nominee. Clay admitted that he considered Seward "his first choice" but could not help but foresee the possibility that "*newcomers*" might "enter the balloting," which would justify his entry. The Kentuckian then predicted, "in that event I will be chosen for these reasons:

1. I am a Southern man, and the cry about sectionalism will be silenced.
2. I am a tariff man; and Pa. must be consulted in that.

3. I am *popular* with the Germans everywhere, and not offensive to the Americans [the Know-Nothings].
4. I have served the party longer than any other man without contemporary reward as others have had.
5. There are elements in my history which will arouse popular enthusiasm and *insure without fail success.*
6. That I will form a Southern wing to the party which is necessary to a safe administration of the government, and thus put down all hopes of *disunion."*

"I think I am the second choice of all the 'old line' candidates' friends," he concluded.[2]

The confidence of Salmon P. Chase, the governor of Ohio, also increased with the approaching convention. One supporter wrote him that the "radical Republicans are rapidly concentrating on you," while others believed that Seward's support had become so weak that he could not even capture New York. Another Republican found Greely "warmly against Seward" and that he was "at present favorable" to Chase. In addition, the Ohio Republican received reports from Indiana, Iowa, and Kansas that his prospects were rising.[3]

Simon Cameron, a Pennsylvania senator, was also enjoying praise as a presidential candidate. Cameron received endorsements from the *Pittsburgh Gazette;* reflecting support from outside his home state, the *New York Herald* also endorsed him. Supporters established a Cameron club in Chicago and in February of 1860 the Pennsylvania Republican state convention endorsed Cameron for president.[4]

The Blair family, which had a prominent following in Maryland and Missouri, thought Edward Bates was the man. Frank Blair, Sr., wrote that "the ultra Republicans on our northern borders from East to West ... incline to Seward's nomination — The middle men & middle states undoubtedly look to Bates as the safest man to prevent secession or to suppress it. This idea may render him the most available candidate, & as such the choice at Chicago — In my opinion he is preferable to Seward in every respect...." His son, Frank Blair, Jr., explained in another letter: "I believe in the good sense of the Black Republican party and because I know that they can elect Bates and don't believe they have another *name* by which they can certainly be saved...." Later he predicted, "I tell you we shall yet get the old man nominated at Chicago and carry the Country for him at the election in November...." If, on the other hand, the Republicans failed to nominate Bates, Blair confessed, "After Bates I say I dont care a d — n —...."[5]

Bates himself expressed substantial optimism. In a diary entry on February 25 he wrote that his "friends have returned [from the Republican convention in Indiana] and report favorably. A large majority of the delegates appointed to the Chicago Convention is made up of 'Bates men' — 20 to 6 or 22 to 4." Bates also recorded that a Pennsylvania delegate "is buoyant and seems confident of my nomination, although the Delegation is under instruction to vote for Senator Cameron. That, he thinks, is a mere compliment, which will be fulfilled by casting one vote — And then, I being the first choice of nearly half of the Delegates (of Pa.) and the second choice of all, will be sure of the united support of all of that delegation. And that, considering the favorable signs in other States, he thinks will make my nomination sure."[6]

Lincoln was far more humble. In fact, he did not even declare himself a candidate while his supporters had been plotting on his behalf. On February 10, with only three months remaining before the convention, Horace White, a *Chicago Press and Tribune* reporter who had attended all of the Lincoln-Douglas debates and had been present for many of Lincoln's speeches during that campaign, wrote him a letter addressed to "Friend Lincoln" in which he advised, "You must get yourself in thinking for the presidency. Do not be surprised if the *Press and Tribune* break ground for you in a few days." As predicted, on February 16, the *Tribune*, recognizing the critical importance of prevailing in the four Northern States the Republicans lost in 1856, namely, Illinois, Indiana, Pennsylvania and New Jersey, advised, "We have no hesitancy in saying that as ... Abraham Lincoln of Illinois is the peer of any man yet mentioned in connection with the Republican nomination, while as regards availability we believe him more certain to carry Illinois and Indiana than anyone else and his political antecedents are such as to commend him heartily to the support of Pennsylvania and New Jersey."[7]

In April, two months later, Judd, who also recognized the importance of Illinois, Indiana, Pennsylvania and New Jersey outlined his strategy to Trumbull. "Cannot a quiet combination between the delegates from New Jersey, Indiana and Illinois be brought about — including Pennsylvania. United actions by these delegates will probably control the convention." But the *Tribune's* endorsement and Judd's strategy would prove pointless if Lincoln did not want the nomination.[8]

Trumbull, who had no personal desire for the presidency but did desire that Lincoln seek the office, finally wrote Lincoln a letter, perhaps a rather blunt one, asking whether Lincoln had any interest in a nomination for which he friends were making substantial plans. "As you request, I will be entirely frank," Lincoln said. "The taste is in my mouth a little."

He then launched into a analysis of the current political situation, although in his typical objective fashion he admitted that his personal self-interest "no doubt, disqualifies me, to some extent, to form correct opinions." In regards to Illinois, Lincoln thought "neither Seward nor Bates" could carry the state "if Douglas shall be on the track." Lincoln believed that Supreme Court justice John McLean, one of the major dissenters in the Dred Scott case, "could carry it with D. on or off—in other words, I think McLean is stronger in Illinois, taking all sections of it, than either S. or B; and I think S. the weakest of the three. I hear no objection to McLean, except his age; but that objection seems to occur to every one; and it is possible it might leave him no stronger than the others."

The Illinois Republicans, Lincoln thought, wanted "something here quite as much as, and which is harder to get than, the electoral vote — the Legislature. And it is exactly in this point that Seward's nomination would be hard upon us." Seward might "gain us a thousand votes in Winnebago," a northern Illinois county, Lincoln surmised, but "it would not compensate for the loss of fifty in Edgar," a southern Illinois county. In other words, Seward was too radical to win Illinois for the Republicans.

Lincoln, indicating how carefully he wished his nomination strategy to proceed, ended the letter with a specific warning to Trumbull:

> A word now for your own special benefit. You better write no letters which can possibly be distorted into opposition, or quasi opposition to me. There are men on the constant watch for such things out of which to prejudice my peculiar friends against you. While I have no more suspicion of you than I have of my best friend living, I am kept in a constant struggle against suggestions of this sort. I have hesitated some to write this paragraph, lest you should suspect I do it for my own benefit, and not for yours; but on reflection I conclude you will not suspect me.
>
> Let no eye but your own see this — not that there is anything wrong, or even ungenerous, in it; but it would be misconstrued.[9]

Finally, Lincoln was in the race. He apparently had become convinced that he would at least have the support of his fellow Republicans in Illinois, and that with Illinois — one of the four doubtful states — supporting him, he had the foundation upon which to build a campaign.

Why Lincoln decided to run is a more difficult question to answer, but his correspondence provides some evidence. In the early part of 1859 his letters bear testament to his deep disappointment with the limited perspectives of his fellow party members. Lincoln's comment that the "Massachusetts republicans should have looked beyond their noses" captures his frustration. Lincoln knew the Republicans needed a candidate who would focus on opposing Douglas and his popular sovereignty. The Republicans in Massachusetts had infuriated immigrants with their restrictions on immigrants' rights. New Hampshire and Ohio Republicans had angered the more conservative members with their attacks on the Fugitive Slave Law, and Kansas Republicans had infuriated other Republicans in not fully rejecting popular sovereignty.[10]

Lincoln discussed the qualifications that he believed a candidate should have in his Ohio and Indiana speeches. A review of his comments in those speeches reveals that Lincoln possessed those qualities. He was not radical in words or actions, and he rightly knew that the Declaration of Independence and opposition to Douglas's philosophy, the expansion of slavery — and not any other issues — were the only bases upon which all the Republicans could unite and win. Douglas's philosophy had brought Lincoln back to politics in 1854 to run for the Senate, and now, Douglas's philosophy had convinced him to run again, this time for a higher office.

However, a week later he wrote a letter marked "PRIVATE" to an Ohio Republican and admitted that with only one state supporting him he held a decidedly weak position entering the convention:

> After what you have said, it is perhaps proper I should post you, so far as I am able, as to the "lay of the land." First then, I think the Illinois delegation will be unanimous for me at the start; and no other delegation will. A few individuals in other delegations would like to go for me at the start, but may be restrained by their colleagues. It is represented to me, by men who ought to know, that the whole of Indiana might not be difficult to get. You know how it is in Ohio. I am certainly not the first choice there; and yet I have not heard that any one makes any positive objection to me. It is just so everywhere so far as I can perceive. Everywhere, except in Illinois, and possibly Indiana, one or another is preferred to me, but there is no positive objection. This is the ground as it now appears.[11]

Seward's understanding of his prospects for nomination were best illustrated by a particular project upon which he had been concentrating. In the weeks just preceding the nomination, Seward put his finishing touches on his farewell speech to the Senate. He had no intention of maintaining his Senate seat when he became a presidential candidate.[12]

Lincoln's confidence must have been shaken just a week later when, on May 9 and 10, the Illinois Republicans gathered at Decatur to nominate delegates to the presidential convention, and candidates for state offices. Lincoln attended the convention and he could gauge his popularity based on the actions of the Republicans in his home state. At the convention, John Palmer, a Lincoln friend and former Democrat, made the motion "That Abraham Lincoln is the choice of the Republican party of Illinois, for the Presidency, and the delegates from this State are instructed to use all honorable means to secure his nomination by the Chicago convention, and to vote as a unit for him."

No sooner had Palmer completed this motion than two Republicans made counter motions. One moved that the convention strike the words "and to vote as a unit for him," while another wanted to strike the words "for him."

In the state where he had made his home for twenty-four years, where he had practiced law for seventeen years, from where he had been elected to Congress, where he had helped form the Illinois Republican party, and where he had battled Douglas, there were Republicans who did not believe that Illinois should support him as a presidential nominee. Although the motions failed, and the convention adopted a resolution that maintained the words "and to vote as a unit for him," this incident served as a warning that even in his home state, he could not assume unanimous support.[13]

While Lincoln had no influence concerning the Republican delegates that each congressional district chose for the national convention, he did have an opportunity to select the four delegates-at-large for the Illinois delegation, and Lincoln made four ingenious selections. Lincoln chose Norman Judd, a former Democrat, two former Whigs, David Davis and Orville Browning, and Gustave Koerner, a German Republican. These four men represented the three major factions of the Republican Party. Davis and Judd, as Lincoln's friends, were predictable decisions. Browning's selection may seem surprising since Browning had confessed to Lincoln his preference for Bates, but Lincoln must have believed that Browning would remain loyal to the will of the state convention, and most importantly, that Browning would, as a friend, remain loyal to him. Koerner's selection surprised even Koerner because he did not even attend the state convention.

The two most unexpected choices — Browning and Koerner — would prove the most crucial. While Judd had already improved Lincoln's chances by lobbying for Chicago as the nominating convention's location, and Davis would serve as the manager for Lincoln's supporters at Chicago, Koerner and Browning, would, at one critical moment, prove decisive.

While Lincoln's supporters had to fight just to maintain unity for Lincoln in Illinois, Seward received far different news prior to the convention. The delegations of New York, Michigan, Wisconsin, Minnesota and California declared for him. He would begin the convention with one hundred eight guaranteed votes — almost half of what he required to secure the nomination — from five different states. Lincoln would begin with a meager twenty-two from only one.

9

Convention Week Begins

Saturday–Tuesday, May 12–15, 1860

As the Republicans descended on Chicago, they found themselves in a far different position than just four years before. As one historian wrote, in 1856 "a hall accommodating two thousand was quite sufficient, now a wigwam holding ten thousand was jammed, and twenty thousand people outside clamored for admittance." In 1856 "the delegates were liberty-loving enthusiasts and largely volunteers, now the delegates had been chosen by means of the organization peculiar to a powerful party." The situation then "seemed but a tentative effort and the leading men would not accept the nomination, while now triumph appeared so sure that every one of the master spirits of the party was eager to be the candidate."[1]

The 466 delegates[2] who traveled to Chicago represented twenty-four states and the three territories: the District of Columbia, Kansas and Nebraska. Six slave states sent representatives: Delaware, Maryland, Virginia, Kentucky, Missouri and even Texas. However, these state delegations did not necessarily represent the opinions of the majority within their states. Of the fifteen delegates from Virginia, ten resided in the area that would later become West Virginia. No delegates represented the other nine slave states of North Carolina, South Carolina, Georgia, Florida, Tennessee, Alabama, Mississippi, Louisiana and Arkansas. While more delegates (eighteen) listed Philadelphia as home, closely followed by New York City with twelve, these proved the exception. The vast majority of delegates traveled from small American towns, towns whose names spoke to the diversity of the nation: Winthrop, Maine; Marquette, Michigan, Zelaski, Ohio, and Mariposa, California. There was also one Pennsylvania delegate who traveled from the relatively unknown town named Gettysburg.

On Saturday, May 12, the festivities began. The Republicans' and the nation's attention focused on a single building in Chicago, what the *Tribune* described as "THE GREAT WIGWAM." In an article infused with civic and party pride, the newspaper described "The Edifice, Its History and Plan," a structure which could hold "10,000 Persons under one Roof."

"The gigantic structure," the *Tribune* declared, stood as "the largest audience room in the United States." The construction of the Wigwam "commenced early in April and pushed rapidly to completion." The "substantial wooden structure" occupied 180 feet of Market Street and 100 feet of Lake Street. According to the *Tribune*, "the entrances are broad and ample" and "the platform is wide and deep" so that it could "accommodate from six to seven hundred persons. It has on either end, as will be seen, ample Committee rooms. In front of the platform is an enclosed space for the music."

To accommodate the spectators, an "immense gallery extending on three sides" added "a judiciously arranged and excellent feature of the Wigwam." For those concerned about observing the convention from these seats, the *Tribune* assured that "the pitch of this is such that from every part a perfect view of the speaker's stand can be gained." The capacity, "based on careful estimates," reached up to "eleven thousand" and to increase its flexibility "its interior was left rough and unplaned, the wall back of the platform being the brick wall of the adjoining store." For evening events, gaslights had been added, which had an "effect" that "was brilliant in the extreme."

"Around the front of the gallery," additional interior decoration included "the coats of arms of the States, and between them wreaths of evergreen. The pillars and supports have been painted white, and wreathed with evergreens, and from each to each have been twined draperies in red, white and blue, with artificial flowers and miniature national flags. The pillars supporting the roof, which form a continuous row along the front of the platform, bear, on the side to the audience, busts of distinguished men, supported by figures of Atlas. The speaker's stand is a double dais or platform on rollers, to be pushed back to the rear of the great stage when the Convention is in session, or brought forward when the great area in front is filled for a mass meeting" and "the brick wall at the rear has been pain[t]ed and divided into arched panels, in which are colossal statuary paintings," while "over the centre of the stage is suspended a large gilt eagle."

In all the preparations for the convention, the committee had incurred a deficit, which it hoped to reduce with a Wigwam dedication ceremony on Saturday night, May 12. The committee set the admission price at twenty-five cents and, according to the *Tribune*, it proved a triumphant success. "Long before the hour announced for the opening of the exercises the rush began and the doorkeepers were busy, and by half-past seven there were from seven to eight thousand persons present. And still they came. Gentlemen and ladies, citizens and strangers, men of all parties, all pressed in. A space had been railed off dividing midway the gallery through its entire length, and in front of this were seats for ladies and gentlemen accompanying ladies. This was filled at an early hour. The platform was also reserved for the same, and there were no vacant seats."

The newspaper declared that "the great hall presents a feature most satisfactory in its acoustic qualities. During some of the speeches last evening we visited the remotest portions of the gallery, and could hear distinctly the fuller tones of the speaker's voice. During the coming week doubtless numbers of our leading Republican orators will enjoy the rare privilege of being listened to by an audience of over ten thousand persons under one roof."[3]

Although the *Tribune* trumpeted the glories of the Wigwam, it also printed a speech that had been delivered at the dedication that must have proved ominous for the Lincoln supporters. The Illinoisans desperately needed Indiana's support, and the speech of Henry S. Lane, Indiana's Republican nominee for governor, a man who would prove pivotal at the convention, but whom historians have not fully credited, provided them with little hope.[4]

It was no accident that the Republicans chose Lane as one of the speakers for the Wigwam dedication; he had impeccable Republican credentials and outstanding abilities. Lane was a ragged veteran of both the Mexican War and many political battles, a man who walked with a cane but who could bring a crowd to its feet with his energetic extemporaneous speaking. He helped found the Republican Party in Indiana and had served as chairman of the 1856 Republican presidential convention in Philadelphia.

Lane possessed another critical strength — Democrats respected him. One prominent Indiana Democrat described Lane as having "political integrity" and a "high sense of personal honor." The biographer of Lane's 1860 gubernatorial opponent wrote of the two candidates: "They easily maintained the most cordial personal relations, and carried away from their repeated contests an increased mutual regard and respect, which lasted through their lives."[5]

However, Lane knew Seward lacked this attribute and the Indiana gubernatorial candidate harbored deep concern over a Seward nomination. Indiana was no Republican bastion. In 1856, in the gubernatorial election, the Democratic candidate won by three percentage points and in the presidential election the Democratic candidate prevailed by ten percentage points. Lane needed a presidential candidate who could attract voters who had previously supported Democratic candidates, and so he arrived in Chicago with two goals. First, he wanted another candidate besides Seward to head the ticket, and second, he wanted a candidate who, like him, respected Democrats.[6]

Despite his position as gubernatorial candidate, though, he had no desire to serve as governor; his real passion was, like Lincoln's, to serve in the United States Senate, and so an interesting arrangement had been made. The Indiana Republicans hoped his popularity would help them win the governor's seat and, if they also captured a majority in the state legislature, the Indiana Republicans would elect Lane senator, and he would resign as governor.[7] .

Having no favorite son to support for president, having agreed before the convention to vote as a block, and having been one of the four northern states won by the Democrats in 1856, Indiana's delegation was in an extremely influential position. Lane, as the gubernatorial nominee, could provide some indication as to which candidate Indiana might support. "Three tremendous cheers" greeted him as he rose to speak and in his opening remarks, Lane heaped praise upon Chicago and its citizens: "I behold the almighty and transforming power of free labor in this city of Chicago, seated as it is, adorned as it is, in its queenly robes beside your crystal lake!" He then succinctly described the foundation of the Republican Party. Lane claimed "to speak in behalf of a great party, but I feel it is no sin to believe in the Declaration of Independence, or to quote the Sermon on the Mount. The grand principles which underlie the noble organization of the Republican party are principles upon which alone may be administered safely these grand institutions of ours, which beautify and adorn our common country. A few great, cardinal ideas represent the whole Republican doctrine — non-extension of slavery into the territories of the United States, and non-interference with slavery, whereso-ever slavery exists by virtue of local law." He could not have provided a better definition of a Lincoln Republican.

Later in his speech, Lane discussed several presidential candidates. He confidently predicted that America will "see a Republican President and a Republican Administration in 1861," but he added, "I know not who that Republican may be" and mentioned a few possibilities, those candidates, no doubt, that he believed were the major contenders: "He may be that distinguished, trusty, and tried statesman of New York, William A. Seward. He may be that man of pure life and spotless integrity, that man of peerless patriotism, who has never yet stained the judicial ermine, John McLean of Ohio. He may be found in the person of another distinguished citizen of Ohio, Salmon P. Chase. He may be found in the iron will man of Massachusetts, Nathaniel P. Banks, whosoever he may be, clothed with the authority and moral power which will go from this Convention, he will be President." But in his entire speech, he never once mentioned Abraham Lincoln.[8]

On the same day, May 12th, one New York newspaper, the *Poughkeepsie Eagle*, which had recognized Lincoln's strength, made an interesting, if not unexpected, suggestion as to who should accept the vice presidential nomination. As one would expect from most New York Republican newspapers, the editor asserted the paper's opinion: "It is now too late to discuss, to much purpose, the claims of the different candidates, nor is it necessary. In our view the people have settled all that already, and the only duty of the Convention will be to carry the popular will into effect, and to give its efficiency. Cavillers may speculate as they please, but we believe the eyes of all disinterested friends of Freedom are now fixed upon one man, that they expect his nomination, and that while it will be the best, it will also prove the strongest that can be made. That man is WILLIAM H. SEWARD. He alone is the personification of the principles of the Republican Party, and we believe his nomination will be hailed with an enthusiasm that has never been equaled since the election of General Jackson, in 1828, or that of General Harrison in 1840." As for other candidates, the editors warned, "While we are persuaded that these results, and a glorious victory will follow the nomination of Senator Seward, we believe the selection of any other candidate would prove a damper that may be followed by fatal consequences."

This newspaper, though, was more vexed by the question of who "shall be selected for Vice President," declaring that "there should be no compromise of principle, but the candidate equally representative of the principles of the party. With this view, and regarding his locality, we consider the Hon. ABRAHAM LINCOLN, of Illinois, as the best selection that could be made for Vice President."

Subtly acknowledging that Seward might not have strong support in the western states, the editors concluded that, with Lincoln, the Republican ticket "could carry every Free State east of the Rocky Mountains, with a sufficient effort, and that, viewing the whole ground, their election could be counted on with far more certainty than that of any other candidates."[9]

The Lincoln men, though, had their sights set on a higher goal. As soon as the Lincoln supporters arrived in Chicago, the lobbying began. As the Illinoisans, led by Judge David Davis, worked the delegations, the rumors and speculations ran rampant, and the Illinoisans repeated these tidbits of information to Lincoln. "Here in great confusion things this evening," one wrote. "Indiana is very willing to go for you, although a portion are for Bates." Some "of the Ohio men are urging you on with great vigor" but the former governor of that state "is for McLean." Pennsylvania "says Cameron or no body." The Pennsylvania and New York "delegates are quarreling." Pennsylvania will support "Seward under no Circumstances." The New York "men tell us to stand firm" and not to support "Cameron." The delegations from New York and Pennsylvania had "both proposed to run you for Vice President" but the Illinoisans had "persistently refused to suffer your name used for Vice President." The writer also noted that Greeley, despised by the pro–Seward New Yorkers, was "working for Bates." While the New Yorkers refused him a place as a delegate, Oregon, with one delegate unable to travel to Chicago, invited Greeley, who gladly accepted and worked tenaciously against Seward. In closing, the writer wrote, "Davis is furious, never saw him work so hard and so quick in all my life."[10] To guide his supporters, Lincoln provided simple, succinct advice: "Be careful to give no offence, and keep cool under all circumstances."[11]

A *New York Tribune* reporter, writing on May 13, concluded: "As yet, there is no clear indication of a preference so decided as to render the nomination of any of the candidates certain. Our correspondent says that it is estimated that Gov. Seward will lead with some eighty-five votes on the first ballot, to sixty for Judge Bates, and that Mr. Chase will hold the third place on the list." The *New York Tribune* also reported that "Mr. Blair, senior, is here, and leads the Bates interest, which is hopeful and earnest. They count up over sixty votes on the first ballot, from nine or ten States." However, the "Seward leaders are also very confident and profess the utmost faith," but the anti–Seward paper found the "Indiana delegation are vehement against him."[12]

The following day, the *New York Tribune* reported that the "weather is beautiful, and the excitement and crowd are increasing. Seward's friends are still hopeful. They hope to get parts of New Jersey, Illinois, and Pennsylvania delegations, but give up on Indiana. They triumphantly ask, if Seward is not the man, why do not his opponents unite upon a substitute?" The correspondent heard that "Mr. Lane, the Republican candidate for Governor of Indiana, says that with Seward he and his party will be inevitably defeated; but with Bates, McLean, or Lincoln, and perhaps others, he can sweep the State. The opponents of Seward insist that he cannot be nominated, since the doubtful States continue solid against him"; he also noted, "Mr. Lincoln, however, seems to be gaining ground...." In another article though, a reporter believed that Lane favored the "nomination of Judge Bates."[13]

Writing on May 15, a *New York Tribune* reporter concluded that "efforts are making to adopt the unit rule in doubtful delegations; if these are successful Seward will be defeated. Everything depends upon the obstinacy and union of Pennsylvania, Ohio, New-Jersey, Indiana, and Illinois." The reporter predicted "The Indiana delegation will vote on the first ballot solid for Bates; Illinois for Lincoln; Ohio for Chase" and "Lincoln may get Wisconsin and Minnesota early, and he threatens Bates in Indiana, and elsewhere."[14]

An *Indianapolis Daily Journal* reporter viewed the situation slightly differently. "Illinois is for Lincoln always and all the time. Indiana leans in the same direction. At a caucus of delegates this noon the expression was in the main for Lincoln. But our men are not hidebound. They will support any man who is sound and reliable and has a decent show of strength. This is a decided effort for Mr. Bates and I think it is stronger than anybody could have suspected."[15]

On May 15, the *New York Times* stated, "The feeling is strong for Mr. Seward, but the main question seems to be who can be elected? Can Mr. Seward?" The reporter astutely noted, "The opinion of the Pennsylvania, New Jersey, Illinois and Indiana Delegations will have great weight in deciding this point."[16] And the Illinoisans were trying to do just that.

Browning's schedule for May 15 provides a good indication as to the intensity of the Illinoisans' efforts. He departed his hometown, Quincy, Illinois, at 5:30 P.M. the previous day and from Galesburg, approximately halfway, he "took a sleeping car, and had comfortable nights rest." He found "a great many going up — long train of cars & all crowded."[17] Upon arriving "in Chicago before breakfast" that morning, he checked in at the Illinois delegation's headquarters at the Tremont House, and then he immediately went to work. He delivered a speech to the Maine delegation "at their solicitation" and "called upon the delegation of New Hampshire" during the day. That evening, after receiving "a message from the Massachusetts delegation," several Lincoln supporters, including Browning, "called upon them at their rooms."[18]

And the rumors continued. A Seward supporter telegraphed Seward: "There is a large lobby of interested creakers — but we feel confident of a favorable result." An Illinoisan informed Lincoln "prospects very good," "we are doing everything," "Illinois men acting nobly" and "Browning doing his duty."[19] Koerner did not share some of the Lincoln supporter's optimism.[20] In fact, far from it. He understood that two candidates held more support than Lincoln. Koerner observed "a Seward delegation, handsomely dressed and with badges and banners, from New York, nearly one thousand strong" that "paraded the streets." The German Republican found "a great many" of the German Republicans "all, strange to say, very enthusiastic for Edward Bates," whom Koerner knew had associated with the anti-immigrant Know-Nothing party. But these Germans exhibited their passion for Bates with "a great display and showed much activity."

Most distressing for Koerner was his conclusion that "the feeling for Seward was decidedly the strongest. Nearly all the German delegates, with the exception of those from Ohio, Missouri and Illinois, considered Lincoln only as a possible candidate, and preferred Seward to Chase, Cameron, or Bates. Carl Schurz [the leading German Republican] was enthusiastic for Seward. When I visited German localities, where, of course, the Presidential question was passionately discussed, I was almost the only one who advocated the claims of Lincoln, not only as the best and purest, but also as the most available candidate."

The Lincoln supporters, Koerner noted, realized that the noise in the Wigwam was more critical than the noise around it, and they implemented a bold strategy. "While the friends of the other candidates held processions and marched around with bands of music, we had made arrangements that the Wigwam should at the earliest opening every morning be filled with Illinoisans. We had them provided with tickets before tickets were distributed to others."[21]

Two Illinois supporters sent another telegram to Lincoln that day: "Moving heaven & Earth nothing will beat us but old fogy politicians" and "the heart of the delegates are with us." In other words, they were not finding their task easy and they had only two days remaining.[22]

The following day, the convention began.

10

The First Day

Wednesday, May 16, 1860

As the delegates picked up the May 16 issue of the *Tribune* that morning, they read a paper in which the editors sought to not only inform the delegates, but to also convince them that of all the candidates, Lincoln should be the party's nominee. The editors admitted, in an article titled "THE SIX STATES" that it "would be offering a premium to political minorities" if one argued "that the six doubtful States, Rhode Island, Connecticut, New Jersey, Pennsylvania, Indiana and Illinois — had the right to designate the candidates of the Chicago Convention." However, the reality of the current state of American politics demanded that the Republican nominee must be acceptable to the constituents of those six states, the editors asserted. Decisions should not be based on the "*opinions*" concerning "the probable action of those States" as opposed "to the positive *knowledge* of the capable and intelligent delegates whom they have sent here." To rely on those mere "opinions," on which the editors were, no doubt, attacking the New Yorkers, "would be rushing blindly and insanely to destruction:"[1]

> The Republicans of these [six] States know what battle they have to fight and the difficulties which stand in the way of success. They are as anxious for a victory over the Sham Democracy as the members of the party elsewhere; and the supposition that they have not representatives here who have not the sense to see and the honesty to declare the true condition of political affairs in their respective localities, is an insult which ought not to be meekly borne.

"If the convention will not listen to entreaties and remonstrances against the pursuit of a line of policy which those States declare to be fatal," the editors argued, "the consequences of the infatuation will be felt when the day for retrieving errors and blunders has gone by."

The editors admitted that they had "yet to learn" which candidate "among the many acceptable candidates before the Convention should receive" the nomination. However, without naming Seward, but clearly referring to the leading candidate, they warned "it is not too much to say that, when" these crucial states "unanimously declare that under the lead of any candidate whom they may point out, defeat is certain," it would be "presumptious [*sic*] and unsafe" for anyone "to challenge the honesty or correctness of their decision."

The editors also took a shot at their competition, such as the Republican newspaper *Chicago Journal,* which supported Seward and opposed Lincoln's nomination, and the *Chicago Times,* which supported the Democratic Party and Stephen Douglas. "For the small blowers and strikers whose incessant drunken babble in bar-rooms and on street corners impugns the deliberate judgment of six Republican State Conventions" the editors contended that they deserved "only the contempt which is bestowed upon ignorance and impudence." Specifically of their competition, the editors wrote, "For the proper reproof of a couple of newspapers in Chicago, of limited circulation and less influence — both of which act upon the hypothesis that the late Republican Convention in this State was an assemblage of knaves and fools who said one thing and meant another — for these, the punishment visited upon them by their few hundred readers will be sufficient."[2]

The editors titled their most crucial article "THE WINNING MAN—ABRAHAM LINCOLN." Here they carefully and logically made their most comprehensive case that the Republicans' only hope lay in nominating the man from Illinois. "In presenting ABRAHAM LINCOLN to the National Republican Convention, as a candidate for the Presidency," they confessed that they were "actuated not by our great love and esteem for the man, by any open or secret hostility to any other of the eminent gentlemen named for that high office, nor by a feeling of State pride or Western sectionalism." Instead, they offered four traits that made Lincoln the right choice: first, "his unexceptionable record"; second, "his position between the extremes of opinion in the party"; third, "his spotless character as a citizen," and finally, "his acknowledged ability as a statesman." These characteristics would, they argued, "in the approaching canvass, give him an advantage before the people which no other candidate can claim."

As for the other candidates, the *Tribune* acknowledged their strengths as well. Seward is "the first choice of perhaps a majority of the rank and file of the party" and Cameron "has claims upon Pennsylvania." Chase possessed "statesman-like qualities, inflexible honesty and marked executive ability" which "entitle[d] him to a high place in Republican esteem." Bates' "pure life and noble aims justly command[ed] the confidence of troops of friends." The "chivalric" Benjamin Wade of Ohio had "extorted the admiration of the North and West. Fessenden "for his gallant service must be gratefully remembered," and McLean, "whose life is without stain, and whose love of country has never been challenged, must be remembered as a strong and unexceptional man." Despite the eminent qualifications and abilities of these candidates, "Illinois claims that Mr. LINCOLN, though without the ripe experience of SEWARD, the age and maturity of BATES and MCLEAN, or the fire of FESSENDEN and WADE, has that rare and happy combination of qualities which, *as a candidate*, enables him to outrank either."[3]

While the editors discussed several other reasons to support Lincoln, two deserve special mention. First, they emphasized his character. "In all the fundamentals of Republicanism, he is radical up to the limit to which the party, with due respect for the rights of the South, proposes to go," and by this they placed Lincoln in the same philosophy as Seward but no further into the realm of the abolitionists. "But nature has given him that wise conservatism which has made his action and his expressed opinions so conform to the most mature sentiment of the country on this question of slavery, that no living man can put his finger on one of his speeches or any one of his public acts as a State legislator or as a member of Congress, to which valid objection can be raised." Here they uncovered one of Lincoln's great strengths. His actions and opinions had been made with "wise conservatism" that was lacking in Seward. He could speak the Republican philosophy in a respectful manner. Lincoln's "avoidance of extremes has not been the result of ambition, which measures words or regulates acts, but the natural consequence of an equable nature and in mental constitution that is never off its balance." Lincoln's actions and philosophy placed him in "the happy mean between that alleged fanaticism which binds the older Anti-Slavery men to Mr. Seward, and that conservatism which dictates the support of Judge Bates. Seward men, Bates men, Cameron men and Chase men can all accept him as their second choice."

Secondly, in referring to his hatred of the anti-immigrant Know-Nothing Party, they noted his strict adherence to the Declaration of Independence. "Without a stain of Know-Nothingism on his skirts, he is acceptable to the mass of the American party who, this year, will be compelled to choose between" the Republican and Democratic candidates. The editors astutely attributed the source of Lincoln's attitude toward immigrants as the Declaration of Independence. "Endeared by his manly defense of the principles of the Declaration of Independence to the citizens of foreign birth, he could command the warm support of every one of them from whom, in any contingency, a Republican vote can be expected."

In closing, though, the editors did acknowledge that their candidate was not the favored one. "Nominated, he would, we believe, be triumphantly elected; but if another, in the wisdom of the Convention, is preferred, we can pledge him to labor, as honest and effective as any that he [had ever] done for himself, for the man of the Convention's choice."[4]

Noon had been selected as the time for the convention to assemble but "before eleven there was a tide flowing toward the Wigwam. Ladies gentle and tender, whose loyal hands had wrought for days on the decorations, waited long and patiently in the crowd to win a good seat where they might reap their well-earned meed. At all the several entrances the rush was tremendous" but "the door keepers were of Roman firmness." Not until 11:30 were the doors "opened slowly, and only to ticket-holders ... in a steady stream." The crowd "spread along the galleries — gentlemen under the protection of ladies." On the lower level where the delegates were to assemble, a sign "'None others admitted'" was "streamed out over the floor." The delegates settled "into eddies of State delegations each about their conspicuously displayed placard elevated above the settees. And so the hall filled up, and when all the ticket-holders were in, the last barrier was removed at the doors, and one grand rush filled, packed and condensed every part of the hall its billows of rushing, excited, humanity had access to."[5]

"Precisely at 12 M. [noon] the gavel of Governor E.D. Morgan, of New York, Chairman of the National Committee, fell, and the Republican Convention was duly constituted which is to nominate the Republican President for 1860."[6]

A New Yorker who had chaired the committee that had organized the convention, called the convention to order and David Wilmot, chosen as the convention's temporary president, spoke to the delegates. Not everyone was pleased with his selection. Lincoln's friend, Orville Browning, described Wilmot as "a dull, chuckle headed, booby looking man, and makes a very poor presiding officer." [7] A prayer was given and Norman Judd from Illinois asked that a Committee on Permanent Organization be assembled. A roll call followed to determine which states would comprise this committee, and in so doing, it highlighted the party's sectional nature. After twenty-seven states had been called, including, surprisingly, Virginia and Texas, a delegate requested "that the names of all the States be called." The chair agreed and called those states who were not represented in the Wigwam: "Tennessee, Arkansas, Mississippi [great laughter], Louisiana, Alabama [laughter and hissing], Georgia, South Carolina, [laughter], North Carolina, Florida [Feeble hisses and much laughter]."

Not all the delegates — especially of the slaveholding states — could claim immediate acceptance. The convention proceeded to form a Committee on Credentials consisting of one delegate from each state, which would have to grapple with the sensitive issue of determining which delegates would be considered legitimate. The convention then adjourned to allow the committees to meet.[8]

At one o'clock that day, the *New York Tribune* reported, "Everything is confusion. Half the Convention are in doubt.... The disorder and want of unity among the opponents of Seward begin to disappear, but they will probably be unable, and will not attempt, to agree upon one candidate, at least at present." The reporter discovered that "Massachusetts having asked the States that protested against Seward whom they could carry, Pennsylvania names McLean, Lincoln, and Cameron; Illinois, Lincoln only" and "Indiana is already divided between Messrs. Bates and Lincoln, with a majority for the latter." The anti–Seward paper predicted that the Texas delegation, which "is all for Mr. Seward ... will be denounced as bogus to-morrow in the Convention." The reporter concluded that "a majority of the Convention is undoubtedly against Mr. Seward, but their difficulty is they have no candidate."[9]

Of all the many newspaper reporters from throughout the North that closely followed the events of the convention, one deserves special mention: Murat Halstead, a thirty-year-old reporter from the Republican *Cincinnati Commercial.* Halstead attended all the political conventions that year and provided copious reports and superb analyses. He had first witnessed the debacle in Charleston where the Democratic Party failed to choose a candidate. He then traveled to Baltimore to report on the Constitutional Union Party convention, and arrived in Chicago just in time for the Republican Party convention's first day.[10]

Despite the naysayers, Halstead found the Seward supporters confidently predicting victory, especially in regard to Pennsylvania. They dismissed "talk of not carrying Pennsylvania" as "all nonsense" because Seward's "friends would spend money enough in the State to carry it against any Democratic candidate who was a possibility." Halstead wrote, "The flood of Seward money promised for Pennsylvania was not without efficacy. The phrase used was, that Seward's friends 'would spend oceans of money.'" The New Yorkers' monetary advantage far exceeded the resources of the Lincoln supporters. In fact, none of Lincoln's friends ever mentioned any financial means that they had available to assist in persuading other delegates.[11]

When the convention reconvened that day, the Committee on Permanent Organization announced a Massachusetts delegate, George Ashmun, as president of the convention, and, in a sign of Seward's strength, Ashmun appointed two well-known Seward supporters, Preston King of New York and Carl Schurz of Wisconsin, to escort him to the chair. It appeared to the Seward supporters like a dress rehearsal for their candidate's coronation.[12]

The Committee on Permanent Organization selected twenty-seven vice presidents (a representative from each delegation) and twenty-six secretaries, the District of Columbia not being represented. The delegates then approved a motion to form a Committee on Resolutions and Platforms, with a representative from each delegation. Shortly thereafter, the members of that committee were announced and, after some more discussion, the convention adjourned until ten o'clock the following morning.[13]

During that day and evening, outside of the Wigwam, reporters and delegates attempted to gauge the current momentum. Halstead wrote that morning that "the current of the universal twaddle this morning is, that 'Old Abe' will be the nominee." One of Lincoln's supporters, echoed this optimism in a telegram to Lincoln: "Prospects fair friends at work night & day tell my wife I am well."[14] Between the two sessions, at 4 o'clock in the afternoon, William Butler, another of Lincoln's supporters, wrote that Iowa, Indiana and New Hampshire "stands [*sic*] as a unite [*sic*] for you," while the Ohio delegation "agreed to cast their first vote for Chase," the second one for Wade" and, "if they found no danger in doing so," the third one for Lincoln "as long as Illinois kept your name before the Convention." Pennsylvania "agreed" to support Wade and then Lincoln and "stick with us as long as your name is kept before the Convention." Butler further speculated that Massachusetts would support him, and recognizing the pivotal role of Indiana, he had also sent for "Lane of Indiana."

"Your friends are doing all that can be done for you," he asserted. "Seward's friends feel a little sore this evening, but Seem to be in good Spirits" and felt assured that all the delegates believed "Seward will not be nominated," except those of the New York delegation. Despite this optimism, though, knowing that no delegates were guaranteed, he admitted, "I think your Chance good yet be prepared for defeat. I am wrighting [*sic*] in the Room where all is fuss and Confusion."[15]

The most significant information in this letter is the intention to consult with Lane, the most influential member of the critical Indiana delegation. Lane had arrived in Chicago believing that Judge John Mclean possessed the qualities necessary for the Republicans to prevail in Indiana. He also considered Bates a strong candidate. Now the Illinoisans had to convince him that Lincoln was his man. With Pennsylvania committed to its favorite son, Cameron, and New Jersey committed to its favorite son, William L. Dayton, the Lincoln supporters needed Indiana; they could not prevail without it.[16]

One of Seward's supporters sent the following telegram to Seward: "There is more opposition by the friends of other candidates than was anticipated, but we still feel confident of success."[17]

Thomas Dudley, a New Jersey delegate, correctly appraised the real difficulty for the anti–Seward forces in regard to the four doubtful states of Illinois, Indiana, Pennsylvania and New Jersey:

> If the four States did not agree, but persisted in putting forward the three candidates, then William H. Seward would be nominated and the party defeated. This was the manner it was presented to them, and certainly a very large majority of all the delegates from the four States so regarded it. The responsibility of the situation was felt, but the difficulty was not an easy one to overcome. Most of the delegates had been instructed, or at least had been elected, with the understanding that they should vote for one of these candidates. To break from them and vote for some one else was not a very easy or pleasant thing to do. This was the situation when the convention assembled on Wednesday.[18]

In assessing the first day's events of the Republican convention, Halstead asserted that for four prospective candidates their campaigns had ended. "The Bates movement, the McLean movement, the Cameron movement, the Banks movement are all nowhere. They have gone down like lead in the mighty waters. 'Old Abe' and 'Old Ben' [Ben Wade of Ohio] are in the field against Seward. Abe and Ben are representatives of the conservatism, the respectability, the availability, and all that sort of thing."[19] The future prospects for Wade and Chase appeared dim because "the Ohio delegation continues so divided as to be without influence." However, Halstead recognized that "if united" the Ohio delegation "would have a formidable influence, and might throw the casting votes between candidates, holding the balance of power between the East and the West."[20] In the end though, he astutely realized that "the question on which every thing turns is whether Seward can be nominated. His individuality is the pivot here, just as that of Douglas was at Charleston."[21] Halstead described the Republicans as "divided into two classes, the 'irrespressibles' and the 'conservatives.'"[22]

Halstead also reported that Greeley remained a humorous target: "The Seward men have badges of silk with his likeness and name, and some wag pinned one of them to Horace Greeley's back yesterday, and he created even an unusual sensation as he hitched about with the Seward mark upon him."[23]

But Greeley found little success. He wrote at 10:40 that night: "As to the Presidency, I can only say that the advocates of Gov. Seward's nomination, who were much depressed last night, are now quite confident of his success. The changes on which their new hopes are based have been effected in the Virginia and New Jersey delegations. I should say that the chances of his nomination are now about even. Mr. Lincoln now appears to have the next best look."[24]

At the Tremont House that day and evening, where the Illinois delegation and other delegations made their headquarters, Halstead found the situation especially intense. "There are now at least a thousand men packed together in the halls of the Tremont House crushing each other's ribs, tramping each other's toes, and titillating each other with gossip of the day; and the probability is, not one is possessed of a single political fact not known to the whole...."[25]

The *Tribune*, in an article titled "O, give me a Cot!," also reported that, for at least some of the delegates, the intensity of the day's events could not be alleviated by the hope of a good night's rest, or by a nice game of billiards:

> In more than one instance, billiard rooms and their tables have come to pay a double debt and bear a double burden. Until a moderate hour for retiring, the markers are busy, and the click of the balls tells of the progress of the game, but at a signal of the clock, mine hosts "take their cue" from the crowd of weary guests, and during the rest of the twenty-four hours, passed on mattresses spread upon the tables, the only "angles" studied, are those of tired humanity wooing "nature's sweet restorer." We looked in, just after midnight, upon one *rancho* of this kind, where one hundred and thirty persons were making this use of billiard tables....[26]

The delegates would need whatever rest they could manage that night, because on the next day May 17, they would choose their candidate for the presidency, or so they thought.

11

The Second Day

Thursday, May 17, 1860

The New Yorkers were jubilant, and for good reason; their day of coronation had come. The years of waiting, campaigning, and caucusing had finally come to a triumphant end. May 17, 1860, would be forever known as the day that President William H. Seward was nominated for the presidency. Everything was ready; everything was set. And yet, somehow, something went wrong. Something went wrong this day and it would forever change the course of American history.

The New Yorkers could not have foreseen the fateful moment. The anticipation and excitement in Chicago had reached a fever pitch. Halstead wrote that "masses of people poured into town last night and this morning, expecting the nomination to be made to-day. All adjectives might be fairly exhausted in describing the crowd. It is mighty and overwhelming; it can only be numbered by tens of thousands. The press about the hotels this morning was crushing. Two thousand persons took breakfast at the Tremont House."[1] Even delegates from other states were in a jubilant mood. The Cincinnati reporter found some of the Missouri delegation "singing songs in their parlor" at two in the morning, while "far down the street a brass band was making the night musical."

Not all were joyful. Halstead also noted that there "was still a crowd of fellows caucusing." He heard the Pennsylvanians affirm that "if Seward were nominated, they would be immediately ruined" and the New Jersey delegates stated the same. The Hoosiers appeared "heart-broken at the suggestion that Seward has the inside track, and thr[e]w up their hands in despair. They [said] Henry S. Lane will be beaten, the legislature pass utterly into the hands of the Democracy." The Illinoisans agonized "at the mention of the name of

Seward, and [said] he is to them the sting of political death. His nomination would kill off Lyman Trumbull and give the legislature into the hands of Democrats."

The Seward supporters brushed all these pessimistic comments aside. When they passed the Tremont House where the Illinoisans and other anti–Seward delegates were staying, "they gave three throat-tearing cheers for Seward." Their parade marched from the Richmond House to the tune of "*O Isn't He a Darling?*" and wearing badges and "splendid" uniforms as they marched with "gay elasticity and jaunty bearing."

The *Chicago Press and Tribune* desperately sounded the alarm over Seward's impending nomination. In an article titled "The Man Who Can Win," the editors pleaded with the Republican delegates to consider the unelectability of the leading candidate. The *Tribune* writers admitted that "we take it for granted that the Republicans desire to succeed in the contest before us." They fully acknowledged that in regard to Missouri, Delaware, Maryland, Virginia and Kentucky the Republicans "have no reason to hope that, in any contingency they can get help from a slave State. The battle must be fought and won by the North."

It was not in the entire North that the battle must be fought, the *Tribune* contended, but rather a "strip of country extending from the Missouri River on the West to the Atlantic Ocean on the East, comprising the southern portions each of Iowa, Illinois, Indiana, Ohio and Pennsylvania, which is mainly populated by emigrants or descendants of emigrants from the slave States. A minority of that people, respectable by reason of their conscientiousness are willing to go with us for restricting the spread of Slavery to the Territories of the United States." These voters were essential for victory, the *Tribune* asserted: "Without their aid, success for any Republican is impossible; and that aid can only be procured by the nomination of a candidate at Chicago, whose antecedents give them assurances that [the] Republican endeavor is to be limited to the platform of the party in the event of success."

Although not specifically named, the *Tribune* argued that Seward's nomination would unquestionably lead to defeat. Republicanism was not "strong enough" at this time to prevail with "the nomination of a candidate who, whatever his fame as a statesman or his eminence as a man, is unacceptable to the voters of that doubtful region." The *Tribune* listed the results from Iowa, Illinois, Indiana, Ohio and Pennsylvania in the 1856 election to "prove that the Republican party has not a majority in one of these States" and to also "prove that the Democracy are in a minority also, and that the balance of power is with that third party which is again called into activity and vigor by the recent nomination of John Bell. They prove, further, that nominations made here by the Convention now in session, must be such, that, while distinctively

Republican, they will command the support of that body of men who do not want to be again driven to take part in a movement like that which defeated Fremont, in 1856."

The nomination of Abraham Lincoln was the solution to the quagmire, the *Tribune* concluded. The editors ingeniously and correctly noted that Lincoln had won the popular vote in Illinois in 1858. Although state legislators determined the final outcome of the senate race, in the race for president, in the crucial border state of Illinois, the popular vote would determine the outcome:

> We assume that the position, antecedents, and record of Mr. Lincoln give him the preference, running qualities alone considered, over every other candidate in the field. Take the contest in Illinois in 1858, when he fought for the State against Douglas. A Republican whose fidelity to his party never was questioned, he canvassed the counties with great ability, and taking the aggregate vote for members of the Legislature, the following was the result:
>
> | | |
> |---|---|
> | Republican | 125,275 |
> | Douglas | 121,190 |
> | Buchanan | 4,683 |

Lincoln, because he was "acceptable, in spite of his Republicanism," had captured "a large majority of that 37,000 men who voted for Mr. Fillmore in 1856, and who, a less popular candidate than Mr. Lincoln being presented to them in 1860, will vote for Mr. Bell. Mr. Lincoln's acceptability, demonstrated by that memorable contest, is not limited to Illinois. The popular qualities which he displayed, and his known conservatism, will have the same influence upon the doubtful vote of Indiana and Pennsylvania which they had here, because in both these States the district of country in which that vote lies, being that belt which we have described, is moved by the same influences that command Southern Illinois."

The *Tribune* had "a calculation which proves that Mr. Lincoln can be elected" that he was "to-day the strongest man in the party. There is no Republican who will refuse him his vote, because he stands fairly and squarely, and long has so stood, on the platform of the party in the organization of which he assisted; and there is no man, no matter how foolishly conservative, professing to be in favor of the limitation of Slavery, who can put his finger on one of Mr. Lincoln's acts or recorded opinions, and say that he proposes that to which any can fairly object. His record is as pure as his life." Lincoln was a "representative Republican, acceptable by reason of his birthplace, political antecedents and constitutional moderation, to that belt of country without the acquiescence of which no man can win; an honest and able statesman, whose purity of character and patriotic motives, partisan malignity has never questioned, we submit that he is the man for the crisis. We commend him to the doubtful States, and also commend their decision to all others as that which the party cannot safely disregard."[2]

The *Tribune* editors were not the only ones who used the May 17 issue of the *Tribune* to call for Lincoln's nomination. Another article titled "Michigan and Wisconsin," signed only by the name "Indiana" and written perhaps by one of the Indiana delegation's leaders, Caleb B. Smith or Lane, attempted to persuade the delegates from those two pro–Seward states. The Hoosier opened with a question: "Should not the delegates of Michigan and Wisconsin consult with those of Indiana and Illinois as to who could carry the latter States?" The author admitted that "Michigan is safe for any Republican, no matter how obnoxious he may be to the Fillmore element" and "so is Wisconsin. But this can not be said of either Indiana or Illinois." The Hoosier questioned whether it was "right or prudent" for "these two radical States to assist in forcing a candidate on their two 'doubtful' neighbors, which may change a 'doubt' into defeat." The author reminded the Michigan and Wisconsin delegates that the "loss of Illinois and Indiana entails the loss of three U.S. Senators" and the state legislatures of Illinois and Indiana. The states under the "pro-slavery party" would then "be so 'Gerrymandered' as to give that party two-thirds of the delegations to the next Congress." The Hoosier closed: "And as Illinois will be entitled to at least sixteen and Indiana to fifteen members, the serious, if not fatal, character of the loss must be apparent to all but the willfully blind and fanatical. There is no blinking these sober, weighty facts. It is better to look them in the face *new*, than after it is too late to remedy the blunder that may be made."[3]

The Massachusetts delegation, while committed to Seward, had some significant concerns, not insofar as how Massachusetts would vote in November, but how the northern states that the Republicans lost in 1856 would vote in November. A New Jersey delegate recalled:

> On Tuesday a committee from Massachusetts and some of the other New England States, with John A. Andrew at its head, visited the delegates from the four doubtful States. Mr. Andrew was the spokesman for his committee. He stated that it was the desire of all that the party should succeed; that he and others from New England were in favor of William H. Seward, but that they preferred the success of the party rather than the election of any particular individual; and when it was made apparent to them that William H. Seward could not carry the doubtful States and that some other man could, they were willing to give up Mr. Seward and go for the man who could make victory certain.

Andrew realized that New Jersey vouched for its native son, William L. Dayton, which would be acceptable to Massachusetts, that Pennsylvania named its favorite son, Simon Cameron, and Illinois and Indiana named Abraham Lincoln. Andrew chastised the four doubtful states for having three candidates, when they must agree on one candidate. Otherwise, New England would "vote for our choice, William H. Seward of New York."[4]

Edward Pierce, a Massachusetts delegate, gave the first indication that Lincoln might be the candidate around which the anti–Seward forces could rally. Pierce stated that "on the request of the Massachusetts delegations to have different candidates who could carry each one of the doubtful states" they contacted the four doubtful states: "Pennsylvania responded, naming three in this order 1 Cameron 2 McLean 3 Lincoln. Here were three states [Illinois, Indiana and Pennsylvania] admitting that they could give their electoral votes for Lincoln."[5]

Lincoln had not been idle either. He sent the following note to his Chicago team: "I agree with Seward in his 'Irrepressible Conflict.'" But possessing an unfounded fear that the Seward supporters might incorporate the 'Higher Law' philosophy into the party platform, he added, "I do not endorse his 'Higher Law' doctrine." Illustrating his intention to win or lose without bartering, Lincoln concluded with "Make no contracts that will bind me."[6]

The convention reassembled at ten o'clock in the Wigwam to consider the credentials of the delegations. Halstead described the crowd as "more dense than ever" and said, "The thing was full yesterday, but it is crammed today." The divisiveness between the pro–Seward and anti–Seward forces became readily evident in the discussion of credentials. The anti–Seward delegates rejected the idea of permitting the Virginia and Texas delegations, supposedly Seward bastions, from voting. After numerous speeches, a vote was taken and it was decided to refer the question on these states and the territories back to the Committee on Credentials. The convention adjourned until three o'clock.[7]

The anti–Seward forces began to caucus with the intention of uniting behind one candidate. Thomas Dudley, a New Jersey delegate, "learned that a sub-convention of the delegates from the four doubtful States had been called at the Cameron rooms in Chicago, and that it was then in session." He immediately "proceeded there at once" and found "much discussion was going on, and it was very evident that nothing could be agreed upon in this sub-convention." Dudley suggested "to Mr. Judd of Illinois that the matter should be referred to a committee of three from each State to be selected by the States. Mr. Judd made this motion and it was carried, and the delegates from each State appointed its committee." Dudley could not recall all the committee members but did remember some notable ones: Judge David Davis of Illinois, Caleb B. Smith from Indiana, David Wilmot, and himself. The subcommittee agreed to meet at Wilmot's rooms that evening at six o'clock, assuming, of course, that the convention did not nominate a candidate before then.

At 3:15 P.M., the convention reassembled, and for the Lincoln delegates, there must have been an overwhelming sense of despair. All their campaigning and all their lobbying had failed. Seward's moment had come. They could only hope that somehow, some way, the balloting could be delayed just one more day.

The delegates had three simple tasks to complete. First, they had to decide which states and which territories would be permitted a vote. Second, they had to approve the platform and finally, they had to nominate a candidate. Little controversy should have occurred with the first two tasks, leaving the delegates ample time to complete the third one.

The Committee on Credentials announced their decision. Texas, Virginia and the territories — Kansas, Nebraska, and the District of Columbia, despite having no electoral votes, would all have the right to vote at the convention. This decision represented another victory for the Seward forces because all these delegates were expected to support the New Yorker. The convention then proceeded to the business of approving the party platform.

The seventeen points of the party platform were read to the entire convention, often interrupted by "tremendous bursts of applause." One delegate rose and opined, "That report is so eloquently unquestionable from beginning to end, and so eloquently carries through with its own vindication, that I do not believe the Convention will desire discussion upon it." The delegates responded with applause and cries of "good, good" and a quick vote approving the platform was expected, and the convention could immediately proceed to nominating a presidential candidate.

But there was at least one delegate who cried out "no, no" and then, the unexpected began. For all the times that Lincoln had stood up for the Declaration of Independence, this time, at this moment, it stood up for him.

First, Joshua Giddings, the firebrand abolitionist from northwest Ohio, rose from his chair. His political career was near its end, and here in the Wigwam in Chicago, he made his last stand and unknowingly helped changed the history of the American people. After hearing the platform read, Giddings, according to his biographer, "at first felt stupefied, then heartsick, for all his worst fears of Republican moral bankruptcy were borne out." The Republicans "branded secession as treason, called the Dred Scott decision a dangerous political heresy, and proclaimed the party's resistance to the extension of slavery," but they had only made the "vaguest mention of the Declaration of Independence." From Giddings' perspective, the "platform committee had all but severed the one tissue of doctrine which connected Giddings' antislavery radicalism to the political process." The Ohioan stated, "Mr. President, I propose to offer, after the first resolution as it stands here, as a declaration of principles, the following:

"That we solemnly reassert the self-evident truths that all men are endowed by their creator with certain inalienable rights, among which are those of life, liberty and the pursuit of happiness; that government are instituted among men to secure the enjoyment of these rights."

After being temporarily interrupted, Giddings continued. "Two hundred years ago the philosophers of Europe declared to the world that human governments were based upon human rights, all Christian writers have sustained that doctrine until the members of this Convention." The nation's founding fathers were "impressed with this all permeating truth,— the right of every human being to live and enjoy that liberty, which enables him to obtain knowledge and pursue happiness, and no man has the power to withhold it from him. Our fathers embraced this solemn truth, laid it down as the chief corner stone, the basis upon which this Federal Government was founded.... It is because these principles have been overturned, uprooted and destroyed by our opponents, that we now exist as a party." Giddings reminded the delegates that in 1856 "at Philadelphia, we prepared and propounded this issue to our opponents. We called on them to meet it. They have not met it. They put forward the supreme court to meet it" but "that court denied those principles." Giddings proposed that the Republicans "maintain the doctrines of our fathers. I propose to maintain the fundamental and primal issues upon which the government was founded. I will detain this Convention no longer. I offer this because our party was formed upon it. It has existed upon it — and when you leave out this truth you leave out the party."

A delegate shot back at Giddings that "the only reply I wish to make on this amendment and the gas expended upon it" was to refer his colleagues to "clause two of the report, which reads as follows: 'that the maintenance of the principles promulgated in the Declaration of Independence and embodied in the Federal Constitution, is essential to the preservation of our republican institutions; and that the Federal Constitution, the rights of the States, and the union of the States, must and shall be preserved.'" Another Republican agreed with Giddings, but he also believed in the "ten commandments" and had no desire to have them "in a political platform." One delegate tried to offer Giddings's amendment again, but before he could attract the attention of the president, another delegate, David Wilmot, stood and began to argue another issue which further delayed the convention.[8]

Wilmot wanted the resolutions to be adopted separately but the delegates yelled out "No," and "Take them in a lot." With this reaction, Wilmot proceeded to attack the 14th resolution. That resolution, in direct refutation of the Know-Nothings and all those who intended to deny citizenship for recent immigrants, stated that the Republicans were opposed to "any change in our Naturalization Laws, or any State legislation" that "abridged or impaired ... the rights of citizenship ... to immigrants from foreign lands." Wilmot wanted "to strike out the words 'State legislation,' because it conflicts[ed]" with another part of the platform which demanded "the right of each State to order and control its own domestic institutions according to its own judgment exclusively." This debate centered upon immigrants' rights versus states' rights, and this was an issue especially sensitive to a group whose support the party desperately needed, namely the German Republicans.[9]

Carl Schurz and Gustave Koerner, both German Republicans, had worked to influence the party's platform. They both "insisted on a resolution denouncing the Massachusetts Amendment" which had been crafted by the anti-immigrant Know-Nothings. Specifically, they had intentionally inserted language that removed the power of the state legislatures to act independently when restricting the rights of citizenship for immigrants. Koerner expressed personal pride in this resolution because the "plan was much stronger than a similar one adopted by the Democrats at Charleston." Others appreciative of the importance of the immigrants' political support and supportive of the Declaration of Independence immediately attacked Wilmot's motion.[10]

Judge Jessup of Pennsylvania, chairman of the Committee on Platform rose to assail Wilmot's motion. "I desire briefly to state to the Convention that the naturalization laws are producing a sad state of feeling among a large number of the Republican party. A great many Republicans are of foreign birth, and they have felt that it was due to them that the Republicans should affirm first, that they do not desire to interfere with the present existing naturalization laws; secondly, that they as a party do not approve of the change of the naturalization laws by the several States, and they do not approve of that legislation which went to impair the rights which the naturalization laws of the Union give to naturalized citizens." Jessup argued that the resolution "is not proposed to interfere with State rights" and he wanted to know if his "colleague from Pennsylvania affirms that he is ready to permit, with his consent, the State legislatures to impair the rights that are guaranteed, under our laws, to emigrants becoming citizens."

Wilmot refused to yield, believing that the 4th resolution of the platform, which supported State rights, preempted the 14th resolution. The 4th resolution, he said, was a broad declaration of State rights — a just declaration of State rights; and under that any State in this — every State in this Union has a perfect power to prescribe qualification of voters. Pennsylvania, Massachusetts or any other State may tomorrow, if it sees fit, by a change of her constitution, not only impair the right of foreign citizens, but may modify and impair the rights vested in native born citizens." He believed that Pennsylvania might "require that any person coming from a foreign land or from another State shall not vote until he has been a resident two years, and on the doctrine of State rights has she not a right to do it! And who has a right to complain?" Wilmot, though, sensed that he did not have strong support, and seeking a respectful manner by which to retreat, he ended his speech stating that if the party supported the right of a state to determine voter qualifications, "I am willing to withdraw my amendment [to loud cheers]."

The German Republicans were outraged at Wilmot's proposal, and although Wilmot had agreed to withdraw it, they were not willing to let the issue pass without comment. Schurz condemned Wilmot's proposal and condemned the right of the states to relegate immigrant citizens to second-class status. "The German Republicans of the Northern States have given you 300,000 votes, and I wish that they should find it consistent with their honor and their safety to give you 300,000 more." Schurz reminded the delegates that the "year 1856 was the year of good feeling; we all joined together in a common cause, and we all fought the common enemy. We did so with honor to ourselves and with confidence to each other. There was no German Republican, I believe, who would have asked for anything more in the Philadelphia platform"; but that resolution had failed to protect the immigrants "from intrechment upon their rights in the States.... They said our rights may be guaranteed to us in a national platform by a general sentence, and nevertheless the Legislatures of the different States may defeat the very purpose for which that national platform was enacted." Schurz questioned, "Of what use, then, is a plank in a platform if its purpose thus can be frustrated by an act of a State Legislature?" Schurz concluded with a powerful declaration that clearly embodied the egalitarian principle of "all men are created equal." To him, and all the other immigrants:

> The question is simply this, on one side there stands prejudice, on the other side there stands right. You please calculate, will prejudice give us more votes or will right give us more votes! Let me tell you one thing, that the votes you get by truckling to the prejudices of people will never be safe; while those votes you get by recognizing constitutional rights may every time be counted upon. Why gentlemen, the German Republicans of the Northern States have been not only among the most faithful, but we have been among the most unselfish members of the Republican party. We never come to you asking for any favor; we never come to you with any pretensions; the only thing we ask of you is this: that we shall be permitted to fight for our common cause; that we shall be permitted to fight in your ranks with confidence in your principles and with honor to ourselves.

The German Republicans were not finished. Having fully accepted the universality of the Declaration of Independence, and yet having been subjected to attacks and insults by the Know-Nothing party and others through the years, the German Republicans, like any immigrants, were especially sensitive to any suggestions that their rights were subject to interpretation. They would not let this issue pass with only one speech. Frederick Hassaureck of Cincinnati, Ohio, immediately followed Schurz and passionately spoke in favor of a national platform that superseded any state legislation. The German Republican announced his full support for the 14th resolution "not because" he was "an adopted citizen" but because he claimed "to be a true American." He claimed "to be an American although I happen to be born on the other side of the Atlantic Ocean. Hassaureck had "felt the spirit of true Americanism" when "as a boy in school" he had "first read of the heroic deeds of the immortal Washington" and when he "first heard of the great Thomas Jefferson, who, upon the altar of God, had sworn eternal hostility to tyranny in every form." As an immigrant who had "suffered the stings and oppressions of despotism," he claimed "to be doubly capable of appreciating the blessings of liberty":

> Gentlemen, if it is Americanism to believe, religiously to believe in those eternal truths announced in the Declaration of Independence, that all men are born equal and free, and endowed by their creator with certain inalienable rights, among which are life, liberty, and the pursuit of happiness, I am proud to be an American. If it is Americanism, gentlemen, to believe that governments are instituted for the benefit of the governed, and not for the benefit of the privileged few — if it is Americanism to believe that this glorious Federation of sovereign States has a higher object and a nobler purpose than to be the mere means of fortifying, protecting and propagating the institution of human servitude — if it is Americanism to believe that these vast fertile Territories of the West are forever to remain sacred, to remain as free homes for free labor and free men, I shall live and die an American.

The German Republican hoped that "this resolution will pass without objection from any side. There are more than 20,000 Republican German votes in the State of Ohio alone; and they shall ever be cast in a solid phalanx for the candidate who is to be nominated by this Convention."[11]

Hassaureck's speech brought the discussion of the platform to a close, and now, despite the unexpected delay, the delegates could approve the platform and proceed to the selection of a presidential candidate. But another delay ensued. George Curtis, a Seward delegate from New York, had witnessed a shocking event and now tried to undo the damage. After the delegates had rebuffed Giddings' motion, the abolitionist — who throughout his career had compromised for the sake of party — now in the twilight of his life refused to compromise again. Giddings' biographer described the abolitionist's reaction: "Giddings rose again, turned on his heel, and, after adjusting his hat, stalked out of the convention. For the only time in his life he felt compelled to sacrifice all party affiliation for an idea. When a delegate tried to stop him, Giddings replied, 'I see that I am out of place here.'"

Curtis "an earnest young delegate from New York," wanted him back. Instead of calling for a vote on the platform, he stated, "I then offer as an amendment to the report, as presented by the committee, the following: That the second clause of the report shall read, 'That the maintenance of the principles promulgated in the Declaration of Independence and embodied in the Federal Constitution'—and then, sir, I propose to amend by adding these words, 'That all men are created equal; that they are endowed by their Creator with certain inalienable rights; that among these are life, liberty, and the pursuit of happiness; that to secure these rights, governments are instituted among men, deriving their just powers from the consent of the governed'—then proceed—'is essential to the preservation of our Republican institutions; and that the Federal Constitution, the Rights of the States, and the Union of the States, must and shall be preserved.'" The delegates responded to this motion with "great applause." "Many gentlemen" were "struggling for the floor" and Giddings decided to wait in the lobby as some delegates made this last, desperate attempt.

A delegate immediately countered Curtis's motion with a question: "Has not that amendment been once voted down?" The chair concurred, considering the new motion "substantially the same proposition already voted upon." Francis Blair, Jr., from Missouri, a Bates supporter, disagreed with the chair's decision because the "amendment which was first offered was to the first clause or section, and the amendment offered now by the gentleman from New York is to the second section, and it [is] an entirely different question." The chair replied, "I took it from the statement of the gentleman from New York, that he offered the same amendment offered before by Mr. Giddings, and voted on." Blair pointed out that Curtis's motion applied to the second resolution and not the first. The chair agreed with this imaginative reasoning and declared the amendment in order.

Curtis questioned whether the delegates were "prepared to go upon the record and before the country as voting down the words of the Declaration of Independence?" The Republican convention of 1856 had not done so, the New Yorker noted, and cautioned whether the delegates "dare to shrink from repeating the words that the great men enunciated" in "Philadelphia in 1776."

An Indiana delegate affirmed "that all the Republicans here are in favor of the Declaration of Independence" and questioned the necessity of publishing it in the platform. He argued that it was already in the platform and read the second resolution to prove his point: "'That the maintenance of the principles promulgated in the Declaration of Independence and embodied in the Federal Constitution is essential to the preservation of our Republican institutions, and that the Federal Constitution, the Rights of the States, and the Union of the States must and shall be preserved.' Does not that endorse it? We believe in the Bible; shall we put it in from the first chapter of Genesis to the last chapter of Revelations? We believe in the Constitution of the United States; shall we put it in from first to last? I say no. I say it is enough for us to assert a belief in, and our confidence in, and firm reliance in the Declaration of Independence and the Constitution."

A Seward supporter from New York insisted that the delegates "mark with great distinctness and in unmistakable terms" that they "endorse the language and that portion of the language of the Declaration of Independence that is moved as an amendment to the second resolution." His demand received cheers and voices: "You shall have it," "We will," and one who responded, "You shall have it if you say no more about it." He retorted, "That, sir, is all I want. I am exceedingly glad that simply the fear of a speech from me should induce gentlemen to vote in that way."

The delegates voted on Curtis's amendment and approved it. While no Seward supporters had spoken on behalf of Giddings' original motion, when Curtis, a known Seward supporter, advocated for it, he brought the full weight of the Seward delegates to bear. Halstead gave him great credit: "It was a great personal triumph for Curtis. His classical features, literary fame, pleasing style as a speaker, and the force of his case, called attention to him, and gave him the ear of the Convention, and gave him the triumph. And the Declaration again became part of the platform of the Republican party."[12] Giddings reentered "the hall amidst thunderous applause to enjoy the last dramatic moment of his public life."[13]

However, not all Republicans expressed support for this change. Bates, who supported the non-extension of slavery but professed no desire for universal equality, scoffed at the platform: "It lugs in the lofty generalities of the Declaration of Independence, for no practical object that I can see, but needlessly exposes the party to the specious charge of favoring negro equality — and this only to gratify a handful of extreme abolitionists, led on by Mr. Giddings."[14] The inclusion of the Declaration of Independence was not simply for show as Bates suggested, though. Seward, Lincoln, Giddings and other Republicans constantly referred to, and believed in, the egalitarian promises of the phrase "all men are created equal." To them, it was not mere hyperbole. Jefferson's words truly embodied their hope for the party's — and the nation's — final goal of full equality for all. Bates completely misunderstood the true inspiration and motivation of many members of his party.

After Giddings returned, the Republicans unanimously adopted the platform and erupted into a celebratory display. One eyewitness described the result: "The delegates and the whole of the vast audience rose to their feet in a transport of enthusiasm, the ladies waving their handkerchiefs and the gentleman their hats, while for many minutes the tremendous cheers and shouts of applause continued, and again and again were renewed and repeated."

For the Seward supporters, the victory vindicated their influence. They fought against the Wilmot provision and had fought for Giddings' amendment, and convincingly won both battles. They were running this convention, and they knew it. It was their platform and now only one battle remained, the nomination of their candidate.

It is important to note, though, that while this was a Seward platform, it was also a Lincoln platform. The four policies that Lincoln had railed against in his letters to the Republicans were all decided in his favor. The Massachusetts suffrage act was repudiated. There was no mention of the Fugitive Slave Law or of Kansas' squatter sovereignty, and the Declaration of Independence had received prominent placement. The platform had proceeded precisely as Lincoln had hoped.

Then came the crucial, decisive moment.

The convention had begun this session at 3:15 that afternoon. Three long hours had passed due to the unexpected discussion on the credentials and especially the platform. One delegate had finally had enough, and made a motion to adjourn, but others shouted "No, No, Ballot, Ballot." The delegate immediately withdrew his motion and moved instead that the convention "now proceed to ballot for a candidate for the Presidency." Another delegate restated the motion to adjourn. The Republicans voted on the motion, and it failed. A delegate then moved that the convention "proceed to ballot for President." An eyewitness described "great disorder" following this motion amidst "cries of 'Ballot, Ballot.'" One delegate, thinking of more personal concerns than of the nomination, called "for a division by ayes and nays, to see if gentlemen want to go without their supper," to which some delegates responded with "derisive laughter, and cries of 'Call the roll.'"

The chair announced "that the papers necessary for the purpose of keeping the tally are prepared, but are not yet at hand, but will be in a few minutes." An unnamed delegate then moved that the "Convention adjourn until ten o'clock to-morrow morning." And this time, for whatever reason, the motion carried, and the delegates adjourned until 10:00 the next morning.[15]

Had Giddings not battled to have the Declaration's language included in the platform, had the German Republicans not fought for the ideals that "all men are created equal," no delay would have ensued, the balloting would have proceeded on May 17, and Seward would have prevailed. But these men had defended the Declaration, and the balloting was suspended for one more day. No Lincoln supporters had contributed to the delay, but they now hoped to profit from it. Now, they had just twenty-fours to change the course of American history.

12

From Dusk to Dawn

May 17–May 18, 1860

"As the great assemblage poured through the streets after adjournment, it seemed to electrify the city. The agitation of the masses that pack the hotels and throng the streets, and are certainly forty thousand strong, was such as made the little excitement at Charleston seem insignificant," Halstead reported. "The cheering of the thousands of spectators during the day indicated a very large share of the outside pressure was for Seward," he believed, for "there is something almost irresistible here in the prestige of his fame." The "confident" Seward men "hoot at the idea that Seward could not sweep all the Northern States, and swear that he would have a party in every slave State in less than a year that would clean out the disunionists from shore to shore." Further:

> The Seward men have been in high feather. They entertain no particle of doubt of his nomination in the morning. They have a champagne supper in their rooms at the Richmond House tonight, and have bands of music serenading the various delegations at their quarters. Three hundred bottles of champagne are said to have been cracked at the Richmond. This may be an exaggeration, but I am not inclined to think the quantity overstated, for it flowed freely as water.

The reporter described the New York delegation leaders, including Thurlow Weed, and George W. Curtis, as " strong men of the State, in commerce, political jobbing, and in literature—first class men in their respective positions, and each with his work to do according to his ability. In the face of such "irrepressibles," the conservative expediency men — Greeley, the Blairs, the Republican candidates for Governor in Pennsylvania, Indiana, and Illinois — are hard pressed, sorely perplexed and despondant."[1]

Halstead found "few men in Chicago who believed it possible to prevent the nomination of Seward. His friends had played their game to admiration, and had been victorious on every preliminary skirmish. When the platform had been adopted, inclusive of the Declaration of Independence, they felt themselves already exalted upon the pinnacle of victory. They rejoiced exceedingly, and full of confidence cried in triumphant tones, 'Call the roll of States.' But it was otherwise ordered. The Chair announced that the tally sheets had not been prepared, and that it would subject the clerks to great inconvenience to proceed to a ballot at that time. The Seward men expressed themselves greatly disgusted, however, and after an uncertain response, very little voting being done either way, the Chair pronounced the motion for adjournment carried. The Seward men were displeased but not disheartened. They considered their hour of triumphing with brains and principle over the results of the caucusing that night, though they knew every hour would be employed against them."

The reporter observed Seward's opponents in a far different mood. They "left the Wigwam that evening thoroughly disheartened. Greeley was, as has been widely reported, absolutely 'terrified.' The nomination of Seward in defiance of his influence would have been a cruel blow."

Two telegrams sent to Seward succinctly captured the New Yorkers' mood: "We have no doubt of favorable result tomorrow"[2] and "Your friends are firm and confident that you will be nominated after a few ballots."[3] However, Halstead recalled, "There was much done after midnight and before the Convention assembled on Friday morning." While the New Yorkers were celebrating, the Illinoisans were lobbying.

The delegates from the four "doubtful" states — Illinois, Indiana, Pennsylvania and New Jersey had not been idle. Realizing the potential influence they could have if united, they had met in the afternoon and decided that three representatives from each of the four states should meet. This Committee of Twelve met for the first time at six o'clock in the evening.[4]

This action represented only a portion of the flurry of activity that engulfed the delegates that night. Pennsylvania and Indiana delegates who were not in the Committee of Twelve were not idle either; they met in a courthouse, hoping to reach consensus on one candidate other than Seward. The Pennsylvanians may have begun to realize that their favorite son, Cameron, had no chance, but they still wanted a Whig. Bates had those qualities and they invited Montgomery Blair to advocate for him. Blair stood before the gathered delegates and told them that with Bates "we could carry Missouri & Maryland," while with "Seward, who was a rawhead," and "bloody to the South we should have the theory of disunion to meet" and "I knew he would be defeated." Seward supporters who heard of this meeting immediately sent word to the New York delegation, and a Lincoln supporter ran to find the Illinois delegation. The Seward delegate arrived in time to hear forty-five minutes of Blair's speech and his response was simple: Seward had money and with his money the Republicans could carry Pennsylvania. Someone told Frank Blair, Jr., about the meeting and he arrived and spoke after the Seward delegate, hoping to pull both of these critical delegations into the Bates column. He argued that the border states would rally to his candidate and that the secession talk would evaporate with Bates as president. Two more Bates supporters spoke guaranteeing, that Missouri would vote Republican, if, of course, Bates was the nominee.[5]

No one had yet spoken for Lincoln, but word had reached the Tremont House and two Illinoisans — Gustave Koerner and Orville Browning — arrived and took center stage. It was an uphill battle, Koerner realized. "The Pennsylvanians had been instructed for Cameron, but about their second choice there was much difference of opinion," he recorded. "The Republican party there was not well organized, and it contained a majority of old-line Whigs and Native Americans." Therefore, "the natural tendency of a majority of the party was to nominate a prominent Whig who had been more or less affiliated with the American party." Under these conditions, Koerner well knew that Bates would "fill the bill." As for the Hoosiers, they were "not instructed; but the Whig party had furnished by far the greatest contingent of the party in that State." When Koerner and Browning arrived, they saw that the Bates' advocates "appeared there in force." Koerner and Browning "heard the last part of Blair's speech" and then they listened to the two speeches for Bates, the last one of which the German Republican described as "a rather able speech for Bates."

It was now Koerner's turn. The German Republican may have felt some intimidation. He described the courthouse as "crowded with many other delegates and with citizens of Chicago." But when Koerner "named Lincoln the cheers almost shook the court house." The German Republican "controverted the idea that Bates could carry Missouri" and stated that "outside of St. Louis and a few German settlements" there was "no Republican presidential candidate" who could prevail in Missouri. Missouri, Koerner concluded, "was for Douglas." He accused "these same gentlemen, led by my friend Blair" of having "made Missouri a Douglas State two years before" and had displayed less than noble allegiance in openly opposing "Lincoln in his race for the Senate." Koerner was "astonished" that his "German friends from Missouri talked of supporting Bates," a man who "had been nominated by the Know Nothings." Bates had also on numerous occasions "supported the Know Nothing ticket" in the St. Louis city elections. "The German Republicans in the other States would never vote" for Bates, Koerner asserted, and he would "advise [his] countrymen to the same effect."

In response, Blair spoke, but "with much less vigor than he had thrown into his first speech." Browning then rose and addressed the audience "from a Whig standpoint; that Lincoln had been a Whig," which would "satisfy the Pennsylvanians and those Indianians who held still to some of the Whig principles." But Browning also claimed that "Lincoln had always opposed Native Americanism," which "would secure him the foreign Republican vote all over the country." Browning "wound up with a most beautiful and eloquent eulogy on Lincoln, which electrified the meeting," according to Koerner. The delegates then entered a "secret session."

Despite Koerner's and Browning's speeches, some Lincoln supporters had lost hope. One took pen and paper at 8:00 P.M. that evening and wrote Lincoln with the words "Confidential Confidential" scrolled at the top of the page. "Dear Lincoln," he penned, "You will remember a long [while] back I said something about a Representative man here for you to be able to meet the N York men upon their system of tactics — they are desperate gamblers and I am well acquainted with their appliances to accomplish an end." Lincoln's men were "too honest to advance your Prospects as surely as I would like to see; Davis is a good judge," and others "are honest & faithful but they are unacquainted with New York" politicians. The writer of the letter had lived among them and had "suffered at their hands." This Lincoln delegate wanted to make deals and promises. "If we could to night say to Ohio, Penna Mass & Iowa," he theorized, and "concentrate" on those delegations with the promise that "each of those states may dispense what ever Patronage they respectively are or would be entitled to from the administration" then the "story would be told to morrow & you would beyond doubt be nominated — But this will not be done as your men (for this purpose) are straw men." He knew Lincoln well and admitted that he had "no relish for such a Game; But it is an old maxium that you must fight the devil with fire, The contest is clearly between you & Seward, neither of the States I have named above realy [*sic*] care any thing for Seward certainly none except Mass & probably Iowa." He attempted to end with some optimism: "We are still hopeful but it is only because we have the man of acknowledge[d] merit — it is not on account of superior skill and management," but "if we are beat this will be the last time I shall ever be heard of in Polatics [*sic*]."[6]

In the hours after this letter was penned, the wind began to change. Koerner and Browning "soon learned" that their speeches had hit the mark. "Indiana would go for Lincoln at the start, and that a large majority of the Pennsylvanians had agreed to vote for him for their second choice," Koerner wrote.[7]

However, the Committee of Twelve had not come to a consensus. They had met again, this time in David Wilmot's rooms. These twelve delegates representing the four crucial states argued and debated for four hours without any resolution. At one point, "the white head of Horace Greeley was thrust into the room." When he asked if the twelve had reached agreement, he was told no. Losing all hope, Greeley telegraphed the following to the New York *Tribune*:

> Gov. Seward Will Be Nominated
>
> Chicago, Thursday, May 17 — 11:40 P.M. — My conclusion, from all that I can gather tonight, is, that the opposition to Gov. Seward cannot concentrate on any candidate, and that he will be nominated. H.G.

Halstead telegraphed a similar message to the *Cincinnati Commercial*, and he believed that "every one of the forty thousand men in attendance upon the Chicago Convention will testify that at midnight of Thursday–Friday night, the universal impression was that Seward's success was certain."

With Greeley's closing of the door, a New Jersey delegate "proposed that they should ascertain, as far as they could, the vote that each of the three candidates, Lincoln, Cameron, and Dayton, could command in the convention." Of these three candidates, Lincoln garnered the most support. A New Jersey delegate offered to drop their support of Dayton, and rally to Lincoln if the Pennsylvanians would also support Lincoln. The Pennsylvanians admitted that they could not speak on behalf of all their delegates, but they intended to "recommend it" if the New Jersey delegates would follow suit. Dudley, one of the New Jersey delegates concluded, "After some discussion it was agreed to, and Abraham Lincoln, so far as this committee of twelve from the four doubtful States was concerned, was agreed upon as the candidate for the Presidency." The committee ended their meeting with the "understanding" that the Pennsylvanians would lobby their delegates for Lincoln and that the New Jersey delegates would attempt to convince their delegation to vote "as a unit for Lincoln." The two New Jersey delegates immediately called for a meeting of their entire delegation at 1 A.M.

The reporters scrambling around the various hotels gathering little tidbits from one person or another began to realize that something was afoot. A *New York Herald* employee made this report at midnight:

> There is very great excitement here pending the ballot to-morrow morning. The friends of Seward are firm, and claim ninety votes for him on the first ballot. A careful survey of the field, after a canvass of the delegation gives him 5 votes from Maine, 9 from Massachusetts, 35 from New York, 3 from New Jersey, 6 from Michigan, 5 from Wisconsin, 4 from Minnesota, 2 from Iowa, 4 from California and 3 Texas — Total 76.
>
> The opposition to Seward is not fixed on any man. Lincoln is the strongest, and may have altogether forty votes. Next Bates, then Chase, Cameron and Wade.

If some effective combination is not made tonight, Seward may be nominated to-morrow. As matters stand such a result is not improbable.

The various delegations still are caucusing.

Ohio decided to-night to give on the first ballot seventeen electoral votes for Chase, four for Lincoln, and two for McLean. When Chase is dropped, Lincoln will be Ohio's next choice. New Hampshire will divide between Lincoln and Chase. Vermont will support Bates or Lincoln. Pennsylvania will stand firm for Cameron, and Illinois and Indiana will vote solid for Lincoln, and he will have scattering votes from several other States on the first ballot, and, from present appearances, will gather strength. His friends are quite sanguine tonight that he will be nominated.

The vote for Seward, on the first ballot, is variously estimated at from seventy-six to ninety electoral votes, three of which he will get from New Jersey.

An effort has been made to night to concentrate the opposition to Seward, from the first ballot on Lincoln; but the friends of other candidates are not included to leave their favorite so soon. It is, therefore, doubtful if a nomination is made before Saturday.

At this same time, the New York *Tribune* also began to notice the change:

MIDNIGHT—Though there is an increased disposition to gather about Mr. Lincoln, no effective combination of opposition is yet formed. Ohio is uncertain, Pennsylvania gives no positive assurances, and when New Jerseys breaks but half goes for Mr. Seward. Part of the Missouri delegation prefer Mr. Seward to Mr. Lincoln.

They want a conservative with whom to make a winning fight, or a straight-out radical for a contest of pure principle.

New England is anxious and doubtful. She is puzzled. They hesitate both to desert Mr. Seward and force him on the doubtful States. They are likely to be much cut up. The Massachusetts delegation have been in a labored conference against, and show an increased disposition to leave Mr. Seward, and go for Mr. Lincoln.

There is no telling what the morrow will bring forth. Probably Mr. Seward — but by no means is that certain tonight. Leading Opposition men are down hearted, and say that with a majority and the convictions of the Convention against Mr. Seward, he is still likely to be nominated. The Seward men are full of hope and joy, but cannot give their figures.[8]

An hour later, the New Jersey delegation met to discuss the results of the Committee of Twelve. According to Dudley, "All of Judge Dayton's friends were present, and after they had informed what had been done by the committee of twelve, they ratified it and agreed that after the complimentary voting was over they would vote for Lincoln."[9]

Still, after these meetings, "there was much done after midnight and before the Convention assembled on Friday morning," Halstead reported. "There were hundreds of Pennsylvanians, Indianians and Illinoisans who never closed their eyes that night. I saw Henry S. Lane at one o'clock, pale and

haggard, with cane under his arm, walking as if for a wager, from one caucus room to another, at the Tremont House. He had been toiling with des-
peration to bring the Indiana delegation to go as a unit for Lincoln." Lane
and others had also "been operating to bring the Vermonters and Virginians
to the point of deserting Seward." When Halstead spoke to Lane, the Hoosier
expressed confidence that Vermont would "cast her electoral vote for any candidate who could be nominated" and he expressed hope that Virginia might
come around to Lincoln as well. Lane had apparently attempted to persuade
the delegates "of those States to consider success rather than Seward, and join
with the battleground States — as Pennsylvania, New Jersey, Indiana, and Illinois insisted upon calling themselves."[10]

With Lincoln requiring a significant number of delegates to counter the
Seward juggernaut, the Vermont delegation, with a meager ten votes, may seem
an odd choice on which Lane should focus. However, the small state held a
special place within the Republican Party: it was the most Republican of them
all. In the 1856 election, Frémont won 78 percent of the vote in Vermont. No
other state came close. Massachusetts came in second, but with 65 percent of
the vote, by a considerably smaller amount. If Lane could convince Indiana —
one of the least Republican states — and Vermont — the most Republican state —
to support Lincoln, he could effectively counter the argument that Lincoln was
only the choice of those states that the Republicans lost four years before.[11]

Despite the intense activity of Lincoln's supporters, the *New York Times*
remained confident that Seward would easily prevail:

> The only thing now remaining is the nomination, and that will be effected
> to-morrow, probably, after ten or twelve ballots. It is impossible to predict
> the result with any certainty, but Mr. Seward's prospects are just now decid-
> edly good. His opponents will find it impossible to unite on any candidate,
> and the general impression is that his nomination is simply a matter of neces-
> sity. The supporters of Mr. Bates have abandoned the field, and most of them
> will at once declare for Mr. Seward.
>
> The only man upon whom there is any hope of uniting is Mr. Lincoln,
> and very little progress is made in the effort. The prospect is that when the
> several States find that they cannot carry their own candidate, they will fall
> back upon Mr. Seward. To this rule there will be exceptions. Part of the Penn-
> sylvania delegation are very bitter in their opposition.... The Vermont dele-
> gation is divided, and for the present more hostile to Mr. Seward than has
> been anticipated. It would be impossible to give an adequate idea of the intense
> excitement pervading the city.

And when dawn finally broke that morning over Chicago, the New Yorkers exuded the confidence that had become their trademark, and the Lincoln
supporters were still hoping for a miracle.[12]

13

The Third Day

Friday, May 18, 1860

"Everything indicates your nomination today sure."[1] So read the telegram that two of Seward's supporters sent to him on the morning of May 18.

The *Chicago Press and Tribune* also realized that today the nomination would come; there would be no miraculous delay that would grant the Lincoln supporters more time. The *Tribune* editors, as opposed to the sentiment of the New Yorkers' telegram, were not confident that their candidate would prevail. And so, in an article titled, "A Last Entreaty," they made one last desperate plea.

First, they attacked the "presumption that the Republicans are to succeed" because "their opponents" are divided. The *Tribune* believed the party should not solely rely on the disruption of their rivals but should prevail "by their own inherent strength and the cohesive power of their principles." Seward supporters could easily argue that, in reference to their candidate, "a man objectionable ... to the six doubtful States, Connecticut, Rhode Island, New Jersey, Pennsylvania, Indiana, and Illinois must be nominated at all hazards" because the division of the Democratic Party, now assured by the disastrous Democratic convention in Charleston, South Carolina, ensured a Republican victory. The *Tribune* rejected this reasoning as "too dangerous to obtain currency among shrewd and sagacious men." It was not prudent, they asserted, to "stake" the party's future on the "contingency of a Democratic disruption, rather than" the party's "certain and reliable strength," which was grounded in the opposition of "the extension of Human Slavery." The *Tribune* editors clearly believed that the New Yorkers had made this case simply to promote the "fortunes" and gratify the "ambition" of the New York candidate. Instead of facing a divided Democratic Party, the *Tribune* believed that

Seward (not specifically named) would "compel the settlement of the disputes and dissensions in the Democratic ranks" and "force" the Republicans to face a "united and unscrupulous party." It was critical, they maintained, that the Republicans capture the six doubtful states, "those six States" which had "cast for Mr. Fillmore in 1856, and now claimed for John Bell and Edward Everett." The loss of these states was the "most fatal feature" of the New Yorkers' argument, according to the *Tribune*.

The *Tribune* admitted that it was "with difficulty" that the "gentlemen from the strong Republican States of Vermont, New York, Michigan, Wisconsin and Minnesota, "should look with distrust upon any representations" of the "six States that we have named, and the difficulties which the nomination of a certain candidate will throw in the way of success. We can conceive that they — coming from localities in which Republicanism has deep and firm roots, cannot understand why it is that Illinois, Indiana and Pennsylvania, populated in part by emigrants, or the descendants of emigrants, from the Slave States, should have the fears by which they are tormented." The editors considered the present course for the Republican Party, the nomination of Seward, to be, "if not the precursor of defeat, at least the opening of a fearful struggle, the end of which is involved in great obscurity and doubt."

Instead, to guide the Republicans in their choice of a presidential nominee, the editors asked the delegates to study "history," specifically "a permanent evidence of the opinion of Indiana and Illinois — which will, to all fair-minds, carry correct knowledge of public opinion in those States. We refer to the Black laws." The *Tribune* editors left no doubt that they found these laws "infamously despotic and unjust" but they also acknowledged that the "Republican party in neither State has ever been able to repeal." These laws had "virtually established" slavery "within the jurisdiction of the two States, and any horseblock in either may any day be made the auction stand at which men are bought and sold." These laws were "a fact — not an opinion of some half mad zealot" which offered "glaring public evidence in the statute book of the true condition, the average enlightenment of the popular mind on this negro question in Indiana and Illinois."

The editors then emphasized the common philosophy of Lincoln and Seward, and the one critical difference between the two men. In highlighting Lincoln's strength — his respect for his opponents that he had displayed in every speech in 1859 and 1860 — and Seward's obvious weakness — his disrespect for his opponents, (a weakness which they described as "obnoxious") — the editors wrote:

> We ask, we entreat, we implore, that a candidate inside of the Republican party, radical up to the extreme limit of the platform, but not obnoxious to the charges which will be urged by the so-called Democracy against one promi-

nent gentleman now in the field and in high favor, may be selected, to the end that a triumph may not be a thing of infinite labor, and prolonged and painful doubt, but a certainty from the moment that the choice of the Convention is declared, let us, speaking in behalf of a larger circle of Republican readers than can be claimed by any other journal west of New York, let us, who have labored so long and, we hope, so acceptably, for the Republican cause, warn the Convention that the voice of the united doubtful States cannot, must not be disregarded. They are six, if not seven, in number. They are as ardently devoted to the general principles of the party as any others.[2]

The *Tribune* also contained articles addressing state delegations:

All Hail Pennsylvanians!

All Pennsylvanians in this city are requested to meet at the Metropolitan Hotel this (Friday) morning at nine o'clock.

Sons of the Keystone State fail not to attend.

By order of E. Poulson,

Ch'n Com. of Arrangements.[3]

Attention! Friends of Seward.

The warm friends of Mr. Seward are requested to meet this morning, at 9 o'clock promptly, at the Richmond House, for the purpose of escorting the New York and Michigan Delegations to the National Convention to the Wigwam.

Turn Out! And let the escort show by its magnitude and enthusiasm the admiration entertained in Chicago for the greatest living American Statesman and Patriot.

By order of the Committee.[4]

The Pennsylvania meeting was especially fortuitous for Lincoln's supporters and ominous for those of Seward. The Keystone state delegates heard, for the first time, the decision of the Committee of Twelve and "agreed to cast their votes for Abraham Lincoln, after giving complimentary votes for Simon Cameron." However, none of the delegates were bound by any of the deals that were made throughout the night and into the morning, something that would not become readily obvious until the voting began.[5]

The convention reassembled at ten o'clock and was opened with a prayer that eerily spoke of the ramifications of the Republicans' nomination on the nation's future: "We entreat thee, that at some future but not distant day, the evils which now invest the body politic shall not only have been arrested in their progress, but wholly eradicated from the system. And may the pen of the historian trace an intimate connection between that glorious consummation and the transactions of this Convention."[6]

After the opening prayer, the nominations began:

> Mr. Evarts, of New York, in the order of business before the Convention, Sir, I take the liberty to name as a candidate to be nominated by this Convention for the office of President of the United States, William H. Seward. [Prolonged applause.]
>
> Mr. Judd, of Illinois, I desire, on behalf of the delegation from Illinois, to put in nomination, as a candidate for President of the United States, Abraham Lincoln, of Illinois. [Immense applause, long continued.]
>
> Mr. Dudley, of New Jersey, Mr. President, New Jersey presents the name of William L. Dayton. [Applause.]
>
> Mr. Reeder, of Pennsylvania, Pennsylvania nominates as her candidate for the Presidency, General Simon Cameron. [Cheers.]
>
> Mr. Cartter, of Ohio, Ohio presents to the consideration of this Convention as a candidate for President, the name of Salmon P. Chase. [Applause.]

Then, Caleb Smith from Indiana, who had been elected chairman of the Indiana delegation, addressed the convention. The previous nominations were all predictable — ones that would have been anticipated prior to the convention, but Indiana fell into a far different category. The delegates knew Indiana's crucial position. The Republicans had lost the state in 1856 and now the state had no favored son seeking the nomination. Smith announced, "I desire, on behalf of the delegation from Indiana, to second the nomination of Abraham Lincoln, of Illinois." [Tremendous applause.] "The uproar was beyond description," Halstead recorded. "Henry S. Lane of Indiana leaped upon a table, and swinging hat and cane, performed like an acrobat. The presumption is he shrieked with the rest, as his mouth was desperately wide open, but ... his individual voice was lost in the aggregate hurricane."

When the screaming subsided, the nominations continued:

> Mr. Blair [Jr.], of Missouri, I am commissioned by the representatives of the State of Missouri to present to this Convention the name of Edward Bates as a candidate for the Presidency. [Applause.]
>
> Mr. Blair, of Michigan, in behalf of the delegates from Michigan I second the nomination of William H. Seward. [Loud applause.]

Then, though, whatever weight Ohio had hoped to hold at the convention quickly dissipated as Corwin of Ohio addressed the convention. "I rise, Mr. President, at the request of many gentlemen, part of them members of this Convention, and many of them of the most respectable gentlemen known to the history of this country and its politics, to present the name of John McLean. [Applause.]" Ohio, unlike Indiana, now admitted that their delegates were not voting as a block and any one of them was free to vote independently. Ohio instantly dropped as a critical state for securing the nomination.

One delegate attempted to end the nominating with a move "to give three cheers for all the candidates presented by the Republican party." The president promptly ruled him "out of order." Iowa had the last comment by announcing that "two thirds of the delegation of Iowa" would "second the nomination of Abraham Lincoln. [Great applause.]"[7] The nominations were closed and the balloting began.

The Seward supporters expected a win on the first ballot, a single knock-out blow. The Lincoln supporters just hoped that Seward would fail to secure enough votes on the first ballot, so that Lincoln would survive to fight in the next one.

The states were called in order from east to west. Maine would announce first, Oregon would announce last, followed by the three territories. The Seward supporters looked to New England to set the tone in favor of their candidate. Immediately, they were shocked. Maine split, providing ten votes to Seward and six to Lincoln. New Hampshire sounded an especially ominous note for the New Yorkers when it divided its votes, giving seven to Lincoln and only one to Seward, Chase, and Frémont. Purely acknowledging its favorite son, Vermont announced all ten of its votes for one of its senators and Massachusetts firmly stood by Seward with twenty-one votes and a paltry four for Lincoln. Rhode Island scattered among four candidates with a majority for McLean. Connecticut also spread its votes, with Bates receiving more than any other candidate. New York, as expected, placed its sizable seventy votes behind Seward.

The next three states followed somewhat predictable patterns. Pennsylvania announced 47½ of its 54 votes for its favorite son, Cameron, while Maryland gave a majority to Bates and three to Seward, and Delaware declared its entire block for Bates. Then came four surprises in a row.

For the Seward supporters and for the Lincoln supporters, nothing gave more concern to one and more hope to the other than the next four announcements. Virginia split, but with fourteen votes for Lincoln, one for Cameron and only eight for Seward. Halstead described this as "the most significant vote" in the first ballot because Virginia was expected to solidly support Seward. "The New Yorkers looked significantly at each other as this was announced." Kentucky spread its votes over six candidates with eight for Chase, who was not expected to receive much support after the first ballot, six to Lincoln and five to Seward. Ohio followed a similar pattern, with thirty-four for Chase, four for McLean and eight for Lincoln. Not one Ohio delegate voted for Seward.

Indiana was next. The question as to whether Indiana's nomination reflected the opinion of just one or some of the delegation would now be answered. A Hoosier declared all twenty-six votes for Lincoln. "The solid vote was a startler," Halstead reported, "and the keen little eyes of Henry S. Lane glittered as it was given. He was responsible for it. It was his opinion that the man of all the land to carry the State of Indiana was Judge John McLean. He also thought Edward Bates had eminent qualifications. But when he found that the contest was between Seward and Lincoln, he worked for the latter as if life itself depended upon success."[8]

After Indiana's declaration, the remaining votes proved anticlimactic. Missouri and Oregon unanimously supported Bates. Illinois solidly backed Lincoln. Texas, Wisconsin, California, Minnesota, Kansas and the District of Columbia all gave a majority to Seward, while Iowa and Nebraska scattered their votes among several candidates. The final tally: Seward had a clear lead with 173½ followed by Lincoln with 102, Cameron 50½, Chase 49, Bates 48, Dayton 14, McLean 12, Collamer 10, Wade 3, Read 1, Sumner 1 and Frémont 1. Seward needed 233 votes — just 59½ more votes to clinch the nomination.

The question for the candidates' supporters now revolved around three states: Vermont, Pennsylvania and Ohio. Would those three states continue to support their favorite sons? Would they throw their support toward another candidate, and, if so, which one? The first ballot seemed to indicate that only two candidates were in the running and the New Yorkers and Illinoisans looked anxiously to these three states.

Inside the Wigwam the thousands of spectators now sensed that the nomination would prove a far more dramatic event than previously expected. A New Yorker quickly sent a telegram to Seward without the same bravado and optimism that had accompanied the previous ones: "First ballot Seward one seventy two — Lincoln hundred two — scattering."[9] Halstead noted, "The division of the first vote caused a fall in Seward stock. It was seen that Lincoln, Cameron and Bates had the strength to defeat Seward, and it was known that the greater part of the Chase vote would go for Lincoln."[10] The chair announced that, no candidate having received a majority of the whole number of votes cast, the convention would proceed to a second ballot.[11]

For Lane, the second ballot would prove whether his words had been persuasive. He "had been operating to bring the Vermonters and Virginians to the point of deserting Seward ... The object was to bring the delegates of those States to consider success rather than Seward, and join with the battleground States — as Pennsylvania, New Jersey, Indiana and Illinois insisted upon calling themselves." Now that Lincoln had survived the first ballot, Lane would know how effective he had been.

"The Convention proceeded to a second ballot," Halstead reported. "Every man was fiercely enlisted in the struggle. The partisans of the various candidates were strung up to such a pitch of excitement as to render them incapable of patience, and the cries of 'Call the roll' were fairly hissed through their teeth."[12]

Maine opened the second ballot as it had opened the first ballot: Seward 10, Lincoln 6. New Hampshire provided two more votes to Lincoln for a total of nine, and one for Seward. Then came Vermont. Now abandoning its favorite son, Vermont announced all ten votes for Lincoln. "This was a blighting blow upon the Seward interest," Halstead reported. "The New Yorkers startled as if an Orsini bomb had exploded." Lane must have smiled again. He had been persuasive.[13]

Massachusetts held fast to Seward with twenty-two votes and only four for Lincoln. Rhode Island and Connecticut scattered their support among several candidates and New York followed with all seventy for their candidate. New Jersey, displaying pointless support for their favorite son, continued to give him ten votes, but the delegation did provide four for Seward, indicating that all fourteen might swing to him on a future ballot.

All eyes turned to the Pennsylvania delegation. That group of men controlled fifty-four votes, the largest block of any state except New York. Their vote would not only numerically improve a candidate's position but it would also provide significant momentum if the Pennsylvania delegates voted together and did not scatter their votes to the wind. The state declared 1 for Cameron, 2½ for McLean, only 2½ for Seward and 48 for Lincoln.

Maryland, Delaware, Virginia and Kentucky all followed. Maryland announced the same votes as on the first ballot, Bates 8, Seward 3. But Delaware made a surprising declaration. All six of its votes moved from the Bates column to the Lincoln column. Virginia held steady with a majority of fourteen to Lincoln, eight to Seward and one to Cameron. Kentucky announced nine for Lincoln (a gain of three), seven for Seward (a gain of two), and six for Chase.

Then came Ohio. Twenty-nine announced for Chase, but the eight delegates who had declared for Lincoln were now joined by six more, while three delegates, for whatever reason, still thought that McLean had a chance.

The next six remained relatively unchanged: Indiana for Lincoln, Missouri for Bates, Michigan for Seward, and Illinois for Lincoln. Seward gained two in Texas as all six supported him and Wisconsin steadfastly declared its ten votes for the New Yorker.

Iowa, though, changed. It still scattered its votes but now declared five for Lincoln, giving him a majority there, and two for Seward, with one vote split between McLean and Chase.

In ending the second ballot, California, Minnesota and the three territories all supported Seward, only Nebraska giving votes to any other candidates. Oregon, with Greeley at the helm, remained a Bates bastion. The final vote: Seward 184½, Lincoln 181, Chase 42½, Bates, 35, Dayton 10, McLean 8, Cameron 2, and Clay 2. Halstead, clearly taking in the excitement wrote, "On this ballot Lincoln gained seventy-nine votes!"[14] He further noted:

It now dawned upon the multitude that the presumption entertained the night before, that the Seward men would have everything their own way, was a mistake. Even persons unused to making the calculations and considering the combinations attendant upon such scenes, could not fail to observe that while the strength of Seward and Lincoln was almost even at the moment, the reserved votes, by which the contest must be decided, were inclined to the latter. There, for instance, was the Bates vote, thirty-five; the McLean vote, eight; the Dayton vote, ten — all impending for Lincoln — and forty-five Chase votes, the greater part going the same way.[15]

Maine opened the third ballot with precisely the same vote that it had made in the first two, Seward 10, Lincoln 6. New Hampshire followed with a repeat of the second ballot, Seward 1, Lincoln 9. Vermont maintained its support of Lincoln with all ten of its votes. The delegates witnessed a slight change in Massachusetts, with four more votes moving to the Lincoln column but still giving Seward 18 to Lincoln's 8. Rhode Island, continuing to appear undecided, spread its support among four candidates but did provide Lincoln with a majority. Connecticut, like its New England neighbor, scattered its votes among several candidates, with Bates and Lincoln receiving the most with four votes: and New York remained faithful to its favorite son.

Then came New Jersey. So far, the state had shown no inclination to follow the Committee of Twelve. In fact, it appeared as if it had no representatives at the meeting at all. On the third ballot, it showed its true hand. Five delegates supported Seward, and one went for Dayton, but eight suddenly switched to Lincoln. It was the first vote for Lincoln from that state, and now with New Jersey in the Lincoln column, all the "battleground" states had professed by their votes that Lincoln was the best, perhaps the only candidate that could prevail within their borders.

Pennsylvania's strength for Lincoln further solidified with four more delegates giving support to him, bringing the state's vote to fifty-two for Lincoln, while two unrealistic delegates still maintained allegiance to McLean.

Next came Maryland. The Blairs had kept the delegates in line for Bates in both Missouri and Maryland, but on this ballot, their grip on Maryland slipped. Two went for Seward and eight jumped to the Illinoisan. On its own, it might have had little significance, but following New Jersey, Lincoln's support in the border states clearly rose.

Delaware's six delegates again announced for Lincoln and Virginia's delegation remained unchanged fourteen to eight votes in Lincoln's favor. Kentucky added four more to the Illinoisans column with fourteen while six votes went to Seward and four to Chase.

Ohio then made an ominous declaration for the New Yorkers. Lincoln's support increased from fourteen to twenty-nine, leaving fifteen for Chase and those two McLean diehards. After this announcement, Halstead reported, "It was whispered about — 'Lincoln's the coming man — will be nominated this ballot.'"

The remaining states and territories all voted in precisely the same manner as they had in the second ballot with the minor exception of one: Oregon broke from the Bates camp and gave four votes to Lincoln and one to Seward.

Halstead wrote:

> When the roll of States and Territories had been called, I had ceased to give attention to any votes but those for Lincoln, and had his vote added up as it was given. The number of votes necessary to a choice were two hundred and thirty-three, and I saw under my pencil as the Lincoln column was completed, the figures 231½ — one vote and a half to give him the nomination. In a moment the fact was whispered, about a hundred pencils had told the same story. The news went over the house wonderfully, and there was a pause. There are always men anxious to distinguish themselves on such occasions. There is nothing that politicians like better than a crisis....

The *Tribune* (incorrectly reporting that 234, not 233, votes were required) described the scene in an article titled "The Four Votes":

> During the progress of the third ballot for President the steady increase of Lincoln's vote raised the expectations of his friends to fever heat that he was about to receive the nomination. When the roll call was completed a hasty footing discovered that Lincoln lacked but 2½ votes of an election. The ballot standing for Lincoln 231½, Seward 180, scattering 34½ — necessary to a choice 234. Before the vote was announced, Mr. R.M. Corwine, of the Ohio delegation, who had voted for Gov. Chase up to that time, and three other delegates, viz: R.K. Enos, John A. Gurley, and Isaac Steese, changed their votes to Lincoln, giving him a majority of the whole Convention, and nominating him. D.H. Cartter, the Chairman of the delegation announced the change of votes, and before the secretaries had time to foot up and announce the result, the vast audience burst forth simultaneously into irrepressible shouts.[16]

"The nerves of the thousands, which through the hours of suspense had been subjected to terrible tension, relaxed, and as deep breaths of relief were taken, there was a noise in the Wigwam like a rush of a great wind in the van of a storm — and in another breath, the storm was there," Halstead reported. "There were thousands cheering with the energy of insanity." From the Wigwam's roof, a man who "was engaged in communicating the results of the ballotings to the mighty mass of outsiders, now demanded by gestures at the skylight over the stage to know what had happened." A secretary "with a tally sheet in his hands, shouted — 'Fire the Salute! Abe Lincoln is nominated!'" Inside the mammoth structure when the cheering "subsided, we could hear that outside, where the news of the nomination had just been announced. And the roar, like a breaking up of the fountains of the great deep that was heard, gave a new impulse to the enthusiasm inside. Then the thunder of the salute rose above the din, and the shouting was repeated with such tremendous fury that some discharges of the cannon were absolutely not heard by those on the stage. Puffs of smoke, drifting by the open doors, and the smell of gunpowder, told what was going on."[17]

THE SCENE IN THE WIGWAM

It is absolutely impossible to describe, as it is equally impossible for one who was not present to imagine, the scene in the Wigwam, when Mr. Lincoln was nominated. Without attempting, therefore, to convey an idea of the delirious cheers, the Babel of joy and excitement, we may mention that stout men wept like children — that two candidates for the gubernatorial chairs of their respective States, who looked to the nomination of Honest Old Abe to carry the Republican cause at home through the storm, sank down in excess of joy. The tumultuous emotions of men all over the platform, who had not closed their eyes during the last forty-eight hours, trembling between hope and fear, — laboring for what they deemed the best interests of the noblest cause under the heavens — acted with electrical effect on the immense auditory. Men of stern coun [sic] countenances and strong nerves, upon rising to speak, were almost disabled by their agitation. Mr. Browning, of Illinois, will pardon us for mentioning his name in this connection.

But the scene is not to be pictured. It is ever memorable to those who witnessed it, and no more can be said.[18]

— *Chicago Press and Tribune*

Many delegates caught up in the moment of excitement jumped "on their chairs" to announce the change in their delegation's vote to Lincoln, Halstead wrote. "A photograph of Abe Lincoln which had hung in one of the side rooms was brought in and held up before the surging and screaming masses. The places of the various delegations were indicated by staffs, to which were attached the names of the States, printed in large black letters on pasteboard. As the Lincoln enthusiasm increased, delegates tore these standards of the States from their places and swung them about their heads."

But not all was well. The coronation had not occurred; the high expectations of the Seward supporters had been dashed by an upstart — a person who had never held office as a Republican, who had not even held public office for over a decade. Not all the delegates were sensitive to the New Yorkers' depression. "A rush was made to get the New York standard and swing it with the rest, but the New Yorkers would not allow it to be moved, and were wrathful at the suggestion."[19] Two telegrams were sent to Seward after the third ballot. The first, without fanfare, conveyed the shocking and depressing news:

"Lincoln nominated third ballot."[20] The second indicated the depth of Seward supporters' disappointment: "Let those who nominated Lincoln — Elect Him. We are against him here."[21] The nomination had been stolen from the man who deserved it, and the Seward supporters were ready to bolt.

14

Aftershock

For the New Yorkers, May 18 became not a bad dream but a dreadful nightmare. The victory that had been so surely within their grasp — that had been preordained, had been snatched from their hands. The confidence that they had exuded just hours before now appeared so false, shallow and misplaced. They now faced the question of whether to support the decision of the majority, or whether to bolt the party.

After Lincoln's nomination, William E. Evarts, chairman of the New York delegation, openly expressed his deep disappointment to the convention delegates. When the cheering for Lincoln subsided, "Evarts finally 'mounted the secretaries' table and handsomely and impressively expressed his grief at the failure of the Convention to nominate Seward — and in melancholy tones moved that the nomination be made unanimous."[1] He admitted that the New York delegation "came to this Convention and presented to its choice one of its citizens, who had served the State from boyhood up, who had labored for and loved it" and "we did our duty to the country and the whole country, in expressing our preference and love for him."

From Seward, the New Yorkers had "learned to love Republican principles and the Republican party. His fidelity to the country, the constitution and the laws, his fidelity to the party and the principle that the majority govern, his interest in the advancement of our party to its victory, that our country may rise to its true glory, induces me to assume to speak his sentiments." Evarts felt compelled, although not with great passion, to move "that the nomination of Abraham Lincoln, of Illinois, as the Republican candidate for the suffrages of the whole country for the office of Chief Magistrate of the American Union, be made unanimous."

John A. Andrew, chairman of the Massachusetts delegation, another delegation that had strongly supported Seward, seconded Evart's motion. In answer to those who now considered abandoning the party, Andrew confessed that "the people of Massachusetts hold in their heart of hearts, next to their reverence and love of the Christian faith, their reverence and love for the doctrine of equal and impartial liberty. We are Republicans," he declared, "by a hundred thousand majority of the old stamp of the revolution."

The Massachusetts Republicans had by:

> affection in our hearts and the judgment of our intellects bound our political generation [to] him, who, by the unanimous selection of the foes of our cause and our men, has for years been the determined standard-bearer of liberty, William H. Seward. Whether in the legislature of his native State of New York, whether as governor of that young and growing imperial commonwealth, whether as senator of the United States, or as a tribune of the people, ever faithful, ever true. In the thickest and the hottest of every battle there waved the white plume of the gallant leader of New York.... As we love the cause, and as we respect our own convictions, and as we mean to be faithful to the only organization on earth which is in the van of the cause of freedom, so do we, with entire fidelity of heart, with entire concurrence of judgment, with the firmest and most fixed purpose of our will, adopt the opinion of the majority of the Convention of delegates, to which the American people have assigned the duty of selection; and as Abraham Lincoln, of Illinois, is the choice of the National Republican Convention, [then] Abraham Lincoln is at this moment the choice of Republicans of Massachusetts.

Andrew predicted a "100,000 majority" and all "13 electoral votes." Against the Democratic Party, he asserted, "and against all those who hold its dogmas, or preach its heresies, with whatever associates, and under whatever lead, Massachusetts comes into the line, and under Abraham Lincoln, of Illinois, we are bound to march with you to victory."[2]

Schurz, from Wisconsin, "again seconded the motion," Halstead noted, "but not so effectively in his speech as his reputation as an orator would have warranted us in expecting." Apparently displaying the universal dejection of the Seward supporters, the German Republican ended his speech with "something of anticlimax in shouting 'Lincoln and victory.'"

Koerner also observed the dejection of the Seward supporters: "William M. Evarts and Carl Schurz, both most deeply affected, while not disguising their regret at the defeat of their favorite, in very beautiful language pledged their States for the support of Lincoln, and predicted that Seward would do all in his power to bring about the success of the party. Their speeches were really a very affecting and interesting part of this memorable convention."[3]

Finally, a member of the Illinois delegation addressed the crowd. Browning had "been requested to make some proper response to the speeches that we have heard from our friends of the other states." He admitted that

"Illinois ought hardly on this occasion to be expected to make a speech, or be called upon to do so" because the Illinoisans "are so much elated at present that we are scarcely in a condition to collect our own thoughts, or to express them intelligently to those who may listen to us." He explained that "in the contest through which we have just passed, we have been actuated by no feeling of hostility to the illustrious statesman from New York, who was in competition with our own loved and gallant son." The Illinois delegates, he said, "were actuated solely by a desire for a certain advancement of Republicanism" because they believed "that we could go into battles on the prairies of Illinois with more hope and more prospect of success under the leadership of our own noble son. No Republican who has a love of freedom in his heart, and who has marked the course of Governor Seward, of New York, in the councils of our nation, who has witnessed the many occasions upon which he has risen to the very height of moral sublimity in his conflicts of his, can do otherwise than venerate his name on this occasion." He ended: "I return to all our friends, New York included, our heartfelt thanks and gratitude for the nomination of this Convention."

Halstead described the Browning's speech as "rather dull" but the "nomination was made unanimous, and the Convention adjourned for dinner and for some, celebration:

> The town was full of the news of Lincoln's nomination, and could hardly contain itself. There were bands of music playing, and processions marching, and joyous cries heard on every hand, from the army of trumpeters for Lincoln of Illinois, and the thousands who are always enthusiastic on the winning side. But hundreds of men who had been in the Wigwam were so prostrated by the excitement they had endured, and their exertions in shrieking for Seward or Lincoln, that they were hardly able to walk to their hotels. There were men who had not tasted liquor who staggered about like drunkards, unable to manage themselves.

Not all was well, though. "The Seward men were terribly stricken down," Halstead observed. "They were mortified beyond all expression, and walked thoughtfully and silently away from the slaughterhouse, more ashamed than embittered. They acquiesced in the nomination, but did not pretend to be pleased with it; and the tone of their conversations, as to the prospect of electing the candidate, was not hopeful. It was their funeral, and they would not make merry."[4]

The delegates returned to the Wigwam later that day to select a nominee for vice president. The majority of delegates, realizing that former Whigs and former Democrats constituted their party, supported a former Democrat, Hannibal Hamlin of Maine, to share the ticket with the former Whig from Illinois.

In making the nomination of Hamlin unanimous, Smith of Indiana, who recognized the fracture that Lincoln's nomination had created and realized the pivotal role that Indiana had played in nominating Lincoln, attempted to placate the New Yorkers. After seconding the motion to "make the nomination of Mr. Hamlin unanimous," Smith stated, on "behalf of my friends of Indiana, I would say that any efforts which we have made to secure the nomination of Abraham Lincoln, of Illinois, we have been animated by no feeling of animosity toward the distinguished son of New York, for in no single State of the Union is the name of William H. Seward more highly honored than in Indiana" and that it was "not that we have loved Seward less, but because we have loved the great Republican cause more." Smith assured the delegates "that the Republican flag will wave in triumph upon the soil of Indiana."[5]

In the closing act of the convention, several delegates addressed the audience, but one deserves special mention. Lane rose and "was received with many cheers." He declared, "Freemen of the United States, you have to-day inaugurated a grand work. No event in the history of the United States, subsequent to the Declaration of Independence, is more sublime and impressive than the event which has this day been inaugurated in this vast presence of the freemen of the United States of America. Into your hands this day is placed the grand responsibility of bearing the torch of civilization in the vanguard of freedom. I ask you to bear it aloft and upward until the whole world shall glow with the light of our illumination. My fellow citizens, the work commenced to-day shall go on, until complete victory shall await our effects in November."

Lane heard that the Seward supporters were castigating the Hoosiers. "The position of many of the states of the West may have been misunderstood," he assured. In referring to Seward's philosophy but carefully avoiding any mention of his character, Lane continued: "We regard to-day William H. Seward as the grandest representative of the liberty-loving instincts of the human heart who exists in the United States. In our heart of hearts we love him, and would make him President to-day if we had the power to do so; but we regard Abraham Lincoln, of Illinois, as an equally orthodox representative of Republican principles, and a most beautiful illustration of the power of free institutions and the doctrines of free labor in the United States." And, like Smith, he predicted: "My fellow citizens, some doubts have been expressed in reference to Indiana. I pledge Indiana by [a] ten thousand majority. I pledge my personal honor for the redemption of that state."[6]

After the convention's conclusion, "the city was wild with delight," Halstead reported. "The 'Old Abe' men formed processions and bore rails through the streets. Torrents of liquor were poured down the hoarse throats of the multitude. A hundred guns were fired form the top of the Tremont House." The train in which Halstead departed Chicago "consisted of eleven cars, every seat full and people standing in the aisles and corners. I never before saw a company of persons so prostrated by continued excitement. The Lincoln men were not able to respond to the cheers which went up along the road for 'old Abe.' Even up to two o'clock in the morning, "at every station where there was a village" the reporter saw "tar barrels burning, drums beating, boys carrying rails; and guns, great and small, banging away. The weary passengers were allowed no rest, but [were] plagued by the thundering jar of cannon, the clamor of drums, the glare of bonfires, and the whooping of the boys, who were delighted with the idea of a candidate for the Presidency who thirty years ago split rails on the Sangamon River — classic stream now and forevermore — and whose neighbors named him 'honest.'"[7]

The *New York Tribune* reported: "Chicago is in a blaze of glory tonight. Bonfires, processions, torchlights, fireworks, illuminations, and salutes, have filled the air with noise and the eye with beauty. 'Honest Old Abe' is the cry in every mouth, and the 'irrepressible conflict' against Slavery and corruptions opens with great promise and immense enthusiasm. It is impossible to exaggerate the good feeling and joy that prevail here. The Illinois delegation resolved that the millennium has come."[8]

Koerner witnessed another side. The evening of May 18, the evening of Seward's defeat, the Lincoln supporter "resorted to the place where the German delegates and German visitors from other States used to congregate. I found them generally very despondent. Seward, or even some other radical Republican, such as Wade or Chase, had been their choice. They believed that Lincoln's nomination would not meet with half the enthusiasm that Seward's would have met with."[9]

Browning had a similar experience. He left Chicago for his hometown on May 19 and happened to share the ride with a former lieutenant governor of New York, Henry R. Selden, for part of the trip. Selden "introduced himself" to Browning and thanked him "on behalf of the New York delegation" for his speech. "I had a good deal of conversation with him upon political subjects," Browning wrote. "He thinks with great effort New York may be carried for Mr Lincoln, but does not regard it as certain. The delegation of that state was greatly devoted to Mr Seward, and are mortified and disappointed."[10]

Trumbull encountered the disappointment of the New Yorkers firsthand when he spoke in New York City on May 19. The Illinois Senator stated that Lincoln "is a giant in stature," to which a New Yorker yelled back, "Not high enough to be President." The Illinois senator replied, "Yes, high enough to be President, and he will be President." Trumbull, like the *Tribune*, noted that Lincoln lost to Douglas in 1858, but that Lincoln "had the popular vote by [a] four thousand majority; and he will more than double it in November. I tell you he will make a clean sweep of every State west of the Alleghanies." Another New Yorker interrupted: "How about poor old Seward?" Trumbull, displaying the character of Lincoln, responded, "Mr. Seward is a statesman and a patriot, and his whole heart is with our great cause."[11]

New Yorkers were not the only ones disappointed by Lincoln's nomination though, even Illinoisans expressed dissatisfaction. Browning confessed in his diary that his "first choice for the Presidency was Mr Bates of Missouri, but under instructions our whole delegations voted for Mr Lincoln." "Many reasons," he claimed, "influenced" him to prefer Bates, "the chief of which, next to his eminent fitness, were to strengthen our organization in the South, and remove apprehension in the South of any hostile purpose on the part of Republicans to the institutions of the South — to restore fraternal regard among the different sections of the Union — to bring to our support the old whigs in the free states, who have not yet fraternized with us, and to give some check to the ultra tendencies of the Republican party." Browning even speculated that Bates "would probably have been nominated if the struggle had been prolonged."[12]

Despite these fears and concerns, the disappointment and dejection, the *Chicago Press and Tribune* editors were ecstatic. The precise result for which they had so fervently hoped, and which they had believed nearly impossible, had come to pass. The May 19 issue was filled with their obvious excitement. The paper reported under an article titled "Our Illumination" and "Great Enthusiasm":

> Last night the *Press and Tribune* building was illuminated from 'turret to foundation' by the brilliant glare of a thousand lights which blazed from windows and doors with a most attractive and beautiful effect. On each side of the counting room door stood a rail — out of the three thousand split by 'honest Old Abe' thirty years ago on the Sangamon river bottoms. On the inside were two more, brilliantly hung with tapers whose numberless individual lights glistened like so many stars in contrast with the dark walnut color of the wood. On the front of the office and over the main door, between the second and third stories, was suspended an immense transparency with this inscription upon it: FOR PRESIDENT, 'HONEST OLD ABE.' — FOR VICE PRESIDENT, HANNIBAL HAMLIN.
>
> Inspired with that pure enthusiasm that every true Republican yesterday felt when their banner was unfurled, they collected in crowds at the several hotels and shouldering rails marched in joyous triumph and through our streets to the cheering music of no less than a score of bands. At dark several of the triumphal processions united, paraded through Clark street, and stopping before our office, rent the air with soul inspiring cheers and exclamations of victory, which awakened a loud response from the honest hearts of one hundred employees of this establishment.

> The Pennsylvanians, in particular, knew no bounds for the expression of their feelings. They at once rallied, several hundred strong, at their headquarters at the Briggs House.... They all assert that Lincoln's nomination will gain them the State by at least 25,000 majority, and their feelings, excited by the certainty of such a glorious victory, carried them almost beyond bounds in the expression of their wild anticipations.

The "inspiration was universal," the *Tribune* reported, "and congratulations were upon the lips of every one who belonged to our ranks. The large warehouse of Huntington, Wadsworth & Parks, on Lake Street, also made a very effective show of variegated lights in every window, while a banner was hung across the street, upon the fold of which was painted: '*For President, Abraham Lincoln.*' Many other buildings were also illuminated, and, as we said before, the enthusiasm was universal, demonstrated by music, cheering, speaking parading, and also by a liberal display of fence rails, and other characteristic emblems of the people's choice."

"Everybody was happy, every heart filled with joy," the *Tribune* editors found, "except the Douglasites. They refused to be comforted."[13]

"The age of purity returns," the *Tribune* declared in an article titled "Nomination of Lincoln":

> After a succession of Presidents, who have not only been subservient to the interests of the Propagandists of Human Slavery, but corrupt to a degree alarming to the truest friends of Republican institutions, the nomination of ABRAHAM LINCOLN— Honest old ABE — by the great Republican party, is a guaranty that the country, wearied and outraged by the malfeasance of those invested with the Federal power, desires a return to the sterling honesty and Democratic simplicity which marked the Administrations of Jefferson, Madison, Adams and Jackson.

The party had chosen well, the *Tribune* asserted, because "Mr. Lincoln is the very soul of integrity. In all his life, now extending over 51 years, there is not an act of commission or omission, by which his thorough uprightness, his exact conscientiousness, his perfect integrity are impaired. The fact is a guarantee that when he goes into the government as its Executive head, the corruption and extravagance which have made the two last Administrations a stench in the nostrils of the American people, and which are fast sapping the foundations upon which our fathers built, will come to a sudden end."

As for his position on slavery, the *Tribune* declared that "Mr. LINCOLN's record" on this issue "is so well known and so clear that it needs no explanation. He is a conservative Anti-Slavery man, against whom no allegation of fanaticism will hold good. Guided by the Constitution and its laws," Lincoln "will command the respect of the North and the South." If "there is an attempt from any quarter whatever to dissolve bonds which tie the States of this Union together, it will be met by more than a Roman firmness which never yet yielded to threats or frowns. That beautiful evenness and integrity of his life, which have made him a man of mark, will not desert him in his promised official career; but will remain the guides and balances in that difficult path which the people will command him to tread."

Even the *Tribune* had to admit, though, "Mr. Lincoln is untried in a merely executive capacity." To this concern, the editors proclaimed that they had "not the smallest fear that he will be unequal to any emergency in which he may be placed. That activity and strength of intellect which have brought him up from a lowly estate to become the head of a great, and we believe, a triumphant party, will be the anchor on which he and the country may depend. In this regard he is eminently safe."

The *Tribune* also argued that Lincoln was superior to his rivals because he obtained his nomination without any deals. "He has no pledges to redeem, no promise to make good," the editors argued, "because "the uprising in his favor has been spontaneous — the outgrowth of a widespread conviction of his fitness and availability." Lincoln had not prevailed through the "work of cliques, or factions" who would now "seek their reward. He goes into the Presidential Chair, clean-handed and pure; and, when President, his distribution of the patronage will be governed by the wants and exigencies of the public service...." Throughout the convention, the *Tribune* continued, "there have been such temptations to lead him into the practices which are unfortunately so common with politicians of less rectitude," but Lincoln "refused all offers of votes which were based upon the promises of future rewards, we have reason to know. With the spirit becoming an honest man, he rejected them all." The *Tribune* concluded the article by predicting that "his nomination will be taken up with the zeal and enthusiasm which foreshadow not only success, but majorities unequalled in the political history of the free States."[14]

As opposed to the *Tribune's* conclusions, some individuals believed that the Republicans had chosen Lincoln for other reasons. Some speculated that Lincoln prevailed because he was more conservative on the slavery issue. Koerner rejected that argument. "Seward was in fact far more conservative on the slavery question than Lincoln," the German Republican wrote. "Besides, his very eminence as a statesman had raised against him in his own State and in his own party dangerous rivalry, and it was very doubtful whether he could carry his own State; and without New York no Republican victory was to be expected."[15] Halstead believed the convention's result was best understood as a "defeat of Seward rather than the nomination of Lincoln." Lincoln triumphed due to his "presumption of availability" as opposed to Seward's "preeminence in intellect and unrivaled fame." It was "a success" by the Lincoln supporters with a candidate who possessed "the ruder qualities of manhood and the more homely attributes of popularity" in contradiction to Seward's "arts of a consummate politician and the splendor of accomplished statesmanship."[16]

Four days after Lincoln's nomination, Greeley explained to his readers in his newspaper, the *New York Tribune*, why Lincoln had been nominated. He admitted, "I went to Chicago to do my best to nominate Judge Bates" because "I deemed Judge Bates the very man to satisfy and attract the great body of conservative and quiet voters who have hitherto stood aloof from the Republican organization, not because they dissent from our principles, because they have been taught to distrust and hate us on other grounds." Greeley further acknowledged that, although "all the world is raining bouquets on the successful nominee," he still believed that "Judge Bates, to whom I never spoke nor wrote, would have been the wiser choice."

Greeley concluded: "Mr. Bates lost the nomination primarily because the Indiana delegation, which was friendly to him when chosen, went over, early in the canvass at Chicago, to Lincoln; and Pennsylvania, by a vote of 60 for Lincoln to 45 for Bates, soon after indicated the former as the ultimate choice. Thenceforward, the only hope of Judge Bates's nomination was in the chance that the Seward men, if beaten, would prefer Bates to Lincoln."

Greeley believed the "candidates for Governor in the great doubtful States — Col. Curtin in Pennsylvania and Gen. Lane in Indiana — were as energetic and efficient as able men must be who felt that life or death for themselves and their party hung on the issue of this struggle. The Indiana delegation — having no candidate in their own State to embarrass their action, and perfectly unanimous in the conviction that to nominate Gov. Seward was to invoke defeat in their State and in the Union — were most efficient in the canvass, while their early adhesion to Lincoln nearly narrowed the contest to him and Gov. Seward." Pennsylvania and Ohio, although possessing far more votes than Indiana, proved less influential, according to Greeley. "Pennsylvania, with Gen. Cameron in the foreground, Ohio with three possible home candidates favored by unequal parts of her delegation, had far less positive weight than their proportional strength entitled them to claim." He considered "the momentous fact that the four conspicuously doubtful States — New Jersey, Pennsylvania, Indiana, and Illinois — unanimously testified that they could not be carried for Gov. Seward, was decisive."

Greeley considered the attitudes of the New Yorkers counterproductive. "Noisy bar-room denunciations of anti–Seward men from this State as ingrates and traitors; claims for Gov. Seward not only of the exclusive leadership but even of the authorship of the Republican party; public boasts that ever so much money could be raised to carry Seward's election and none at all for that of anybody else, with triumphant queries — 'If you don't nominate Seward, where will you get your money?' — these were the weapons only of the lowest stratum of New York politicians, yet they had a most damaging effect." The anti–Seward had "had no faith that elections were or could be honestly carried by" money "and no belief that any considerable sum was needed for that purpose." In reference to Lincoln's reputation as a railsplitter, Greeley wrote, "If it was, they preferred to earn it by splitting rails at fifty cents a day to having it seem to influence their choice of a candidate for President."[17]

The New Yorkers disagreed with Greeley. Just as they pinned a Seward badge on him at the convention, they now pinned the blame on him for Seward's defeat. In the pro–Seward *New York Times*, the Republican competitor to Greeley's *Tribune*, Seward supporter Henry Raymond, who had lobbied for Seward at the convention, alleged that the "main work of the Chicago Convention was the defeat of Gov. Seward," and the "nomination which it finally made was purely an accident, decided far more by the shouts and applause of the vast concourse which dominated the Convention, than by any direct labors of any of the delegates." Raymond believed that the "great point aimed at was Mr. Seward's defeat; and in that endeavor, Mr. Greeley labored harder and did tenfold more, than the whole family of Blairs, together with all the Gubernatorial candidates, to whom he modestly hands over the honors of the effective campaign."

In response, Greeley again gave the credit to others. He admitted that he "did what he could" to defeat Seward but his main focus had been "strenuously urging that the Delegations from Pennsylvania, New-Jersey, Indiana and Illinois, must be regarded as authority as to who could and could not" win their states. "The Delegations from those States, with the candidates for Governor in Pennsylvania and Indiana, whose representations and remonstrances rendered the nomination of Gov. Seward, in the eyes of all intelligent, impartial observers, a clear act of political suicide, were nowise instructed or impelled by me. They acted on views deliberately formed long before they came to Chicago."[18]

John S. Bobbs, an Indiana delegate, wrote on May 19th: "Mr Lincoln owes his nomination to a prevailing opposition to Mr. Seward among the delegations from the Free States bordering the slave states." He acknowledged that the "delegates were divided in their preferences" but the people of Indiana held "too great prejudice" toward Seward, and the delegation rallied together to "vote as a unit for Mr. Lincoln in order to defeat Mr. Seward ... Indiana having no candidate of her own was in a position to make her vote decisive."[19]

Edward Pierce, a member of the Massachusetts delegation, wrote decades later: "This is certain — that Mr Lincoln's nomination was perfectly assured without bargins — and if any were made, they were made in face of an inevitable result, to gain points after the election." The "problem" for the Republicans was which "candidate, reliable and true, would carry the four free states lost in 1856. Pennsylvania, New Jersey, Indiana and Illinois. It was honestly felt that it was hazardous to present to them Seward or even Chase. The names left for a choice were Judge McLean, Bates and Lincoln. Illinois, Penn & N.J. three of the four had 'favorite sons,' Lincoln, Cameron & Dayton." What made the difference from Pierce's perspective was "the unanimous support of one of the four." Indiana, he recalled, had no "favorite son." The Hoosiers' support "put Lincoln altogether ahead of McLean and Bates; and besides strong anti-slavery men had prejudices against McLean and a distrust of Bates which was not felt about Lincoln." Pierce did "not see how the convention after this could avoid nominating Lincoln — who was a true man, obnoxious to no section — and according to testimony from the four free states lost in 1856, altogether likely to carry them."

However, Pierce had heard the many comments concerning the bartering of Lincoln's nomination and sought to quash all those rumors: "No bargain was necessary to secure his nomination and none had any effect if it was made, to secure it. Doubtless after the election, persons who wanted to have positions and influence did what they could to magnify them by claiming that they, for a few considerations promised, gave essential support, and were now entitled to payment." On this issue, he concluded, "'Bargain and Sale' are favorite terms among a certain order of politicians who often resort to them for explanations of results where better motives controlled."[20]

Raymond was completely wrong; Koerner and Halstead were both correct in some points, and incorrect in others, while Bobbs, Greeley and Pierce came closer to the truth. Lincoln had prevailed for three main reasons: his advocacy for the non-extension of slavery, his adherence to the Declaration of Independence, and his character. However, his attacks on the spreading of slavery were only significant in terms of making him a viable candidate. All the major candidates shared this philosophy. It was the one common denominator among all the major candidates and among the party members. While this position was not pivotal in determining Lincoln's success over the other major candidates, it was necessary for him to hold to this philosophy to be considered.

Secondly, any candidate who would succeed at the 1860 convention must have demonstrated unequivocal support for the Declaration of Independence. The majority of delegates held that one document in the highest esteem above all else. Again and again the delegates reminded themselves of its importance. The *Chicago Press and Tribune* believed it so vital that it published Lincoln's

Lewistown speech on the Declaration in its May 15 issue before the convention even began. The German Republicans displayed almost a religious fervor toward it. The delegates placed it as the first document mentioned in the draft platform and then, due to Giddings, they overwhelmingly added the Declaration's entire first paragraph to the platform. Had Lincoln's Columbus speech become his public philosophy, he would not have stood a chance. Fortunately, the Columbus speech proved an anomaly. However, while the Republicans' passion toward the Declaration did not favor either Seward or Lincoln, both of whom had praised it numerous times, it did prove the first strike against Bates due to his association with Know-Nothings.

After maintaining faithfulness toward the Declaration, Lincoln's third advantage lay in his character. This advantage was most vividly displayed by the faithfulness of the Republicans in his home state. Lincoln had achieved this support by earning the respect of a vast cross section of Republicans after the 1854 Kansas-Nebraska Act. Former Democrats such as Trumbull and Judd, both of whom opposed him for the Senate in 1855, former Free Soilers such as Owen Lovejoy, and former Whigs such as Davis, all steadfastly supported Lincoln in the 1858 senatorial campaign. Men who despised each other on a personal or political level, such as Davis and Lovejoy, had nothing but kind words for Lincoln. This admiration even seemed to extend to the entire state itself in 1858 when the Republicans, with Lincoln at the head of their ticket, lost the election in the state legislature but won a majority of the popular vote. And, it was this admiration that enabled Lincoln to gain the support of a majority of the Republican delegates at the Illinois state convention. These delegates not only agreed to vote as a block, but to vote as a block for him. He accomplished something within his home state that eluded Governor Chase of Ohio, who quickly found himself behind Lincoln because he could not even command all the delegates from his own state.[21]

Seward, the expected nominee, stood as Lincoln's most significant opponent. In retrospect, the race was fought between the supporters of these two men. Here, Seward lost the nomination in the border states — the four states the Republicans lost in 1856: Illinois, Indiana, Pennsylvania and New Jersey. However, these states did not support Lincoln because he held a more conservative philosophy than Seward. As Republicans, there was no difference in the two men's philosophy on slavery, a point which Douglas clearly understood when he linked the "House Divided" speech and the "Irrepressible Conflict" speech in his essay. Bates also viewed the two men in the same regard when he wrote that Lincoln "is as fully committed as Mr. Seward, is to the extremist doctrines of the Republican party." Lincoln concurred with these sentiments when he, in his New England speeches and in his written statement to his supporters, admitted his approval of Seward's "Irrepressible

Conflict" speech. Instead of philosophy, the two men differed in another critical aspect.[22]

Indiana held the most influential place of all the four border states because no Hoosier sought the presidency. The Hoosiers could rightly claim objectivity in suggesting a candidate. This objectivity proved critical with the Committee of Twelve and with the convention as a whole. When Illinois *and* Indiana declared for Lincoln, Pennsylvania and New Jersey had no choice but to yield to the other two.

Three individuals, whom historians have not fully acknowledged, proved decisive in bringing Indiana into the Lincoln fold. Lane deserves the most credit for lobbying the Hoosiers to support Lincoln, and Koerner and Browning share credit for finishing the job. Koerner, Browning and the Committee of Twelve also deserve recognition for persuading the Pennsylvanians to support Lincoln.[23]

Lane never made any definitive statements as to why he supported Lincoln over Seward. However, an examination of Lane's and Lincoln's characters uncovers two vital characteristics that they shared. First, both men passionately supported the Declaration of Independence. Since the Alton debate in 1858, Lincoln continually spoke in favor of the Declaration of Independence with only one exception. Lane began his speech at the Wigwam dedication with a rousing speech in favor of the Declaration of Independence and then spoke of it again in his last speech at the convention. Second, and most important, they shared the same character. These two men avoided the inflammatory language that had become Seward's trademark and were therefore respected by most Republicans, and even by some Democrats. Lane must have used these three points to convince at least three delegations — Indiana, Vermont and Virginia — to support Lincoln. Lane could win in Indiana, and since Lincoln was like him, Lincoln could also prevail in Indiana. Lane saw in Lincoln a Lane Republican or, to put it another way, he saw himself as a Lincoln Republican.

Some historians have speculated that the Indiana delegates and other states supported Lincoln because of promised offices. This theory fails on one crucial point. The proponents of this theory assume that, above all, the Republican delegates sought to acquire cabinet positions and other patronage instead of selecting a candidate who would win. The leaders of the Indiana delegation, Lane and Caleb Smith, who eventually received the position of secretary of the interior, never made any mention that a cabinet position had been promised for supporting Lincoln. In fact, although Smith hoped for a cabinet position and had "reason to believe that a place will be offered" to him, he admitted after the convention, in regard to a cabinet post, "I have no promises from any one authorized to speak for Mr. Lincoln...."[24]

Like Smith, Cameron received a cabinet position. There is some evidence that Davis spoke with one of the Pennsylvania delegates about a post for Cameron, but best evidence suggests this occurred *after* the Pennsylvania delegation decided for Lincoln. Furthermore, Davis pledged only access to Lincoln, not any position. Pennsylvania, like Indiana, sought the most electable candidate who supported the ideals of the Republican Party, as demonstrated by the concerted efforts of Illinois, Indiana and Pennsylvania.[25]

In fact, Lincoln dispersed cabinet positions not on the basis of events at the convention, but rather on the basis of maintaining party unity. Seward, his main opponent, accepted the office of secretary of state, the highest cabinet position. Another opponent, Bates, became attorney general. Montgomery Blair and Welles, who opposed and worked against Lincoln's nomination until the bitter end, also received appointments. All these actions demonstrated Lincoln's magnanimity and keen political wisdom, and not any convention bargains.

Lincoln prevailed over Seward that May due to his character. He correctly understood the Declaration of Independence as encapsulating the party's ultimate goal and non-extension of slavery as the issue upon which all Republicans could unite, and he spoke on behalf of both with far more respect toward the Republicans' opponents than had Seward. His note to "stay cool and give offence to no one" exemplified his character. Seward too often spoke without considering the reactions of others, which created for Seward a distasteful reputation in the border states where the Republicans did not constitute an overwhelming majority. Lane and others recognized this weakness, and saw in Lincoln a person who spoke with respect for the immediate goals of the Republican Party and the nation's ultimate goal as defined by the Declaration of Independence.

The May 19 issue of *New York Times* described it best: "Great inquiry has been made into the history of Mr. Lincoln. The only evidence ... is that he had a stump canvass with Mr. Douglas, in which he was beaten. He is not very strong" in the West "but is unassailable in his private character."[26]

Seward's supporters held a huge advantage in experience, prestige and money. All Lincoln's supporters had was his character and, in the end, it was all they ever needed.

After the convention, attention then switched, not to Springfield, Illinois, where Lincoln's acceptance was all but expected, but to Auburn, New York. Numerous Seward supporters wrote to their leader expressing anguish, disappointment and anger. Seward was so confident of his nomination that he had drafted a resignation speech for his Senate seat. Now he might quit the party and run an independent campaign. Precedence had been set with the split in the Democratic Party and with the sudden formation of the Constitutional Union Party.

"Dear and honorable Sir! Unthankfulness has in all ages been a predominant vice of mankind, but the last event at Chicago has made it the predominant <u>Infamy</u> of modern times," one supporter wrote. "I since have struggled with myself (and am still struggling), if I should not go before the People, the self-judging, independent people, and present Your name as the only-one to conquer the land at the election day. Why? Are the People Sheep? Shall they share and shelter the paid ingratitude?"[27] Another supporter sent a Philadelphia newspaper article with the following assessment: "Respectable mediocrity has carried off the prize habitually for a whole generation, while the great and towering minds by which parties have been created, and policy shaped, have been shelved and consigned to ignoble seclusion."[28] A third supporter wrote: "I am greatly disappointed for the honor of our country in the personal preference unexpectedly given to an undisciplined statesman for the post of honor." Yet he urged Seward to remain Republican: "We will not faint, or tire, but labor on, to secure the best interests of all classes, both bond & free...."[29]

Some of his other supporters also took the high road and encouraged Seward to remain engaged in the nation's politics. These supporters included Charles Francis Adams, the son of John Quincy Adams: "For a long time past it has been an impression strongly fixed in my mind that no statesman of the first class is likely to be called to the Presidency at any moment excepting perhaps in that of an extreme peril of the state. I had hoped indeed that your case might prove an exception.... Your services are more necessary to the cause than they ever were and your own reputation will gain more of permanency from the becoming manner with which you meet this disappointment, than it would from all the brilliancy of the highest success. I trust you will indulge no notions of retirement — but on the contrary reserve your part in the van of the great merriment of opinion just the same as if nothing had happened."[30]

Although Seward's biographer wrote that the senator realized "how fortunate it was that he did not keep a diary," because it would have been filled with "all his cursing and swearing after the day the news came," Seward never mentioned an independent candidacy, nor did he make any negative comments publicly about Lincoln. He accepted defeat, accepted Lincoln's nomination and agreed to campaign for the Republicans in 1860.[31]

The *Tribune* editors were cognizant of these apprehensions and, in the May 19 issue, sought to sooth the Seward supporters' fears. The greatest uncertainty with which the diehard Seward supporters were grappling was not Lincoln's character, but his philosophy. The fact that the border states and the slave states constituted some of Lincoln's most fervent backers only fostered the belief that he was marginal on the slavery issue and on the issue of equality. In fact, four of the six slave states overwhelmingly supported Lincoln over Seward. The *Tribune*'s editors addressed this concern directly, not with their words, but with those of Lincoln. They did not chose Lincoln's "Cooper Union" speech or any of his speeches from 1859 and 1860. Instead, they conspicuously placed on the May 19 issue a speech which Lincoln had delivered in the small town of Lewistown, Illinois, two years before — a speech in which Lincoln pointed to the document for which Giddings was prepared to leave the party, which the German Republicans embraced as their shield, and which the Republicans had claimed as their cornerstone. The last three sentences of this speech were especially poignant for the Seward Republicans: "I charge you to drop every paltry and insignificant thought for any man's success. It is nothing; I am nothing; Judge Douglas is nothing. *But do not destroy that immortal emblem of Humanity — the Declaration of American Independence.*"[32]

Epilogue

They clearly chose the wrong man. Democrats, southerners and slave-holders were supporting human bondage, were openly assaulting the promises of the Declaration of Independence, and sought to spread slavery from coast to coast. At a time like this, they should have chosen a candidate who responded to these attacks with attacks of his own. A candidate who freely insulted the party's enemies, who put them in their place, who threatened and belittled all those who opposed them. They should have chosen the firebrand.

Or, to view it from another perspective, they chose the right man. They chose a candidate who, as a lawyer and as a candidate, in his words and his actions, in his personal and his political life, treated all those whom he encountered with respect and dignity — a man who found his guiding principle not in hatred or revenge, but in the words "all men are created equal," and saw his opponents not as Democrats or southerners or slaveholders, but as his fellow countrymen, his fellow citizens, his fellow Americans.

Instead of selecting a man who attacked individuals, the Republicans chose a man who attacked an idea — an idea that all men are not created equal, that the Declaration of Independence was not his nation's cornerstone, that this was not the "last, best hope of earth."

Appendix A:
After the Convention

Orville Browning (1806–1881) was appointed to the United States Senate in 1861 to complete the term of Stephen Douglas. Browning's conservatism that led him to prefer Bates as a presidential candidate also led him to oppose the Emancipation Proclamation. He attempted to persuade Lincoln to modify it. Lincoln refused. At the beginning of the Grant administration in 1869, he left the Republican Party and became a Democrat.

Stephen Arnold Douglas (1813–1861) was nominated for president by the Democratic Party in 1860, but relatively early in the campaign he turned his focus to the southern states and campaigned not so much for himself, but against secession, his greatest fear.

As for Lincoln's Inaugural Address, Douglas stated, "I indorse it," and he made two famous quotes in the last year of his life. First, in Chicago, he replied to those who wished to know where he stood on secession:

"There are only two sides to the question. Every man must be for the United States or against it. There can be no neutrals in this war, only patriots — and traitors."

Second, as he was dying, his wife asked him if he had any words for his sons. He told her, "Tell them to obey the laws and support the Constitution of the United States." Four hours later, he died.

David Davis (1815–1866) originally approved of the Emancipation Proclamation, and Lincoln appointed him to the United States Supreme Court. When Davis, like Browning, later recommended that Lincoln alter the Emancipation Proclamation, Lincoln also refused to follow Davis' advice. Davis served on the Supreme Court until 1877, served in the United States Senate for one term, and retired to Bloomington, Illinois.

Joshua Giddings (1795–1864) became consul general to Canada in the Lincoln administration and praised the issuance of the Emancipation Proclamation.

Norman Judd (1815–1878) accompanied Lincoln on his railroad trip to Washington, D.C., in 1861. Lincoln nominated him as minister to Prussia, and after his return to the United States, Judd was elected to the United States House of Representatives in 1866 and 1868.

Gustave Koerner (1809–1896) served as minister to Spain during the Lincoln administration. At the end of the Civil War, he returned to the United States. In 1865, he was given the honor of serving as one of Lincoln's pallbearers.

Henry Smith Lane (1811–1881) won election as the Republican gubernatorial candidate in 1860. As planned, the state legislature elected him senator two days after he became governor. He served one term. Lane was one of Lincoln's most loyal senators. He supported the Emancipation Proclamation and voted in favor of the Thirteenth Amendment, which outlawed slavery.

William Henry Seward (1801–1872) served as secretary of state, the most revered cabinet post, in Lincoln's administration and became the president's closest advisor. When, in 1862, some New Yorkers formed a group to again promote his future political aspirations, Seward responded, "I neither look for, nor should it be offered to me, would I never hereafter accept, any reward." He continued as secretary of state under President Andrew Johnson. In 1869, after eighteen years of continuous public service, from senator to secretary of state, Seward, the man who had been so close to obtaining the presidency, made his 1862 statement a reality. He walked away from Washington, D.C., and from public life forever. Three years later, he passed away at his home in Auburn, New York.

Abraham Lincoln (1809–1865) became the sixteenth president of the United States and led the ship of state through the storm of civil war by the moral compass of the Declaration of Independence.

Appendix B:
Is He One of Us?

On November 2, 1860, with an unprecedented number of four major candidates from which to choose, the Americans headed to the polls and initiated a revolution. The Republicans swept all eleven states that they had carried in 1856, plus three of the four crucial ones that had eluded them four years before: Illinois, Indiana and Pennsylvania. Even in the fourth crucial state — New Jersey — the Republicans won a majority, four of the seven electoral votes. In nominating Lincoln, in terms of electability, the Republicans had chosen well.

But for some delegates, especially those who had supported Seward, this victory might have proved bittersweet. They must have wondered whether Lincoln abided by the sentiments of the Declaration of Independence, or whether their party had compromised on their most cherished beliefs simply for the sake of victory. The Emancipation Proclamation must have given them great hope. But it was a speech he delivered just a little over three years after he was nominated that must have convinced them that they he was one of them, that for the first time in American history they had a president who firmly believed that "all men are created equal" meant "all men." In this speech at Gettysburg, Pennsylvania, Lincoln cleverly pointed the Americans back to the Declaration of Independence as the nation's cornerstone when he began with the words "Four score and seven years ago" (1776).

Four score and seven years ago our fathers brought forth upon this continent, a new nation, conceived in Liberty, and dedicated to the proposition that all men are created equal.

Now we are engaged in a great civil war, testing whether that nation, or any nation so conceived, and so dedicated, can long endure. We are met on a great battle-field of that war. We have come to dedicate a portion of that field, as a final resting place for those who here gave their lives, that that nation might live. It is altogether fitting and proper that we should do this.

But, in a larger sense, we can not dedicate — we can not consecrate — we can not hallow — this ground. The brave men, living and dead, who struggled here, have consecrated it, far above our poor power to add or detract. The world will little note, nor long remember, what we say here, but it can never forget what they did here. It is for us, the living, rather, to be dedicated here to the unfinished work which they who fought here, have, thus far, so nobly advanced. It is rather for us to be here dedicated to the great task remaining before us — that from these honored dead we take increased devotion to that cause for which they gave the last full measure of devotion — that we here highly resolve that these dead shall not have died in vain — that this nation, under God, shall have a new birth of freedom — and that government of the people, by the people, for the people, shall not perish from the earth.

Notes

Chapter 1

1. Lincoln to Anson G. Henry, November 19, 1858, in *The Collected Works of Abraham Lincoln*, ed. Roy Basler (New Brunswick, NJ: Rutgers University Press, 1953), 3:339.

2. Lincoln to William H. Henderson, February 21, 1855, in *The Collected Works*, 2:306–307.

3. Ibid., 2:459.

4. Lincoln to M.M. Inman, November 20, 1858, in *The Collected Works* 3:341.

5. Basler, ed., *The Collected Works* 2:282 and 4:67.

6. Ibid., 2:249–276.

7. Two justices filed dissenting opinions on the Dred Scott decision: Judge Benjamin R. Curtis and Judge John McLean. Curtis' last term on the court was 1857; he would resign due to an ongoing dispute with Taney over the Dred Scott decision. Ironically, although Lincoln agreed with Curtis, the justice did not agree with Lincoln. Curtis would oppose the Emancipation Proclamation and the Lincoln administration while serving as a lawyer in Civil War Washington.

8. Basler, ed., *The Collected Works* 2: 398–409.

9. Or could be interpreted as the "epilogue" of the Declaration of Independence.

10. William H. Herndon and Jesse W. Weik, *Abraham Lincoln: The True Story of a Great Life* (New York: D. Appleton, 1896), 2:86.

11. Basler, ed., *The Collected Works* 2: 546–547.

12. Ibid., 3:22.

13. Ibid., 3:500.

14. Ibid., 3:501.

15. Timothy S. Good, *The Lincoln-Douglas Debates and the Making of a President* (Jefferson, NC: McFarland, 2007), 173–174. The following were Lincoln's specific quotes concerning "superior" and "inferior." Ottawa: "There is a physical difference between the two, which in my judgment will probably forever forbid their living together upon the footing of perfect equality, and inasmuch as it becomes a necessity that there must be a difference, I, as well as Judge Douglas, am in favor of the race to which I belong having the superior position." Freeport: none. Jonesboro: none. Charleston: "And inasmuch as they cannot so live, while they do remain together there must be the position of superior and inferior, and I as much as any other man am in favor of having the superior position assigned to the white race." Galesburg: "[T]he inferior races are our equals." Quincy: "And inasmuch as they cannot so live, while they do remain together there must be the position of superior & inferior. I am as much as any other man in favor of having the superior position assigned to the white race." Alton: none.

16. Basler, ed., *The Collected Works* 2:301–304.

17. Herndon and Weik, 2:127.

18. Abraham Lincoln to M.M. Inman, No-

vember 20, 1858, in *The Collected Works* 3:341.

19. Abraham Lincoln to H.D. Sharpe, December 8, 1858, in *The Collected Works* 3:344.

Chapter 2

1. Seward wrote the following in 1855: "'The underground railroad works wonderfully. Two passengers came here last night. Watch [the family dog] attacked one of them." Frederick W. Seward, *Seward at Washington as Senator and Secretary of State, 1861–1872* (New York: Derby and Miller, 1891), 258.

2. *Congressional Globe*, 31st Congress, 1st Session, Appendix, 260–269, March 11, 1850.

3. Endorsement on the Margin of the *Missouri Democrat*, May 17, 1860, in *The Collected Works of Abraham Lincoln,* ed. Roy Basler (New Brunswick, NJ: Rutgers University Press, 1953), 4:50. Seward's reaction to the publicity of his speech is best described by one his biographers, Glyndon G. Van Deusen: "Seward's mood in the midst of all this publicity was mainly one of elation.... 'I know,' he declared, 'that I have spoken words that will tell when I am dead, and even while I am living, for the benefit and blessing of mankind, and for myself this is consolation enough.'" Glyndon G. Van Deusen, *William Henry Seward: Lincoln's Secretary of State, the Negotiator of the Alaska Purchase* (New York: Oxford University Press, 1967), 126–128.

4. George E. Baker, *Life of William Seward, with Selections from His Works* (New York: J.S. Redfield, 1855), 392.

5. William H. Herndon and Jesse W. Weik, *Abraham Lincoln: The True Story of a Great Life* (New York: D. Appleton, 1896), 2:68; Timothy S. Good, *The Lincoln-Douglas Debates and the Making of a President* (Jefferson, NC: McFarland, 2007), 29–30.

6. Van Deusen, 194.

7. Ibid., 194.

8. G.E. Baker, ed., *The Works of William H. Seward* (Boston, 1884), 4:289–302.

9. New York *Evening Post*, November 15, 1858.

10. Niven, *Gideon Welles*, 283–285.

11. Endorsement on the Margin of the *Missouri Democrat*, May 17, 1860, in *The Collected Works*, 4:50.

Chapter 3

1. Glyndon G. Van Deusen, *William Henry Seward* (New York: Oxford University Press, 1967), 211–213.

2. William H. Herndon and Jesse W. Weik, *Abraham Lincoln: The True Story of a Great Life* (New York: D. Appleton, 1896), 2:9–11.

3. Abraham Lincoln to Anson S. Miller, November 19, 1858, in *The Collected Works of Abraham Lincoln,* ed. Roy Basler (New Brunswick, NJ: Rutgers University Press, 1953), 3:340.

4. Abraham Lincoln to Eleazar A. Paine, November 19, 1858, in *The Collected Works* 3:340.

5. Abraham Lincoln to M.M. Inman. November 20, 1858, in *The Collected Works* 3:340.

6. Abraham Lincoln to B. Clarke Lunday, in *The Collected Works* 3:342.

7. Abraham to Alexander Sympson, December 12, 1858, in *The Collected Works* 3:346.

8. Abraham Lincoln to Lyman Trumbull, December 11, 1858, in *The Collected Works* 3:344–345; and Lincoln to Trumbull, February 3, 1859, 3:355–356.

9. Abraham Lincoln to Thomas J. Pickett, April 16, 1859, in *The Collected Works* 3:377.

10. Abraham Lincoln to Samuel Galloway, July 28, 1859, in *The Collected Works* 3: 394–395.

11. There is some confusion as to the spelling of Israel Washburn's name. In some references it is spelled with an "e" at the end. The most common form seems to be without an "e." His brother, Elihu Washburne, Republican congressman from Illinois, spelled his last name with an *e*.

12. Representative Israel Washburn Jr. of Maine, speech in House of Representatives, January 10, 1859.

13. Abraham Lincoln to Elihu B. Washburne (as spelled in the *The Collected Works*), January 29, 1859, in *The Collected Works* 3:351.

14. Abraham Lincoln to Joshua F. Speed, August 24, 1855, *The Collected Works* 2:320.

15. *Congressional Globe*, 35th Congress, 1st Session, May 5, 1858, pp. 1964–1965. Trumbull voted against the bill because no evidence of Oregon's population existed. Douglas, following his doctrine of popular sovereignty, voted for the bill because the citizens of Oregon supported it.

16. Lincoln again urged that the Republicans not follow Douglas: "Our only serious danger is that we shall be led upon the ground of Judge Douglas, on the delusive assumption that it is a good way of whipping our opponents, when in fact, it is a way that leads straight to final surrender." He insisted that "the Republican party should not dally with Judge Douglas when it knows where his proposition and his leadership would take us...." Lincoln reminded his audience to "never forget that we have before us this whole matter of the right and wrong of slavery in this Union, though the immediate question is as to its spreading out into new Territories and States."

17. Abraham Lincoln Speech at Chicago, March 1, 1859, *The Collected Works* 3:365–370.

18. The reporter was Robert Hitt, who had attended all the Lincoln-Douglas debates as one of the reporters for the *Chicago Press and Tribune*.

19. Abraham Lincoln To Henry L. Pierce and others, April 6, 1859, *The Collected Works* 3:374–376.

20. With this principle as the party's foundation, he believed it essential that the Republicans not compromise, especially any compromise with Douglas. To the Republican governor Salmon P. Chase, Lincoln thanked him "as being one of the very few distinguished men, whose sympathy we in Illinois did receive last year, of all those whose sympathy we thought we had reason to expect.... Had we thrown ourselves into the arms of Douglas, as re-electing him by our votes would have done, the Republican cause would have been annihilated in Illinois, and, as I think, demoralized, and prostrated everywhere for years, if not forever." But having not compromised, "'we are clean,'" he wrote, and believed that "the Republican star gradually rises higher everywhere" (Abraham Lincoln to Salmon P. Chase, April 30, 1859, *The Collected Works* 3:378).

21. Abraham Lincoln to Mark W. Delahay, May 14, 1859, *The Collected Works* 3:378–379.

22. Abraham Lincoln to Theodore Canisius, May 17, 1859, *The Collected Works* 3:380.

23. Abraham Lincoln to Joshua F. Speed, August 24, 1855, *The Collected Works* 2:320.

24. Abraham Lincoln to Salmon P. Chase, June 9, 1859, *The Collected Works* 3:384.

25. Abraham Lincoln to Salmon P. Chase, June 20, 1859, *The Collected Works* 3:386.

26. Abraham Lincoln to Nathan Sargent, *The Collected Works* 3: 388.

27. Victor Emmanuel had become the symbol of Italian unity. Abraham Lincoln to Colfax, *The Collected Works*, 3:390–391. Finally, to an Ohio Republican he wrote, "Two things done by the Ohio Republican convention — the repudiation of Judge Swan, and the 'plank' for repeal of the Fugitive Slave Law — I very much regretted." Lincoln believed "these two things" would be "viewed by many good men, sincerely opposed to slavery, as a struggle against, and in disregard of, the constitution itself. And it is the very thing that will greatly endanger our cause, if it be not be kept out of our national convention." Lincoln also found "another thing our friends are doing which gives me some uneasiness. It is their leaning towards 'popular sovereignty.'" He opposed this practice because "Douglas' popular sovereignty, accepted by the public mind, as a just principle, nationalizes slavery, and revives the African Slave-trade, inevitably." Lincoln considered "taking slaves into new territories, and buying slaves in Africa, are identical things — identical rights or identical wrongs — and the argument which establishes one will establish the other. Try a thousand years for a sound reason why congress shall not hinder the people of Kansas from having slaves, and when you have found it, it will be an equally good one why congress should not hinder the people of Georgia from importing slaves from Africa"(Abraham Lincoln to Samuel Galloway, July 28, 1859, *The Collected Works* 3:394–395).

Chapter 4

1. Harry V. Jaffa and Robert W. Johannsen, eds., *In the Name of the People: The Speeches and Writings of Lincoln and Douglas in the Ohio Campaign of 1859* (Columbus: Ohio State University Press, 1959), 58–84.

2. Douglas also assaulted the proposition that the Republicans most often raised in objection to his policy: the morality of slavery: "It is no answer to this argument to say that slavery is an evil or a crime, and therefore the people should not be permitted to ruin themselves for inflicting such a curse upon them." He maintained that "it is the right of every

people to judge for themselves whether it be an evil or not. It is their right to judge whether it be a crime. It is the right of every community to judge for themselves the character and nature of every institution it is proposed to adopt."

In response to the Republican charge that the Dred Scott decision undercut his position, Douglas argued: "We are told by the Republicans on every stump that this doctrine of popular sovereignty is dead. They say Judge Taney killed it — that it had its throat cut by the Dred Scott decision — that popular sovereignty has no longer a breath of life in its body...." Douglas completely rejected this attack. "There is not one word of truth in the whole statement." The Dred Scott decision, Douglas asserted, states that "the federal government cannot interfere in the Territory with slavery, either for it or against it, and that is the affirmance precisely of my doctrine and your doctrine and the Democratic doctrine of popular sovereignty."

Chapter 5

1. Harry V. Jaffa and Robert W. Johannsen, eds., *In the Name of the People: The Speeches and Writings of Lincoln and Douglas in the Ohio Campaign of 1859* (Columbus: Ohio State University Press, 1959), 234–280.

2. For a detailed discussion of Lincoln's visit to Dayton, see Lloyd Ostendorf's *Mr. Lincoln came to Dayton* (Dayton, Ohio: The Otterbein Press, 1959), 11–25.

3. Ibid., 281–285. Lincoln attacked the biblical justification for slavery. The Kentuckians "are trying to show that slavery existed in the Bible times by Divine ordinance." However, he said, "Douglas is wiser than you, for your own benefit, upon that subject. Douglas knows that whenever you establish that slavery was right by the Bible, it will occur that that slavery was the slavery of the white men — of men without reference to color.... [Douglas] makes a wiser argument for you [because he] makes the argument that the slavery of the black man, the slavery of the man who has a skin of a different color from your own, is right. He thereby brings to your support Northern voters who could not for a moment be brought by your own argument of the Bible-right of slavery" (281–282). Lincoln also asserted that Douglas' popular sovereignty

would inevitably lead to the reopening of the African slave trade: "Douglas says that it is the sacred right of the man who goes into the Territories to have slavery if he wants it." If slavery were to be accepted, Lincoln asked, "Is it not the sacred right of the man that don't go there equally to buy slaves in Africa, if he wants them?" He gave a challenge: "If any man can show how the people of Kansas have a better right to slaves because they want them than the people of Georgia have to buy them in Africa, I want him to do it.... I think it cannot be done.... If it is popular sovereignty for the people to have slaves because they want them, it is popular sovereignty for them to buy them in Africa because they desire to do so."

4. Ibid., 295.

5. Ibid., 303–304.

6. It is believed that during his journey through Ohio and Indiana, Lincoln took time to put onto paper some of his ongoing thoughts on the issue of slavery. This passage bears further proof of the cause that continued to fuel Lincoln's passion for politics. "We know Southern men declare that their slaves are better off than hired laborers amongst us," he wrote. "How little they know whereof they speak! There is no permanent class of hired laborers amongst us. Twentyfive [*sic*] years ago, I was a hired laborer. The hired laborer of yesterday labors on his own account to-day; and will hire others to labor for him to-morrow." Lincoln believed "Advancement — improvement in condition — is the order of things in a society of equals. As Labor is the common burthen [burden] of our race, so the effort of some to shift their share of the burthen [burden] on to the shoulders of others, is the great, durable, curse of the race." Lincoln considered the burden of labor, from a biblical perspective, as "originally a curse for transgression upon the whole race, when, as by slavery, it is concentrated on a part only, it becomes the double-refined curse of God upon his creatures."

He summarized the issue: "Free labor has the inspiration of hope; pure slavery has no hope. The power of hope upon human exertion, and happiness, is wonderful. The slavemaster himself has a conception of it; and hence the system of tasks among slaves. The slave whom you can not drive with the lash to break seventy-five pounds of hemp in a day, if you will task him to break a hundred, and promise him pay for all he does over, he will break you a hundred and fifty. You have substituted hope for the rod. And yet perhaps it does not occur to you, that to the extent of your gain in the case, you have given up the slave system, and adopted the free system of labor."

7. *Cincinnati Daily Gazette*, September 19, 1859; *Ohio Statesman*, September 20, 1859, as reprinted in *Abraham Lincoln: A Press Portrait*, ed. Herman Mitgang (Athens: University of Georgia Press, 1989), 141.

8. Roy Basler, ed., *The Collected Works of Abraham Lincoln* (New Brunswick, NJ: Rutgers University Press, 1953), 3: 469–470.

Chapter 6

1. Michael J. Dubin, *United States Presidential Elections, 1788–1860: The Official Results by County and State* (Jefferson, NC: McFarland Press, 2002), 135. The conclusion of the Milwaukee speech is worth noting: "It is said an Eastern monarch once charged his wise men to invent him a sentence, to be ever in view, and which should be true and appropriate in all times and situations. They presented him with the words: 'And this, too, shall pass away." How much it expresses! How chastening in the hour of pride!— how consoling in the depths of affliction! 'And this, too, shall pass away.' And yet let us hope it is not quite true. Let us hope, rather, that by the best cultivation of the physical world, beneath and around us; and the intellectual and moral world within us, we shall secure an individual, social, and political prosperity and happiness, whose course shall be onward and upward, and which, while the earth endures, shall not pass away" (Roy Basler, ed., *The Collected Works of Abraham Lincoln* (New Brunswick, NJ: Rutgers University Press, 1953), 3: 481–482).

2. Abraham Lincoln to William E. Frazer, November 1, 1859, in *The Collected Works* 3: 491.

3. Abraham Lincoln to James A. Briggs, November 13, 1859, in *The Collected Works* 3: 494.

4. Lincoln's reasons for visiting Kansas were best expressed in a letter to a Kansas Republican, Mark Delahay. Delahay had invited Lincoln before, and Lincoln had to turn down the invitation. Lincoln wrote: "I find it impossible for me to attend your Republican convention at Ossawatan [Ossawatomie] on the

18th. It would have afforded me much personal gratification to see your fine new country, and to meet the good people who have cast their lot there; and still more, if I could thereby contribute any thing to the Republican cause" (Abraham Lincoln to Mark Delahay, May 14, 1859, in *The Collected Works* 3:378–379).

5. Ibid., 3:496–497. In writing of this speech, two papers indicated that popularity to which the debates had propelled Lincoln: "The Hon. Abe Lincoln, who beat Douglas on the popular vote for U.S. Senator at the last election in Ill., addressed the citizens of Elwood on Wednesday evening last, upon National politics," the *St. Joseph Weekly Free Democrat*, a Republican paper, wrote. Another Republican paper concurred: "Hon. Abe Lincoln, of Illinois, who stirred up Douglas with a sharp stick until he squealed, is now stumping it in the Territory. He speaks at Troy today, at Atchison to-morrow, and at Leavenworth on Saturday," according to the *Kansas Chief* (Fred W. Brinkerhoff, *The Kansas Tour of Lincoln the Candidate*, Kansas Historical Quarterly (1944)).

6. Lincoln to Delahay, 3:497–502.

7. Abraham Lincoln to Norman B. Judd, December 14, 1859, in *The Collected Works* 3:509. Lincoln also corresponded with another Illinois Republican on this matter: "Judd has started East to attend the sitting of the National committee, at N.Y. the 21st. Previous to going he wrote that soon after his return he would call the State Committee together; and he wished me to see some of the members, including yourself, upon a matter which I can tell you better when I see you, than I can write about it. In a general way I may say it was relative to whether Delegates to the National convention shall be appointed, by general convention, or by districts. Perhaps it would be as well to make no committal on this, till we have a conference." Lincoln, most likely, would advocate for a convention but, displaying his mode of operation, preferred to discuss the matter in person before suggesting a course of action (*The Collected Works* 3:509–510).

8. Abraham Lincoln to Jackson Grimshaw, December 15, 1859, in *The Collected Works* 3:510.

9. Abraham Lincoln to Jesse W. Fell, Enclosing Autobiography, December 20, 1859, in *The Collected Works* 3:511–512.

10. Glyndon G. Van Deusen, *William Henry Seward: Lincoln's Secretary of State, the Negotiator of the Alaska Purchase* (New York: Oxford University Press, 1967), 174. George H. Baker, ed., *The Life of William H. Seward, with Selections from his Works* (New York: J.S. Redfield, 1855).

11. Browning, 395.

12. Harold Holzer, *Lincoln at Cooper Union: The Speech that Made Abraham Lincoln President* (New York: Simon and Schuster, 2004), 26.

13. *New York Times*, January 26, 1860.

14. David L. Smiley, *Lion of White Hall: The Life of Cassius Clay* (Gloucester, MA: Peter Smith, 1969), 60–62, 164; Cassius M. Clay, *The Life of Cassius Marcellus Clay: Memoirs, Writings, and Speeches, Showing His Conduct in the Overthrow of American Slavery, the Salvation of the Union, and the Restoration of the Autonomy of the States* (New York: Negro Universities Press, 1969), 82–85.

15. Basler, ed., *The Collected Works*, 3:527–547.

Chapter 7

1. On March 7, 1860, recalling Lincoln's visit to New Hampshire, a Democratic paper, *The New England Patriot*, like Douglas, made a connection between the philosophies of Seward and Lincoln in an editorial titled "It Means Disunion": "The 'irrepressible conflict' doctrine of the black republicans means disunion or it means nothing. This doctrine, false, dangerous, revolutionary and treasonable, was first proclaimed by Abraham Lincoln of Illinois in his speech accepting the nomination for Senator in the great contest in which he was so completely overthrown by Douglas. He stated it very briefly in these words: 'I BELIEVE THAT THIS GOVERNMENT CANNOT ENDURE PERMANENTLY HALF SLAVE AND HALF FREE.' In other words, SLAVERY MUST BE ABOLISHED IN THE SLAVE STATES, OR THE GOVERNMENT AND THE UNION MUST BE OVERTHROWN. This is the doctrine of the black republican party, and every intelligent man must see that it is the very essence of Garrison abolitionism" (as quoted in Edwin L. Page, *Abraham Lincoln in New Hampshire* (Boston: Houghton Mifflin Company, 1929), 11–12).

2. According to the editors of *The Col-lected Works*, the newspaper summaries of his speeches at Meriden, Connecticut; Woonsocket, Rhode Island; and Norwich and Bridgeport, Connecticut, indicate that Lincoln delivered the same speeches at these towns that he delivered at New Haven, Connecticut (Basler, *The Collected Works*), 4:13.

3. John Niven, *Gideon Welles: Lincoln's Secretary of the Navy* (New York: Oxford University Press, 1973), 288–289.

4. Ibid.

5. Basler, ed., *The Collected Works*, 4:8–27. I have chosen the *Evening Press* version, believing that the Republican version would prove more accurate.

6. Ibid., 3:555.

7. Ida Tarbell, *The Life of Lincoln* (New York: The Macmillan Company, 1917), 1:341–342.

Chapter 8

1. Koerner concluded, "I am pretty certain that, had the Convention been held at any other place, Lincoln would not have been nominated." Thomas J. McCormack, ed., *Memoirs of Gustave Koerner, 1809–1896: Life-sketches Written at the Suggestion of His Children* (Cedar Rapids, IA: Torch Press, 1909), 79–80.

2. David L. Smiley, *Lion of White Hall: The Life of Cassius M. Clay* (Gloucester, MA: Peter Smith, 1969), 165.

3. Frederick J. Blue, *Salmon P. Chase: A Life in Politics* (Kent, OH: Kent State University Press, 1987), 120.

4. Erwin Stanley Bradley, *Simon Cameron, Lincoln's Secretary of War: A Political Biography* (Philadelphia: University of Pennsylvania Press, 1966), 138–142.

5. William Ernest Smith, *The Francis Preston Blair Family in Politics,* vol. 1 (New York: Macmillan Company, 1933), 465, 468.

6. Howard K. Beale, ed., *The Diary of Edward Bates, 1859–1866* (Washington, D.C.: Government Printing Office, 1933), 102, 108.

7. James C.Y. Chu, "Horace White: His Association with Abraham Lincoln, 1854–60," *Journalism Quarterly* (Spring 1972): 58. An Iowa delegate had written on February 2, 1860, "I am for the man who can carry Pennsylvania, New Jersey, and Indiana...." (James S. Pike, *First Blows of the Civil War* (Canbury, NJ: The Scholar's Bookshelf, 2007), 484).

8. Norman Judd to Lyman Trumbull, April 2, 1860, as quoted in Reinhard Luthin, "Pennsylvania and Lincoln's Rise to the Presidency," 67.

9. Abraham Lincoln to Lyman Trumbull, April 29, 1860, in *The Collected Works of Abraham Lincoln,* ed. Roy Basler (New Brunswick, NJ: Rutgers University Press, 1953), 4:45–46.

10. Abraham Lincoln to Mark W. Delahay, *The Collected Works* 4:49.

11. Abraham Lincoln to Lyman Trumbull, April 29, 1860, *The Collected Works* 4:47–48.

12. Glyndon G. Van Deusen, *William Henry Seward: Lincoln's Secretary of State, the Negotiator of the Alaska Purchase* (New York: Oxford University Press, 1967), 222.

13. *Illinois State Journal,* May 12, 1860.

Chapter 9

1. James F. Rhodes as quoted in William Ernest Smith, *The Francis Preston Blair Family in Politics* (New York: Macmillan Company, 1933), 1:473–474.

2. Each state was permitted twice as many delegates as the number of electoral votes. However, the following states were not able to find enough acceptable individuals to fill their allotted number: Maryland — eight electoral votes and eleven delegates; Virginia — fifteen electoral votes and twenty-three delegates; Kentucky — twelve electoral votes and twenty-three delegates; and Oregon — three electoral votes and five delegates (Paul M. Angle and Earl Schenck Miers, *Fire the Salute! Abe Lincoln Is Nominated: Murat Halstead Reports the Republican National Convention in Chicago, May 16, 17, & 18, 1860* (Kingsport, TN: Kingsport Press, Inc., 1960), 19).

3. *Chicago Press and Tribune,* May 14, 1860.

4. Goodwin claims that Lane was from Pennsylvania. He was from Indiana (Doris Kearns Goodwin, *Team of Rivals: The Political Genius of Abraham Lincoln* (New York: Simon and Schuster, 2005), 242).

5. David Turpie, *Sketches of My Time* (Bobbs-Merrill, 1903), 202; John W. Holcombe and Hubert Skinner, eds., *Life and Public Services of Thomas A. Hendricks, with Selected Speeches and Writings.* (Indianapolis: Carlon and Hollenbeck, 1885), 208–209.

6. Michael J. Dubin, *United States Gubernatorial Elections, 1776–1860: The Official Results by State and County* (Jefferson, NC: McFarland, 2003), xlii; Michael J. Dubin, *United States Presidential Elections, 1776–1860: The Official Results by County and State* (Jefferson, NC: McFarland, 2002), 135.

7. Graham Andrew Barringer, "The Life and Times of Henry S. Lane," Ph.D. diss., Indiana University, 65. Bates described him as "a zealous man and powerful on the stump" (Beale, 102).

8. *Chicago Press and Tribune,* May 14, 1860.

9. *Auburn Daily Advertiser,* May 14, 1860.

10. Jesse K. Dubois to Abraham Lincoln, Sunday, May 13, 1860, Abraham Lincoln papers at the Library of Congress; William Butler to Abraham Lincoln, Monday, May 14, 1860, Abraham Lincoln papers at the Library of Congress.

11. Abraham Lincoln to Mark W. Delahay, *The Collected Works of Abraham Lincoln,* ed. Roy Basler (New Brunswick, NJ: Rutgers University Press, 1953), 4:49.

12. *New York Tribune,* May 14, 1860.

13. Ibid., May 15, 1860.

14. Ibid., May 16, 1860.

15. *Indianapolis Daily Journal,* May 16, 1860, as quoted in Roll, *The Nomination of Abraham Lincoln in 1861,* 7.

16. *New York Times,* May 15, 1860. The newspaper also reported on this day that "The chances appear to be, that the superior tact of Seward's friends, and the distracted state of the Opposition will carry him through successfully."

17. Theodore Calvin Pease and James G. Randall, *The Diary of Orville Hickman Browning,* vol. 1, *1850–1864* (Springfield: Illinois State Historical Library, 1925), 406.

18. Ibid., 406–407.

19. Jesse K. Dubois to Abraham Lincoln, Tuesday, May 15, 1860, Abraham Lincoln papers at the Library of Congress.

20. Elbridge Gerry Spaulding telegram to William H. Seward, May 15, 1860, William H. Seward papers at the University of Rochester.

21. Thomas J. McCormack, ed., *Memoirs of Gustave Koerner, 1809–1896: Life-sketches Written at the Suggestion of His Children* (Cedar Rapids, IA: Torch Press, 1909), 84–85.

22. Jesse K. Dubois and David Davis to Abraham Lincoln, Tuesday, May 15, 1860, Abraham Lincoln papers at the Library of Congress.

Chapter 10

1. "Hon. Mr. Morse said that if Stephen A. Douglas was not elected the next President, William H. Seward would be — a sentiment which may be safely commended to the consideration of weak kneed Republicans" (*Chicago Daily Journal*, May 15, 1860).

2. *Chicago Press and Tribune*, May 16, 1860: "Mr. Seward has many friends here, both among the delegates and among other leading members of the Republican party who are in attendance to witness the deliberations of the Convention; and it is hoped, though not certain, that he, being recognized Leader of the Party of Freedom of the Nation, will be selected as its Standard-Bearer for the coming struggle. We believe him to be a man for the times, because he truly represents the spirit and sentiments of the Party — the spirit and sentiments that have made the Party what it is, and upon and by which the Party must ultimately either conquer or fall" (*Chicago Daily Journal*, May 15, 1860).

3. The *Tribune* also noted Lincoln's humility in that "by his own motion, he is not a candidate." They contended that Lincoln had "never sought, directly or indirectly, for the first or second place on the ticket. The movement in his favor is spontaneous. It has sprung up suddenly and with great strength, its roots being in the conviction that he is the man to reconcile all differences in our ranks, to conciliate all the now jarring elements, and to lead forward to certain victory." This was an assertion that the editors knew was untrue. Many of Lincoln's supporters had been maneuvering for his nomination for well over six months. However, they concluded this point by stating that Lincoln had "put forth no personal effort for success." On this point, discounting the publication of the debates and in accepting speech requests, they were closer to the truth.

As for Lincoln's record on specific policies, the editors argued, it was so acceptable to the party that he had "no new record to make." As a former Whig, Lincoln would have "nothing to explain for the satisfaction of New Jersey, Pennsylvania and the West ... [Lincoln's] opinions and votes on the Tariff will be acceptable to all sections except the extreme South, where Republicanism expects no support." He was also, according to the *Tribune,* accepted on the issues of "the improvement of the rivers and

harbors ... the Homestead bill, and to the speedy construction of the Pacific Railroad."

The *Tribune* men also found Lincoln's past an asset. Lincoln was "a Southern man by birth and education," opposed "sectionalism" and was a candidate "around whom all opponents of the extension of Human Slavery, North and South can rally." He was also "a man of the people" because he had attained "his position" not due to "family influence, the partiality of friends or the arts of the politician. All his early life a laborer of the field, in the sawmill, as a boatman on the Wabash, Ohio, and Mississippi, and as a farmer in Illinois, he ha[d] that sympathy with the men who toil *and vote* that [would] make him strong": his role as "a valiant soldier in the Black Hawk war, a student in a law office, bending his great powers to overcome the defects of early training; then a legislator, and at last a brilliant advocate, in the highest courts." With the exception of his service in the Black Hawk war, in which he participated but witnessed no military action, the editors correctly appreciated some of the source of his humility which guided him in his personal relations and his public actions.

In closing, they maintained Lincoln's strength was rooted in his reputation for honesty and in his electability. "Mr. LINCOLN is an honest man," they declared. The editors alleged "that in his life of 51 years, there is no act of a public or private character, of which his most malignant enemy can say, 'this is dishonest,' 'this is mean'.... His escutcheon is without a blemish."

They concluded: "Mr. LINCOLN *can be elected,* if placed before the people with the approbation of the Convention to meet tomorrow. In New England, where Republicanism pure and simple is demanded, and where he has lately electrified the people by his eloquence, his name would be a tower of strength. New York, who clings with an ardent embrace to that great statesman, her first choice, would not refuse to adopt Mr. LINCOLN as a standard bearer worthy of the holy cause. Pennsylvania, satisfied with his views in regard to the present necessity of fostering domestic interests, and the constitutional moderation of his opinions upon slavery, would come heartily into his support."

4. "We present our candidate, then, not as the rival of this man or that, not because the West has claims which she must urge; not be-

cause of a distinctive policy which she would see enforced; not because he is the first choice of a majority; but because he is that patriot in whose hands the interests of the government may be safely confided" (*Chicago Press and Tribune*, May 16, 1860).

5. The *Tribune* continued to display local pride for the building that was to house the convention. In an article titled "THE GREAT WIGWAM," the newspaper declared that "everybody, citizens and strangers, delegates or outsiders (unless by very pressure of the crowd too emphatically *outsiders*), all fell in love with the Great Wigwam yesterday, and its praises were on more than half a score thousand tongues, since its vast area and admirable arrangement give to that number of spectators a sight few of them will ever forget, a sight and hearing of the most remarkable political Convention in spirit, enthusiasm, and inevitable destiny of result that ever assembled in the history of our politics."

6. Following the practice that the *Tribune* had used for the Lincoln-Douglas debates, the newspaper promised, with their "corps of phonographic reporters," to present a "verbatim report with a fullness and completeness of detail that leaves nothing to be supplied" (*Chicago Press and Tribune*, May 17, 1860).

7. Theodore Calvin Pease and James G. Randall, *The Diary of Orville Hickman Browning*, vol. 1, *1850–1864* (Springfield: Illinois State Historical Library, 1925), 407.

8. This debate led to an interesting interchange between two delegates. In the discussion on the Committee on Credentials, Greeley proposed that the discussion on the credentials of the delegates should be laid before the convention, and then referred to the Committee on Credentials. Cartter, a delegate from Ohio, responded: "I move an amendment; I move to amend the proposition of the gentleman from Oregon or New York, Mr. Greeley, I am not such which [laughter], that instead of each delegation presenting their credentials here, they present them to the Committee on Credentials" (Johnson 83–99).

Greeley replied, "I accept the amendment of the gentleman from Maryland or Rhode Island, I am not particular which" [laughter and applause].

9. *New York Tribune*, May 17, 1860.

10. Halstead was somewhat idealistic, believing the convention system corrupt, and hoped to prove his theory with evidence from all the conventions. Despite his opinion, his descriptions of the conventions are not only the most detailed but, for the most part, objective.

11. William B. Hesseltine, *Three Against Lincoln: Murat Halstead Reports the Caucuses of 1860* (Baton Rouge: Louisiana State University Press, 1960), 162.

12. Halstead found some humor on this occasion: "The Hon. George Ashmun, the presiding officer, was escorted to his Chair by Preston King and Carl Schurz, the one short and round as a barrel and fat as butter, the other tall and slender. The contrast was a curious one, and so palpable that the whole multitude saw it, and gave a tremendous cheer" (Hesseltine, 145).

13. The convention received the following invitation before it adjourned: "To the Honorable Members of the National Republican Convention–Gentlemen: In compliance with the wishes of the citizens, we are, through the courtesy of the Committee, permitted to occupy the 'Wigwam' this evening for an exhibition drill, to which we beg to return an invitation to the members of your honorable body. We shall feel highly honored by the presence of all who can find leisure to attend. Tickets of admission will be found at the headquarters of the different delegations. I have the honor to be, your obedient servant, E.E. Ellsworth, Commander, U.S. Zouave Cadets" (Johnson, 106). Ellsworth had studied in Lincoln's law office, and both Lincolns thought highly of him. At the beginning of the Civil War, the young man led a detachment to take Alexandria, and specifically a secession flag that Lincoln could see from the White House. As Ellsworth walked down the stairs of the Alexandria Hotel with the flag in the hotel, he was shot and killed. His body lay in state at the White House. Lincoln wrote to his parents: "Our affliction here is scarcely less than your own." He referred to their son as "my young friend, and your brave and early fallen child" (Mark Neely, *The Lincoln Encyclopedia* (New York: Da Capo Press, 1982), 103).

14. Jesse K. Dubois to Abraham Lincoln, Wednesday, May 16, 1860, Abraham Lincoln papers at the Library of Congress.

15. William Butler to Abraham Lincoln, Wednesday, May 16, 1860, Abraham Lincoln papers at the Library of Congress.

16. Hesseltine, 166.

17. Elbridge Gerry Spaulding telegram to William H. Seward, May 16, 1860, William H. Seward papers at the University of Rochester.

18. Thomas H. Dudley, "The Inside Facts of Lincoln's Nomination," *Century Illustrated Monthly Magazine* (1890): 478.

19. Paul Angle and Earl Schenck Miers, eds., *Fire the Salute! Abe Lincoln Is Nominated* (Kingsport, TN: Kingsport Press, 1960), 6. Angle and Miers wrote, "Halstead slipped badly in classifying Senator Benjamin Franklin Wade as a conservative. He was radically anti-slavery."

20. Ibid., 14.

21. Ibid., 12.

22. Ibid., 13.

23. Ibid., 7.

24. *New York Tribune*, May 17, 1860.

25. Angle and Miers, 6.

26. *Chicago Press and Tribune*, May 17, 1860.

Chapter 11

1. William B. Hesseltine, ed., *Three Against Lincoln: Murat Halstead Reports the Caucuses of 1860* (Baton Rouge: Louisiana State University, 1960), 148.

2. *Chicago Press and Tribune*, May 17, 1860.

3. Ibid.

4. Thomas H. Dudley, "The Inside Facts of Lincoln's Nomination," *Century Illustrated Monthly Magazine* (1890): 477–479.

5. Douglas L. Wilson and Rodney O. Davis, *Herndon's Informants: Letters, Interviews and Statements about Abraham Lincoln* (Urbana: University of Illinois Press, 1998), 684.

6. Endorsement on the Margin of the *Missouri Democrat*, *Collected Works* 4:50.

7. Hesseltine, 150.

8. Charles W. Johnson, ed., *Proceedings of the First Three Republican National Conventions* (Minneapolis: 1893), 133–137.

9. Ibid., 137.

10. Thomas J. McCormack, ed., *Memoirs of Gustave Koerner, 1809–1896: Life-sketches Written at the Suggestion of His Children* (Cedar Rapids, IA: Torch Press, 1909), 87.

11. Although Koener delivered no speech on this issue, he apparently had to take action to prevent Wilmot's motion from receiving more support. The Massachusetts delegation sat directly in front of the Illinois delegates and John A. Andrews, whom Koerner described as "one of the foremost Republicans of New England, fiery, energetic, and most eloquent, and soon to be governor of Massachusetts," ignored the discussion on this motion until he noticed "Massachusetts was mentioned as being the State whose action was disapproved." Andrews "turned round to Boutwell, who sat on his left, and exclaimed: 'That will never do! This is aimed at our State.' And with that he rose, and called out: 'Mr. President!'" Koerner, recognizing that "great influence" he held feared the result had "he been recognized by the chair. But Boutwell, as a member of the platform committee, who had become convinced that this very section was all-important to keep the German Republicans in line, at once laid hands on Andrews's shoulders and sought to push him down, while I, sitting right behind him, took hold of his coattails and held him down; and while he was looking round with the greatest astonishment, seeming to ask for an explanation, the vote was taken on the resolution and the next one was read. Andrews was greatly excited, but Boutwell and I succeeded in quieting him." Koerner described the whole event as "rather comical" (McCormack, 89–90).

12. Hesseltine, 155–156.

13. James Brewer Stewart, *Joshua R. Giddings and the Tactics of Radical Politics* (Cleveland: Press of Case Western Reserve University, 1970), 272–273.

14. Howard K. Beale, ed., *The Diary of Edward Bates, 1859–1866* (Washington, D.C.: Government Printing Office, 1933), 129.

15. Johnson, 124, 140–143.

Chapter 12

1. William B. Hesseltine, ed., *Three Against Lincoln: Murat Halstead Reports the Caucuses of 1860* (Baton Rouge: Louisiana State University, 1960), 158–160.

2. Edwin Denison Morgan telegram to William H. Seward, May 17, 1860, William H. Seward papers at the University of Rochester.

3. Elbridge Gerry Spaulding telegram to William H. Seward, May 17, 1860, William H. Seward papers at the University of Rochester.

4. Thomas H. Dudley, "The Inside Facts of Lincoln's Nomination," *Century Illustrated Monthly Magazine* (1890): 478.

5. William Ernest Smith, *The Francis Preston Blair Family in Politics* (New York: Macmillan Company, 1933), 476–477.

6. Mark W. Delahay to Abraham Lincoln, Thursday, May 17, 1860, Abraham Lincoln papers at the Library of Congress.

7. Thomas J. McCormack, ed., *Memoirs of Gustave Koerner, 1809–1896: Life-sketches Written at the Suggestion of His Children* (Cedar Rapids, IA: Torch Press, 1909), 87–89; William Ernest Smith, *The Francis Preston Blair Family in Politics,* vol. 1 (New York: Macmillan Company, 1933), 476–477; Marvin Cain, *Lincoln's Attorney General: Edward Bates of Missouri* (Columbia: University of Missouri Press, 1965), 111. Both Smith and Cain contend that this meeting occurred on May 15. However, Koerner claims it occurred on May 17. Browning, who mentions numerous details of his campaigning that week, makes no mention of the event, but there is a page missing from his diary for May 17. Koerner, being an eyewitness, is by far the most reliable source. After 11:00 PM the *New York Tribune* received this report: "Illinois, Indiana, and Pennsylvania say that with this platform, and Mr. Seward, they are beaten beyond all hope in the latter States by 20,000 to 50,000."

8. All newspaper articles are from *Chicago Press and Tribune,* May 21, 1860.

9. Dudley, 478. John Palmer, an Illinoisan who was not a delegate, wrote a slightly different version. Davis told Palmer that after visiting the New Jersey delegation, he found that they "were insisting that Seward should have the first place on the ticket and Lincoln the second, and asked me to go and see them." Palmer confessed uncertainty as to how to convince them, but said that he "determined upon my line of conversation while on the way. When introduced to the delegation, they suggested that Mr. Seward be nominated for the presidency, and Mr. Lincoln be given the vice-presidency, when I told them that there were forty thousand Democrats who would vote the Republican ticket, but who would not consent to do so if two old Whigs were placed upon the ticket." Davis, who apparently accompanied Palmer on this visit, "was asked if there was as much party feeling, as much prejudice, in the minds of the Democratic-Republicans" as Palmer had indicated. Davis answered, "You must take a Democrat for one of these offices." Palmer concluded that, at least

with this delegation, the Lincoln supporters "escaped the responsibility of two old Whig party men being placed upon the ticket; and thus Mr. Lincoln and Mr. Seward were brought face to face as candidates for the presidency" (John M. Palmer, *Personal Recollections of John M. Palmer* (Cincinnati: The Robert Clarke Company, 1901), 81). Some historians have given credence to Addison G. Proctor's recollection of the convention (Addison G. Proctor, *Lincoln and the Convention of 1860: An Address before the Chicago Historical Society, April 4, 1918* (Chicago: Chicago Historical Society), 1918.) Proctor, claiming to be the youngest delegate at the 1860 convention, gave a speech in 1918 detailing events that occurred with the Kansas delegation. However, Proctor describes personal visits by Greeley, Lane, and Cassius Clay. But Clay was not in Chicago at the time — he was in Kentucky during the entire convention. Proctor's memory concerning Kansas' support for Seward may be understandable, but detailing an entire conversation with a man who was not there is inexcusable. I therefore do not give any veracity to his account. Goodwin, though, believes Proctor was a reliable source (Goodwin 262, 264).

10. Hesseltine, 160–162.

11. Michael J. Dubin, *United States Presidential Elections, 1788–1860: The Official Results by County and State* (Jefferson, NC: McFarland, 2002), 135.

12. Lincoln's supporters could take solace from one item in the *Chicago Press and Tribune* that morning: "Mr. Volk's studio in the Portland Block, corner of Dearborn and Washington streets is open to visitors from 9 A.M. to 5 P.M., where may be seen his statues of Senator Douglas, busts of Hon. Abraham Lincoln, and other works." At least Mr. Volk thought that Lincoln had a chance, and thus maybe his bust of Lincoln would instantly become a collector's item.

Chapter 13

1. Preston King and William M. Evarts telegram to William H. Seward, May 18, 1860, William H. Seward papers at the University of Rochester. The *New York Times* of May 18 reported, "Our Special Correspondent remains of the opinion that the strength of Mr. Seward in the Convention is such that he will, in all

likelihood, be nominated on the 10th or 11th ballot to-day. The elements of opposition remain incoherent; a last effort to concentrate upon Mr. Lincoln having failed last evening. Mr. Bates is now abandoned."

2. The editors further argued: "They recognize the necessity for success, that the good name of the country, imperiled by the disgraceful Administration now in power, may be restored; that the Union, now threatened by the Democracy, may be preserved; that the Republican organization, upon which the hopes of the country now hang, may be kept from the dissolution which a defeat foreshadows. They case seventy-five electoral votes. They are potent, and their approbation of the nominee, not only here at Chicago, but at the polls in November, must be secured, else an inglorious and fatal defeat stares us in the face. For the sake of all that the party would accomplish we entreat the Convention to act with the prudence, wisdom and foresight which the crisis demands. We believe that all will yet be well" (*Chicago Press and Tribune*, May 18, 1860). The Illinoisans also heard a rumor either late on the evening of the 17th or in the early morning of the 18th Lincoln was considering coming to Chicago. Fearing that his presence, when all other candidates were absent, might ruin all chances for his nomination, two Lincoln supporters sent him the following telegraph: "Do not come without we telegraph you" (Jesse K. Dubois and William Butler to Abraham Lincoln, Friday, May 18, 1860, Abraham Lincoln papers at the Library of Congress).

3. *Chicago Press and Tribune*, May 18, 1860.

4. Ibid.

5. Thomas H. Dudley, "The Inside Facts of Lincoln's Nomination," *Century Illustrated Monthly Magazine* (1890): 478.

6. Charles W. Johnson, ed., *Proceedings of the First Three Republican National Conventions* (Minneapolis: 1893), 143.

7. Ibid., 148–149.

8. William B. Hesseltine, ed., *Three Against Lincoln: Murat Halstead Reports the Caucuses of 1860* (Baton Rouge: Louisiana State University, 1960), 166.

9. Elbridge Gerry Spaulding telegram to William H. Seward, May 18, 1860, William H. Seward papers at the University of Rochester.

10. Hesseltine, 165–166.

11. Johnson, 151.

12. Hesseltine, 161, 162, 168.

13. "Vermont's example was more important than her numerical strength, for it disclosed the inmost thoughts of a group of intelligent, high-principled men, who were moved by an unselfish purpose and a solemn responsibility. Lincoln had now become the cynosure of the conservatives with a first-class radical endorsement to boot, and he deserved both distinctions" (Horace White, *The Life of Lyman Trumbull* (New York: Houghton Mifflin Company, 1913), 106).

14. Hesseltine, 168.

15. Ibid., 169.

16. *Chicago Press and Tribune*, May 19, 1860. The newspaper had mistakenly printed 331? for Lincoln. This writer corrected it in the text.

17. Paul Angle and Earl Schenck Miers, ed., *Fire the Salute! Abe Lincoln Is Nominated* (Kingsport, TN: Kingsport Press, 1960), 45.

18. *Chicago Press and Tribune*, May 19, 1860.

19. Hesseltine, 170–172.

20. Edwin Denison Morgan to William H. Seward, May 18, 1860, William H. Seward papers at the University of Rochester.

21. Gilbert C. Davidson telegram to William H. Seward, May 18, 1860, William H. Seward papers at the University of Rochester.

Chapter 14

1. William B. Hesseltine, ed., *Three Against Lincoln: Murat Halstead Reports the Caucuses of 1860* (Baton Rouge: Louisiana State University, 1960), 170–172.

2. Charles W. Johnson, ed., *Proceedings of the First Three Republican National Conventions* (Minneapolis: 1893), 155–157.

3. Thomas J. McCormack, ed., *Memoirs of Gustave Koerner, 1809–1896: Life-sketches Written at the Suggestion of His Children.* (Cedar Rapids, IA: Torch Press, 1909), 91.

4. Hesseltine, 172–174.

5. Johnson, 162–163.

6. Ibid., 165–166.

7. Hesseltine, 177.

8. *New York Tribune*, May 19, 1860.

9. McCormack, 92.

10. Theodore Calvin Pease and James G. Randall, eds., *The Diary of Orville Hickman Browning*, vol. 1, *1850–1864* (Springfield: Illinois State Historical Library, 1925), 408.

11. *New York Times*, May 21, 1860.

12. Pease and Randall, 407–408. In regard to Lincoln's nomination, Bates wrote in his diary: "I think they will soon be convinced, if they are not already, that they have committed a fatal blunder. They have denationalized their Party; weakened it in the free states, and destroyed its hopeful beginnings in the border slave states" (Howard K. Beale, ed., *The Diary of Edward Bates, 1859–1866* (Washington, D.C.: Government Printing Office, 1933), 131.

13. *Chicago Press and Tribune*, May 19, 1860.

14. Ibid.

15. McCormack, 92.

16. Hesseltine, 176–177.

17. *New York Tribune*, May 22, 1860.

18. Ibid., May 25, 1860.

19. Dr. John S. Bobbs to Simon Cameron, May 19, 1860, Cameron papers, as quoted in Reinhard H. Luthin's "Indiana and Lincoln's Rise to the Presidency" (*Indiana Magazine of History* 38 (December 1942): 385–405).

20. Wilson and Davis, eds., *Herndon's Informants: Letters, Interviews, and Statements about Abraham Lincoln* (Chicago: University of Illinois Press, 1998), 683–684.

21. One interpretation suggests that the Republicans chose Lincoln because the former Know-Nothings would find him more acceptable than Seward. The Know-Nothings proved significant in the 1856 election and Seward had gained their ire by his support for immigrant rights. This interpretation fails on two fronts. First, if the Republicans considered the Know-Nothing support that critical, they should have rallied to Bates who had been associated with the movement. Secondly, the case of Indiana and Illinois illustrates the Republicans' lack of concern with the former Know-Nothings. In the 1856 election, the Republican presidential candidate lost by 10 percent of the vote and the Know-Nothings' candidate, Millard Fillmore, garnered 10 percent. However, at the Indiana state Republican convention in April 1860, where Lane was chosen as the gubernatorial nominee, a historian noted that "not a Fillmore man was an officer." In fact, no Fillmore men were on the committee on resolutions, on the state ticket, on the electoral ticket, or on the State Central Committee, nor were any delegates to the presidential convention. The historian concluded: "Truly may it be said that this was a straight Repub-

lican convention." The Indiana Republicans were not about to lower their standard to include any Know Nothings, a policy that exactly mirrored the sentiment of Abraham Lincoln.

In Illinois in 1856, the Republican presidential candidate lost by 4 percent of the vote while the Know-Nothings attracted 15 percent. At the Illinois state Republican convention which nominated Lincoln as presidential candidate, the very first resolution of the platform rejected the Know-Nothings with the following language: "We are in favor of giving full and efficient protection to all the rights of all classes of citizens, at home and abroad, without regard to the place of their birth.... The State Legislatures should pass no law discriminating between native born and naturalized citizens in the exercise of the right of suffrage" (Charles Zimmerman, "The Origin and Rise of the Republican Party in Indiana from 1854 to 1860," *Indiana Magazine of History* (1917), 385; Michael J. Dubin, *United States Presidential Elections, 1788–1860: The Official Results by County and State* (Jefferson, NC: McFarland, 2002), 141; *Illinois State Journal*, May 11, 1860).

22. Howard K. Beale, ed., *The Diary of Edward Bates, 1859–1866* (Washington, D.C.: Government Printing Office, 1933), 129.

23. Some have given joint credit to Lane and the Pennsylvania gubernatorial nominee Andrew Curtin. Curtin undoubtedly assisted in denying Seward's nomination by professing that Seward could not carry Pennsylvania, but the Pennsylvania delegation proved less influential by supporting Cameron on the first ballot. The Hoosiers, led by Lane, proved far more influential by unanimously declaring for Lincoln on the first ballot.

24. Caleb B. Smith to William Schouler, "confidential," December 1, 1860, as quoted in Reinhard H. Luthin's "Indiana and Lincoln's Rise to the Presidency," 393.

25. Willard L. King, *Lincoln's Manager: David Davis* (Cambridge, MA: Harvard University Press, 1960), 140–141; Luthin, *Pennsylvania and Lincoln's Rise to the Presidency*, 70. The most reliable evidence comes from Alexander K. McClure, who was present for the Pennsylvania delegation discussion. Halstead reported that the "Pennsylvanians declare, if Seward were nominated, they would be immediately ruined," and on the night be-

fore the nomination "there were hundreds of Pennsylvanians, Indianans, and Illinoisans who never closed their eyes that night." Further, "It was reported, and with a well-understood purpose, that the Republican candidates for Governor in Indiana, Illinois, and Pennsylvania would resign if Seward were nominated."

26. *New York Times*, May 19, 1860.

27. M. Langenschwartz letter to William H. Seward, May 20, 1860, William H. Seward papers at the University of Rochester.

28. Frank M. Coxe to William H. Seward, May 22, 1860, William H. Seward papers at the University of Rochester.

29. Henry Dana Ward to William H. Seward, May 21, 1860, William H. Seward papers at the University of Rochester.

30. C.F. Adams to William H. Seward, May 22, 1860, William H. Seward papers at the University of Rochester.

31. Glyndon G. Van Deusen, *William Henry Seward: Lincoln's Secretary of State, the Negotiator of the Alaska Purchase* (New York: Oxford University Press, 1967), 22.

32. *Chicago Press and Tribune*, May 19, 1860. This also appeared in the *New York Tribune* on May 23, 1860.

Bibliography

Books

Allen, Howard W., and Vincent A. Lacey, eds. *Illinois Elections, 1818–1990: Candidates and County Returns for President, Governor, Senate, and House of Representatives*. Carbondale: Southern Illinois University Press, 1992.

Angle, Paul M. *Here I Have Lived: A History of Lincoln's Springfield, 1821–1865*. Springfield, IL: Abraham Lincoln Association, 1935.

_____, and Earl Schenck Miers, eds. *Fire the Salute! Abe Lincoln Is Nominated*. Kingsport, TN: Kingsport Press, 1960.

Baker, G.E., ed. *The Works of William H. Seward*. Boston, 1884.

Baringer, William E. *Lincoln's Rise to Power*. Boston: Little, Brown, 1937.

Basler, Roy, ed. *Abraham Lincoln: His Speeches and Writings*. New York: Da Capo Press, 1949.

_____. *The Collected Works of Abraham Lincoln*, New Brunswick, NJ: Rutgers University Press, 1953.

Beale, Howard K., ed. *The Diary of Edward Bates, 1859–1866*. Washington, D.C.: Government Printing Office, 1933.

Beveridge, Albert. *Abraham Lincoln, 1809–1858*. Vols. 1 and 2. New York: Houghton Mifflin, 1928.

Blaine, James G. *Twenty Years of Congress: From Lincoln to Garfield, with a Review of the Events which Led to the Political Revolution of 1860*. Vols. 1 and 2. Boston: Rand, Avery, 1884.

Blue, Frederick J. *Salmon P. Chase: A Life in Politics*. Kent, OH: Kent State University Press, 1987.

Boritt, Gabor. *Lincoln and the Economics of the American Dream*. Champaign: University of Illinois Press, 1994.

Bradley, Erwin Stanley. *Simon Cameron, Lincoln's Secretary of War: A Political Biography*. Philadelphia: University of Pennsylvania Press, 1966.

Brown, William Garrott. *Stephen A. Douglas*. Boston: Houghton, Mifflin, 1902.

Cain, Marvin. *Lincoln's Attorney General: Edward Bates of Missouri*. Columbia: University of Missouri Press, 1965.

Carr, Clark Ezra. *Stephen A. Douglas: His Life, Public Services, Speeches and Patriotism*. Chicago: A.C. McClurg Co., 1909.

Current, Richard N. *The Lincoln Nobody Knows*. New York: Hill and Wang, 1958.

Dittenhoefer, Abram J. *How We Elected Lincoln: Personal Recollections*. Philadelphia: University Press of Pennsylvania, 2005.

Donald, David Herbert. *Liberty and Union*. Lexington, Mass.: Heath and Company, 1978.

_____. *Lincoln*. New York: Simon and Schuster, 1995.

_____. *Lincoln Reconsidered*. New York: Vintage Books, 1947.

_____. *"We Are Lincoln Men": Abraham Lincoln and His Friends*. New York: Simon and Schuster, 2003.

Dubin, Michael J. *United States Gubernatorial Elections, 1776–1860: The Official Results by State and County*. Jefferson, NC: McFarland, 2003.

_____. *United States Presidential Elections, 1788–1860: The Official Results by County and State*. Jefferson, NC: McFarland, 2002.

Fehrenbacher, Don. *Chicago Giant: A Biography of "Long John" Wentworth*. Madison, WI: American History Research Center, 1957.

_____. *Prelude to Greatness: Lincoln in the 1850s*. Stanford: Stanford University Press, 1962.

Foner, Eric. *Free Soil, Free Labor, Free Men: The Ideology of the Republican Party before the Civil War*. Oxford: Oxford University Press, 1970.

Freehling, William W. *The Road to Disunion: Secessionists at Bay, 1776–1854*. New York: Oxford University Press, 1990.

Gardner, William. *Life of Stephen A. Douglas*. Boston: Roxburgh Press, 1905.

Going, Charles Buxton. *David Wilmot Free Soiler: A Biography of the Great Advocate of the Wilmot Proviso*. New York: D. Appleton and Company, 1924.

Goodwin, Doris Kearns. *Team of Rivals: The Political Genius of Abraham Lincoln*. New York: Simon and Schuster, 2005.

Guelzo, Allen C. *Abraham Lincoln: Redeemer President*. Grand Rapids, MI: Wm. B. Eerdman's, 1999.

Harper, Robert S. *Lincoln and the Press*. New York: McGraw-Hill, 1951.

Herndon, William H., and Jesse W. Weik. *Abraham Lincoln: The True Story of a Great Life*. Vols. 1 and 2. New York: D. Appleton and Company, 1896.

Hesseltine, William B., ed. *Three Against Lincoln: Murat Halstead Reports the Caucuses of 1860*. Baton Rouge: Louisiana State University, 1960.

Holcombe, John W., and Hubert M. Skinner. *Life and Public Service of Thomas A. Hendricks, with Selected Speeches and Writings*. Indianapolis: Carlon and Hollenbeck, 1885.

Jaffa, Harry V. *Crisis of the House Divided*. Chicago: University of Chicago Press, 1959.

_____, and Robert W. Johannsen, eds. *In the Name of the People: Speeches and Writings of Lincoln and Douglas in the Ohio Campaign of 1859*. Columbus: Ohio State University Press, 1959.

Johannsen, Robert W. *The Frontier, the Union, and Stephen A. Douglas*. Urbana: University of Illinois Press, 1989.

_____. *Stephen Douglas*. Urbana: University of Illinois Press, 1973.

Johnson, Charles W., ed. *Proceedings of the First Three Republican National Conventions*. Minneapolis: 1893.

King, Willard L. *Lincoln's Manager: David Davis*. Cambridge, MA: Harvard University Press, 1960.

Kolchin, Peter. *American Slavery, 1619–1877.* New York: Hill and Wang, 1993.

Logsdon, Joseph. *Horace White: Nineteenth Century Liberal.* Westport, CT: Greenwood, 1971.

Luthin, Reinhard H. *The First Lincoln Campaign.* Gloucester, MA: Peter Smith, 1964.

Magdol, Edward. *Owen Lovejoy: Abolitionist in Congress.* New Brunswick, NJ: Rutgers University Press, 1967.

McCormack, Thomas J., ed. *Memoirs of Gustave Koerner, 1809–1896: Life-sketches Written at the Suggestion of His Children.* Cedar Rapids, IA: Torch Press, 1909.

McPherson, James M. *Abraham Lincoln and the Second American Revolution.* New York: Oxford University Press, 1991.

_____. *Battle Cry of Freedom: The Civil War Era.* New York: Oxford University Press, 1988.

Miers, Earl Schenck. *Lincoln Day by Day: A Chronology, 1809–1865.* Dayton, OH: Morningside Press, 1991.

Miller, William Lee. *Arguing About Slavery: The Great Battle in the United States Congress.* New York: Alfred A. Knopf, 1996.

Mitgang, Herbert, ed. *Abraham Lincoln: A Press Portrait.* Athens: University of Georgia Press, 1989.

Monaghan, Jay. *The Man Who Elected Lincoln.* Indianapolis and New York: Bobbs-Merrill, 1956.

Moore, William F., and Jane Ann Moore. *Owen Lovejoy: His Brother's Blood, Speeches and Writings, 1838–1864.* Chicago: University of Illinois Press, 2004.

Neely, Mark E., Jr. *The Abraham Lincoln Encyclopedia.* New York: Da Capo Press, 1982.

Newton, Joseph Fort. *Lincoln and Herndon.* Cedar Rapids, IA: The Torch Press, 1910.

Nicolay, Helen. *Lincoln's Secretary: A Biography of John G. Nicolay.* New York: Longmans, Green and Company, 1949.

Nicolay, John G., and John Hay, eds. *Complete Works of Abraham Lincoln.* Vols. 1–12. Lincoln Memorial University, 1894.

Niven, John. *Gideon Welles: Lincoln's Secretary of the Navy.* New York: Oxford University Press, 1973.

Oates, Stephen. *With Malice Toward None: The Life of Abraham Lincoln.* New York: New American Library, 1977.

Ostendorf, Lloyd. *Mr. Lincoln Came to Dayton.* Dayton, OH: Otterbein Press, 1959.

Palmer, John M. *Personal Recollections of John M. Palmer: The Story of an Earnest Life.* Cincinnati: Robert Clarke Company, 1901.

Pease, Theodore Calvin, and James G. Randall. *The Diary of Orville Hickman Browning.* Vol. 1, *1850–1864.* Springfield: Illinois State Historical Library, 1925.

Potter, David M. *The Impending Crisis, 1848–1861.* New York: Harper and Row, 1976.

Proctor, Addison G. *Lincoln and the Convention of 1860: An Address before the Chicago Historical Society, April 4, 1918.* Chicago: Chicago Historical Society, 1918.

Randall, J.G. *Lincoln: The Liberal Statesman.* New York: Dodd, Mead, 1947.

Randall, Ruth Painter. *Colonel Elmer Ellsworth.* Boston: Little, Brown, 1960.

Ransom, Roger L. *Conflict and Compromise: The Political Economy of Slavery, Emancipation, and the American Civil War.* Cambridge: Cambridge University Press, 1990.

Ray, P. Orman. *The Convention That Nominated Lincoln: An Address Delivered before the Chicago Historical Society on May 18, 1916, the Fifty-Sixth Anniversary of Lincoln's Nomination for the Presidency.* Chicago: University of Chicago Press, 1916.

Roske, Ralph J. *His Own Counsel: The Life and Times of Lyman Trumbull.* Reno: University of Nevada Press, 1979.

Seward, Frederick W. *Seward at Washington, as Senator and Secretary of State: A Memoir of His Life, with Selections from His Letters, 1846–1861.* New York: Derby and Miller, 1891.

Shaw, Albert. *Abraham Lincoln: His Path to the Presidency.* Review of Reviews, 1930.

Smith, William Ernest. *The Francis Preston Blair Family in Politics.* Vols. 1 and 2. New York: Macmillan Company, 1933.

Smith, Willard H. *Schuylar Colfax: The Changing Fortunes of a Political Idol.* Indianapolis: Indiana Historical Bureau, 1952.

Sparks, Edwin Erle. *The Lincoln-Douglas Debates of 1858.* Springfield: Illinois State Historical Library, 1908.

Stamp, Kenneth M. *The Peculiar Institution: Slavery in the Ante-Bellum South.* New York: Alfred A. Knopf, 1956.

Stewart, James Brewer. *Joshua R. Giddings and the Tactics of Radical Politics.* Cleveland: Press of Case Western Reserve University, 1970.

Tarbell, Ida M. *The Life of Abraham Lincoln.* Vols. 1 and 2. New York: Macmillan, 1917.

Taylor, John M. *William Henry Seward: Lincoln's Right Hand.* New York: Harper-Collins, 1991.

Thomas, Benjamin. *Abraham Lincoln: A Biography.* New York: Alfred A. Knopf, 1952.

_____. *Portrait for Posterity: Lincoln and His Biographers.* New Brunswick, NJ: Rutgers University Press, 1947.

Trefousse, H.L. *Benjamin Franklin Wade: Radical Republican from Ohio.* New York: Twayne Publishers, 1963.

Trefousse, Han L. *Carl Schurz: A Biography.* Knoxville: University of Tennessee Press, 1982.

Turner, Justin G., and Linda Levitt Turner. *Mary Todd Lincoln: Her Life and Letters.* New York: Fromm International, 1987.

Turpie, David. *Sketches of My Time.* Bobbs-Merrill, 1903.

Van Deusen, Glyndon G. *Thurlow Weed: Wizard of the Lobby.* Boston: Little, Brown, 1947.

_____. *William Henry Seward.* New York: Oxford University Press, 1967.

Wakefield, Sherman Day. *How Lincoln Became President.* New York: Wilson-Erickson, 1936.

Weed, Thurlow. *Life of Thurlow Weed Including His Autobiography and a Memoir.* Boston: Houghton Mifflin, 1884.

White, Horace. *The Life of Lyman Trumbull.* New York: Houghton Mifflin, 1913.

Wills, Garry. *Lincoln at Gettysburg: The Words That Remade America.* New York: Simon and Schuster, 1992.

Wilson, Douglas L. *Lincoln before Washington: New Perspectives on the Illinois Years.* Champaign: University of Illinois Press, 1997.

_____, and Rodney O. Davis *Herndon's Informants: Letters, Interviews and Statements about Abraham Lincoln.* Urbana: University of Illinois Press, 1998.

Articles/Speeches

Auchampaugh, Philip G. "The Buchanan-Douglas Feud." *Journal of the Illinois State Historical Society* 25 (April–July 1932): 5–48.

Bailey, Louis J. "Caleb Blood Smith." *Indiana Magazine of History* (September, 1933): 213–239.

Basler, Roy P. "Abraham Lincoln's Rhetoric." *American Literature* 11 (May 1939): 167–182.

Blegen, Thoedore. "Campaigning with Seward in 1860." *Minnesota History* (1927): 150–171.

Bromley, Isaac H. "Historic Moments: The Nomination of Lincoln." *Scribner's Magazine,* November 1893.

Chu, James C.Y. "Horace White: His Association with Abraham Lincoln, 1854–1860." *Journalism Quarterly* 49 (Spring 1972): 51–60.

Dudley, Thomas H. "The Inside Facts of Lincoln's Nomination." *Century Illustrated Monthly Magazine* (1890): 477–479.

Fehrenbacher, Don E. "The Historical Significance of the Lincoln-Douglas Debates." *Wisconsin Magazine of History* 42 (Spring 1959): 193–199.

_____. "Lincoln, Douglas, and the 'Freeport Question.'" *American Historical Review* 66 (April 1961): 599–617.

Hesseltine, William B. "The Pryor-Potter Duel." *Wisconsin Magazine of History* (June 1944): 400–409.

Krug, Mark M. "Lyman Trumbull and the Real Issues in the Lincoln-Douglas Debates." *Journal of the Illinois State Historical Society* 57 (Winter 1964): 380–396.

Luthin, Reinhard. "Pennsylvania and Lincoln's Rise to the Presidency." *Pennsylvania Magazine of History and Biography* (January 1943): 61–82.

Roll, Charles. "Indiana's Part in the Nomination of Abraham Lincoln for President in 1860." *Indiana Magazine of History* 25 (March 1929): 1–13.

Sharp, Walter Rice. "Henry S. Lane and the Formation of the Republican Party in Indiana." *The Mississippi Valley Historical Review* 7 (September 1920): 93–112.

Strevey, Tracy E. "Joseph Medill and the *Chicago Tribune* in the Nomination and Election of Lincoln." *Papers in Illinois History and Transactions for the Year 1938* (1939): 39–63.

Zimmerman, Charles. "The Origin and Rise of the Republican Party in Indiana from 1854 to 1860." *Indiana Magazine of History* (1917): 349–412.

Index